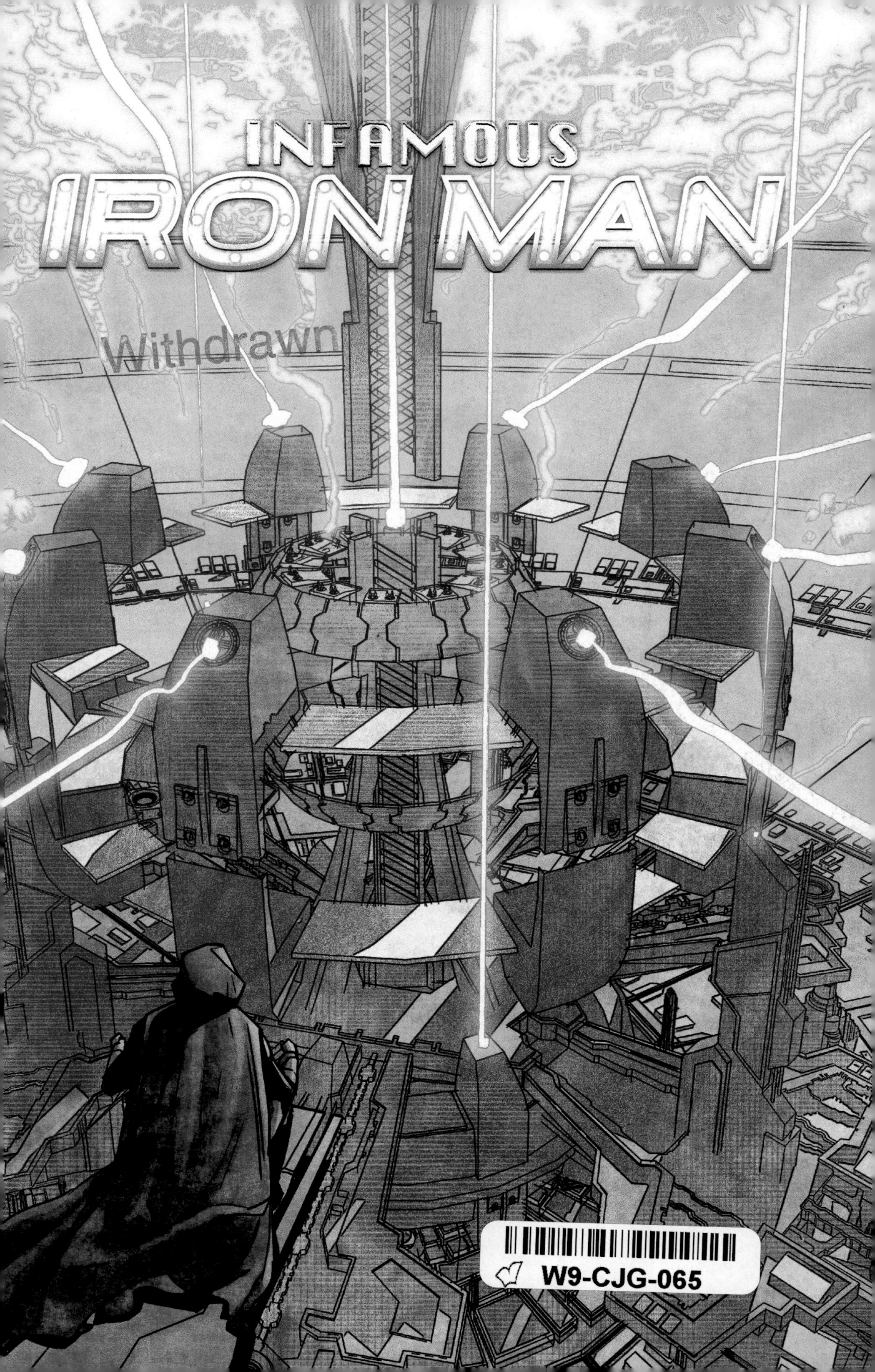
INFAMOUS
IRON MAN

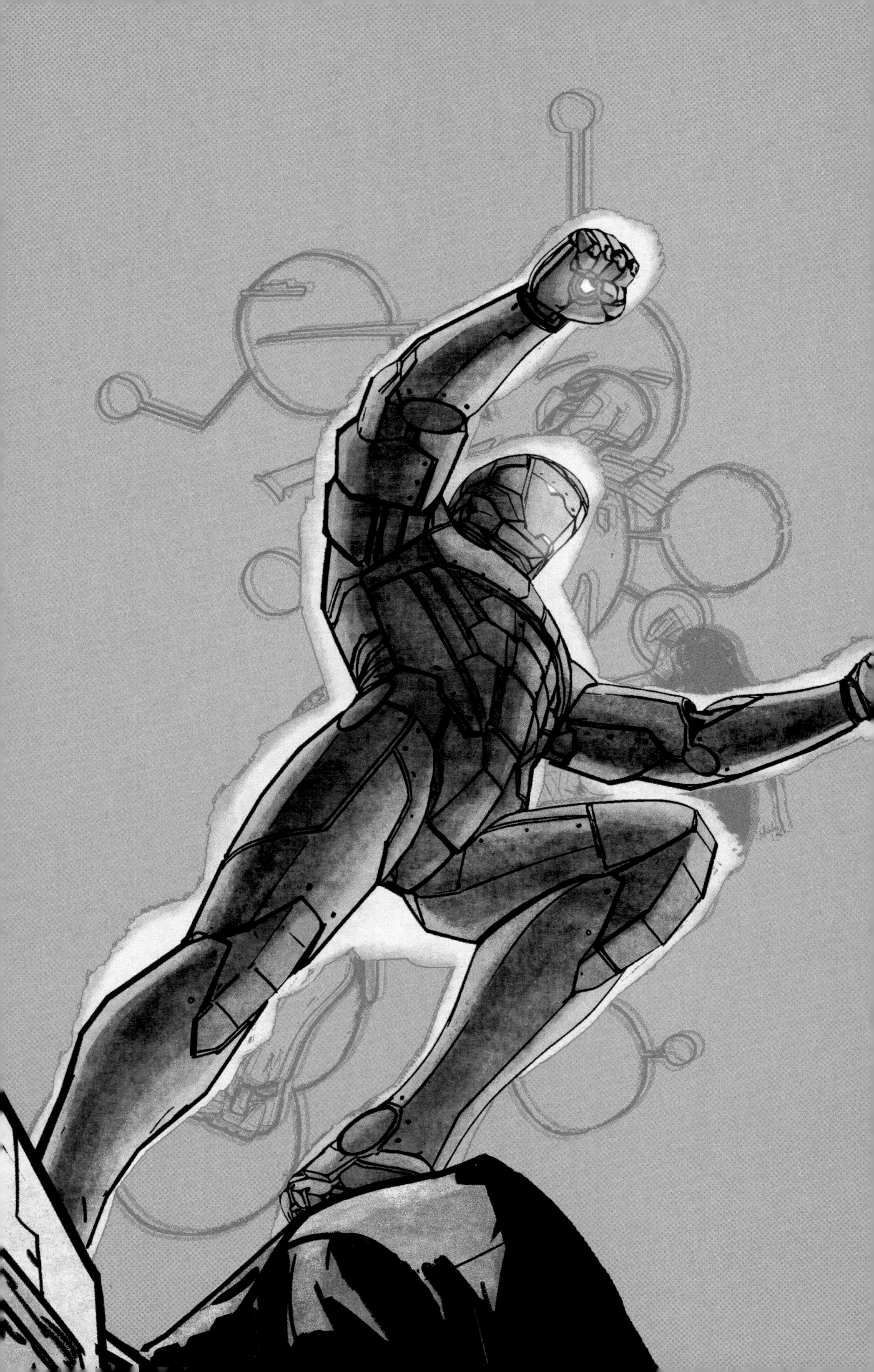

INFAMOUS

IRON MAN

THE ABSOLUTION OF DOOM

BRIAN MICHAEL BENDIS
WRITER

ALEX MALEEV
ARTIST

MATT HOLLINGSWORTH
COLOR ARTIST

VC's CLAYTON COWLES
LETTERER

ALEX MALEEV
COVER ART

ALANNA SMITH
ASSISTANT EDITOR

TOM BREVOORT
EDITOR

COLLECTION EDITOR: **JENNIFER GRÜNWALD**
ASSISTANT EDITOR: **CAITLIN O'CONNELL**
ASSOCIATE MANAGING EDITOR: **KATERI WOODY**
EDITOR, SPECIAL PROJECTS: **MARK D. BEAZLEY**
VP PRODUCTION & SPECIAL PROJECTS: **JEFF YOUNGQUIST**
SVP PRINT, SALES & MARKETING: **DAVID GABRIEL**
BOOK DESIGNER: **ADAM DEL RE**

EDITOR IN CHIEF: **AXEL ALONSO**
CHIEF CREATIVE OFFICER: **JOE QUESADA**
PRESIDENT: **DAN BUCKLEY**
EXECUTIVE PRODUCER: **ALAN FINE**

IRON MAN CREATED BY STAN LEE, LARRY LIEBER, DON HECK & JACK KIRBY

NFAMOUS IRON MAN VOL. 2: THE ABSOLUTION OF DOOM. Contains material originally published in magazine form as INFAMOUS IRON MAN #7-12. First printing 2017. ISBN# 978-1-302-90625-2. Published by MARVEL WORLDWIDE, NC., a subsidiary of MARVEL ENTERTAINMENT, LLC. OFFICE OF PUBLICATION: 135 West 50th Street, New York, NY 10020. Copyright © 2017 MARVEL No similarity between any of the names, characters, persons, and/or institutions n this magazine with those of any living or dead person or institution is intended, and any such similarity which may exist is purely coincidental. **Printed in the U.S.A.** DAN BUCKLEY, President, Marvel Entertainment; JOE QUESADA, hief Creative Officer; TOM BREVOORT, SVP of Publishing; DAVID BOGART, SVP of Business Affairs & Operations, Publishing & Partnership; C.B. CEBULSKI, VP of Brand Management & Development, Asia; DAVID GABRIEL, SVP of Sales & larketing, Publishing; JEFF YOUNGQUIST, VP of Production & Special Projects; DAN CARR, Executive Director of Publishing Technology; ALEX MORALES, Director of Publishing Operations; SUSAN CRESPI, Production Manager; STAN LEE, hairman Emeritus. For information regarding advertising in Marvel Comics or on Marvel.com, please contact Vit DeBellis, Integrated Sales Manager, at vdebellis@marvel.com. For Marvel subscription inquiries, please call 888-511-5480. **lanufactured between 9/29/2017 and 10/30/2017 by QUAD/GRAPHICS WASECA, WASECA, MN, USA.**

0 9 8 7 6 5 4 3 2 1

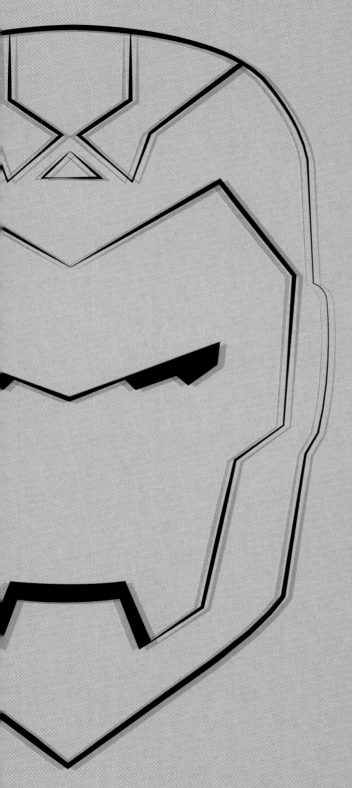

Victor Von Doom has lived a lifetime of devious infamy as Doctor Doom — but recent events, including the sudden, almost fatal incapacitation of Tony Stark, A.K.A. Iron Man, have inspired Doom to dedicate his life to more heroic pursuits...as the INFAMOUS IRON MAN.

Victor recently discovered that his mother, the dark arts master Cynthia Von Doom, was not dead as he had believed. She claimed she wanted to rekindle their relationship now that Victor was turning over a new leaf — but there's a dark version of Reed Richards whispering in her ear at every turn, and his intentions are still unknown.

Meanwhile, a S.H.I.E.L.D. operation led by Ben Grimm, A.K.A. the Thing, continues to pursue Victor, believing his motives for taking out a number of other dangerous villains to be less than honorable.

7

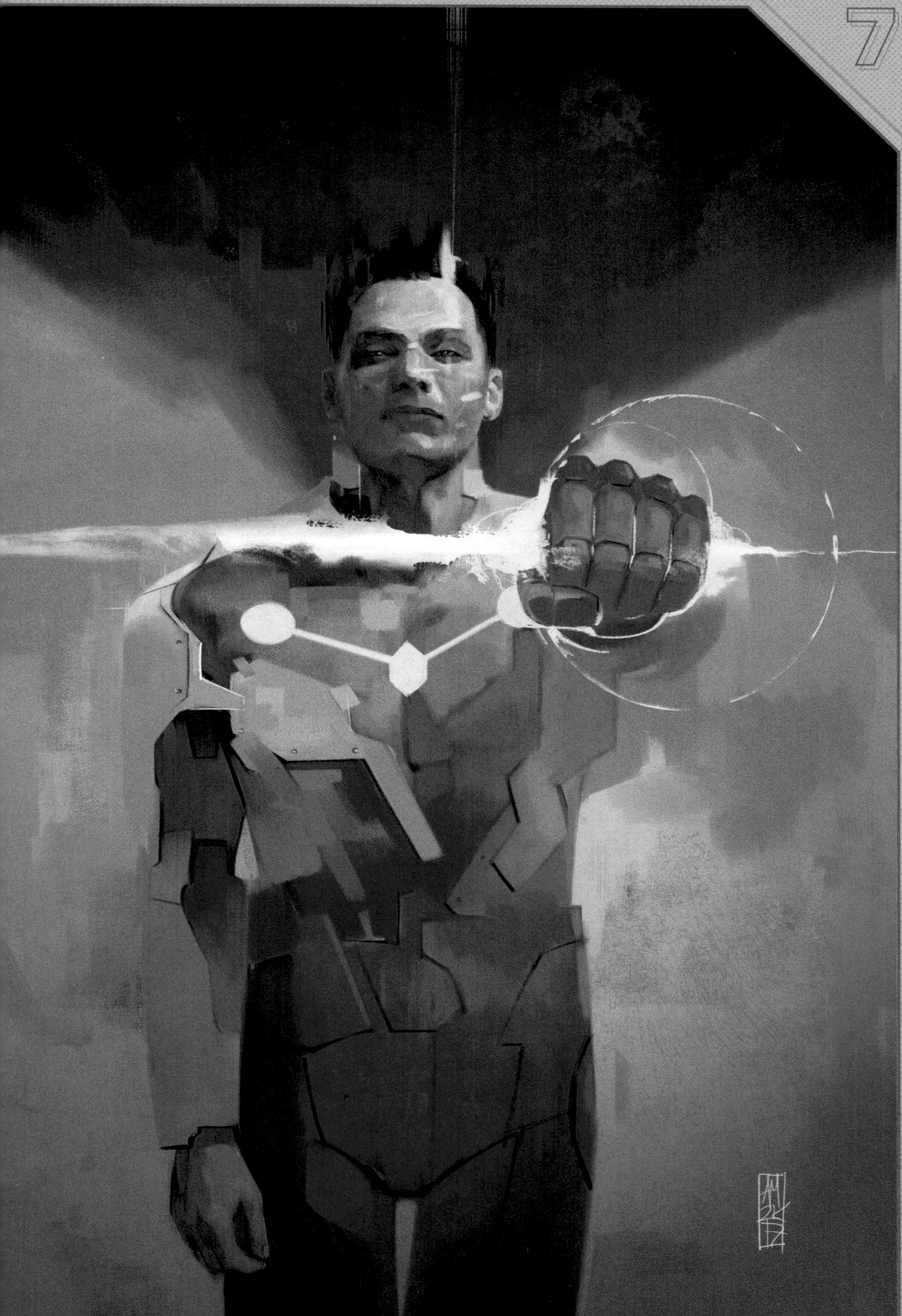

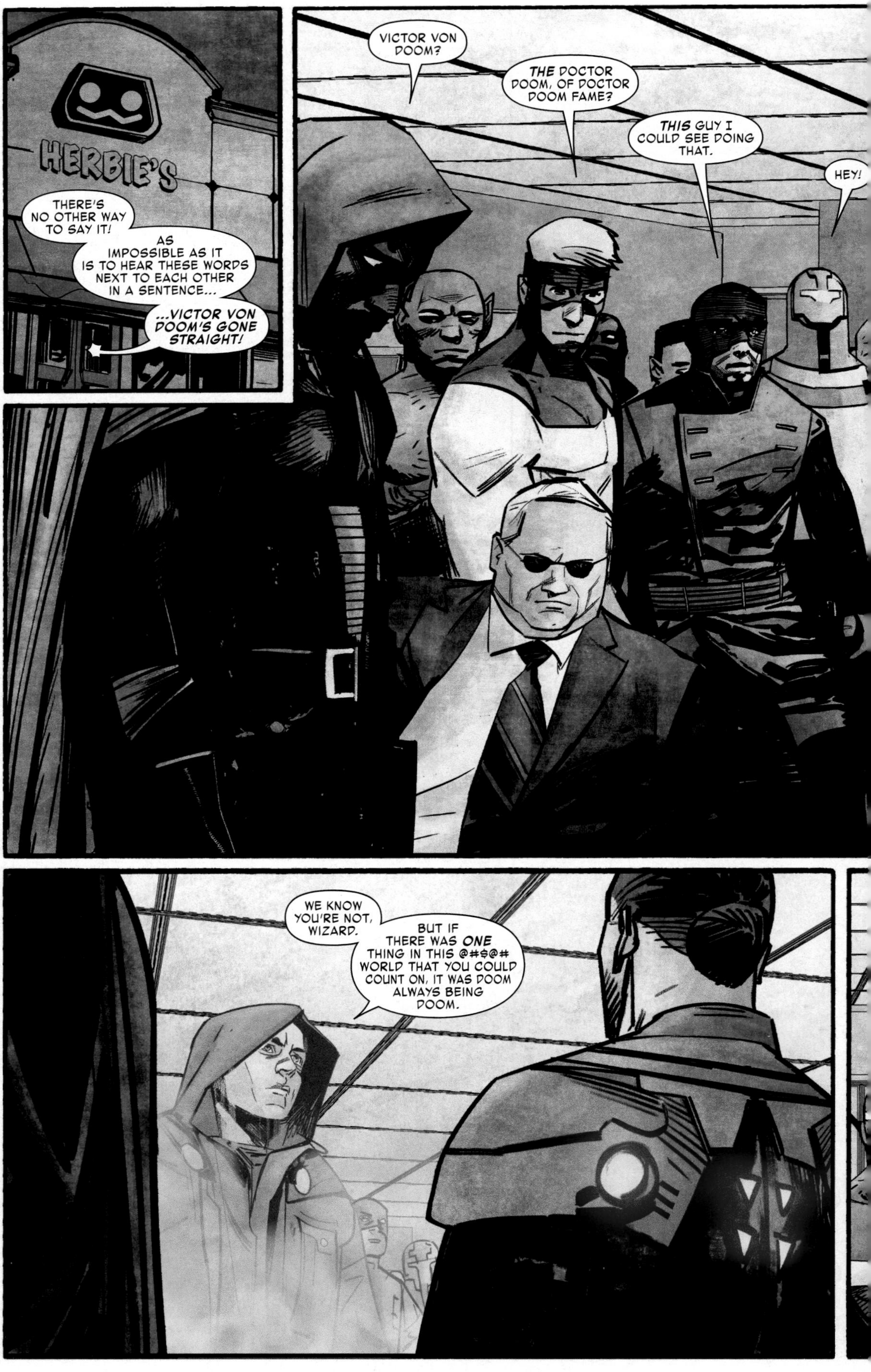

HERBIE'S
THERE'S NO OTHER WAY TO SAY IT!
AS IMPOSSIBLE AS IT IS TO HEAR THESE WORDS NEXT TO EACH OTHER IN A SENTENCE...
...VICTOR VON DOOM'S GONE STRAIGHT!
VICTOR VON DOOM?
THE DOCTOR DOOM, OF DOCTOR DOOM FAME?
THIS GUY I COULD SEE DOING THAT.
HEY!
WE KNOW YOU'RE NOT, WIZARD.
BUT IF THERE WAS ONE THING IN THIS @#$@# WORLD THAT YOU COULD COUNT ON, IT WAS DOOM ALWAYS BEING DOOM.

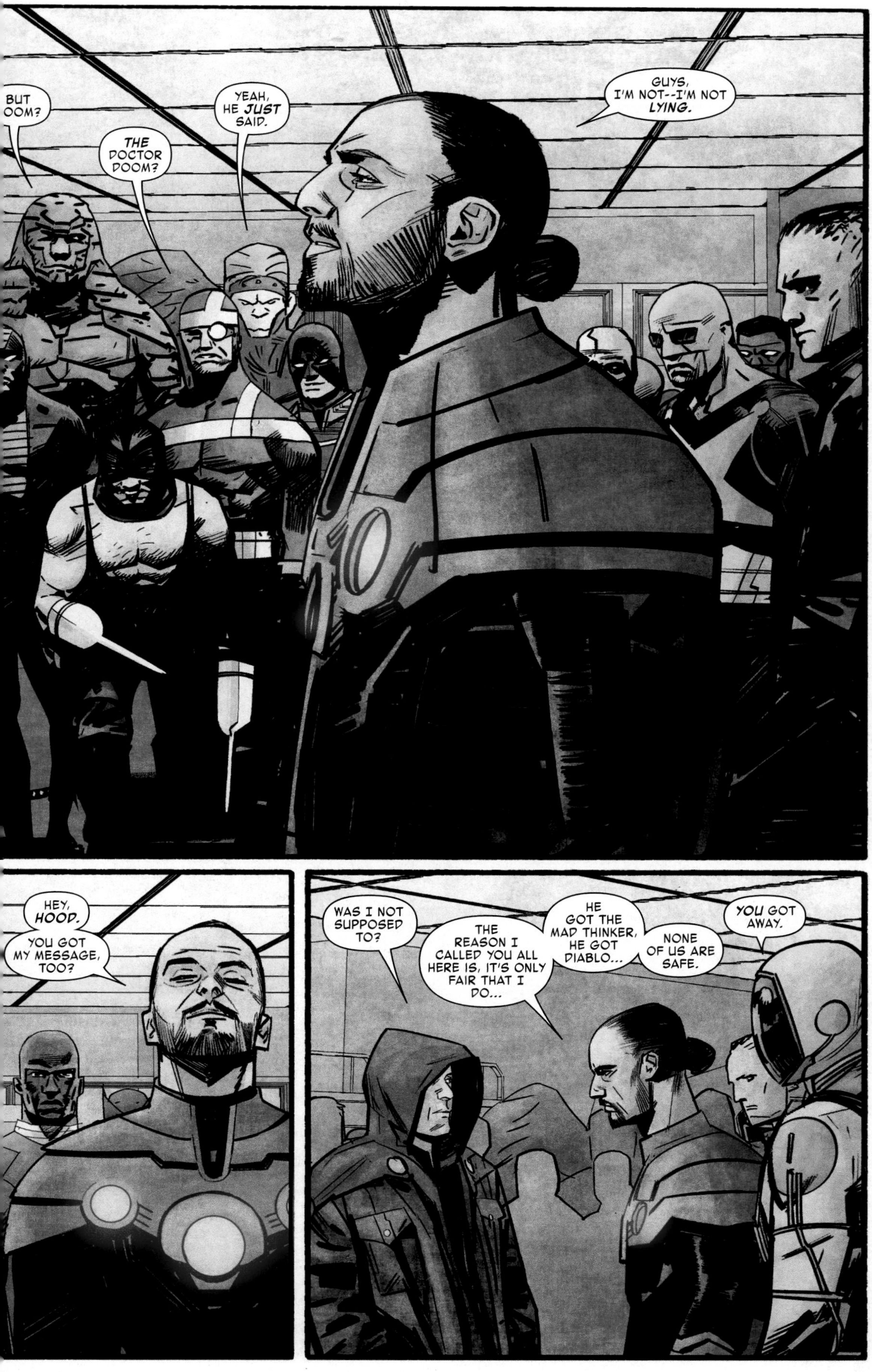
BUT
OOM?
THE DOCTOR DOOM?
YEAH, HE JUST SAID.
GUYS, I'M NOT--I'M NOT LYING.
HEY, HOOD.
YOU GOT MY MESSAGE, TOO?
WAS I NOT SUPPOSED TO?
THE REASON I CALLED YOU ALL HERE IS, IT'S ONLY FAIR THAT I DO...
HE GOT THE MAD THINKER, HE GOT DIABLO...
NONE OF US ARE SAFE.
YOU GOT AWAY.

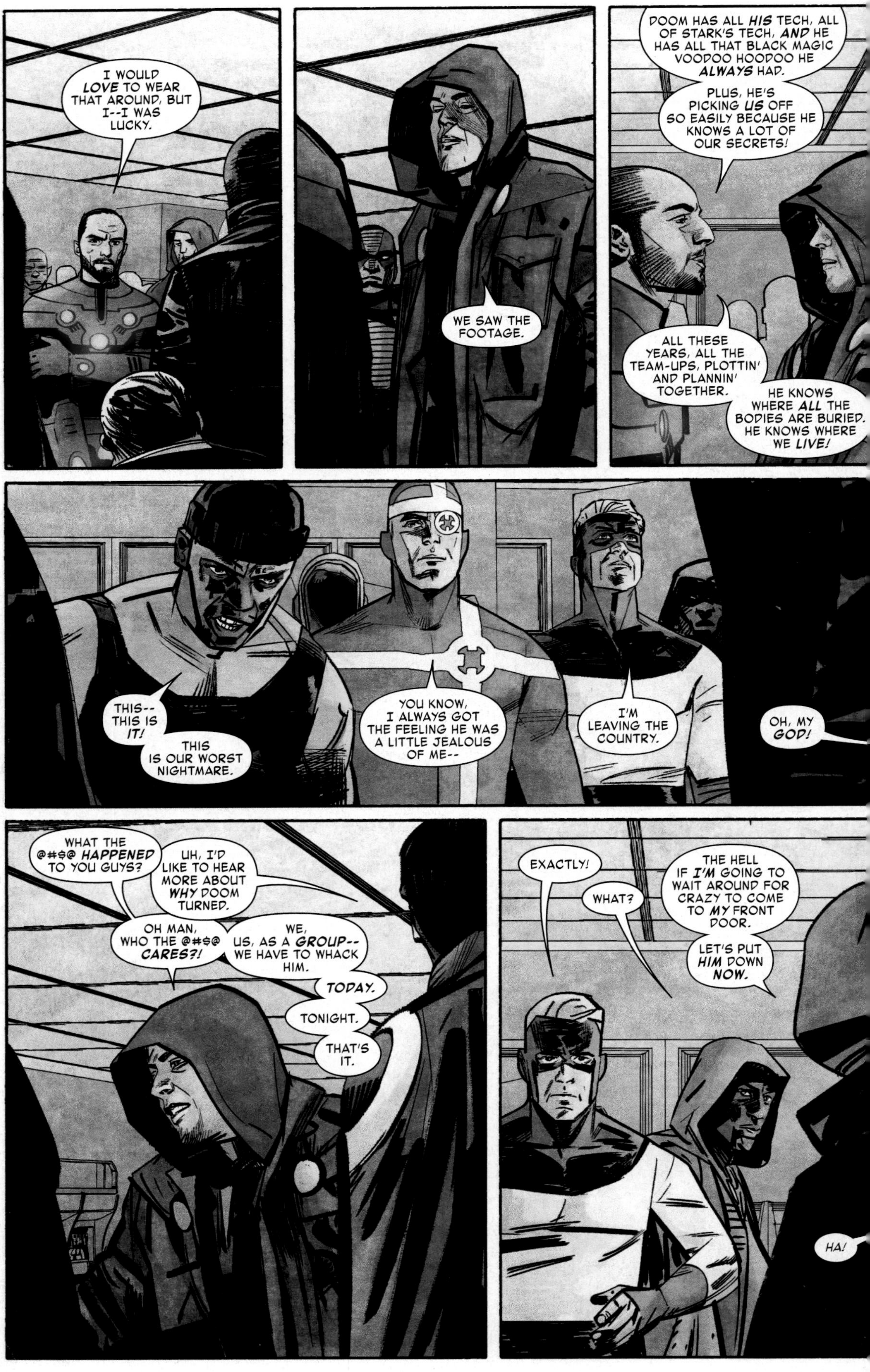
I WOULD LOVE TO WEAR THAT AROUND, BUT I--I WAS LUCKY.
WE SAW THE FOOTAGE.
DOOM HAS ALL HIS TECH, ALL OF STARK'S TECH, AND HE HAS ALL THAT BLACK MAGIC VOODOO HOODOO HE ALWAYS HAD.
PLUS, HE'S PICKING US OFF SO EASILY BECAUSE HE KNOWS A LOT OF OUR SECRETS!
ALL THESE YEARS, ALL THE TEAM-UPS, PLOTTIN' AND PLANNIN' TOGETHER.
HE KNOWS WHERE ALL THE BODIES ARE BURIED. HE KNOWS WHERE WE LIVE!
THIS-- THIS IS IT!
THIS IS OUR WORST NIGHTMARE.
YOU KNOW, I ALWAYS GOT THE FEELING HE WAS A LITTLE JEALOUS OF ME--
I'M LEAVING THE COUNTRY.
OH, MY GOD!
WHAT THE @#$@ HAPPENED TO YOU GUYS?
UH, I'D LIKE TO HEAR MORE ABOUT WHY DOOM TURNED.
OH MAN, WHO THE @#$@ CARES?!
WE, US, AS A GROUP-- WE HAVE TO WHACK HIM.
TODAY.
TONIGHT.
THAT'S IT.
EXACTLY!
WHAT?
THE HELL IF I'M GOING TO WAIT AROUND FOR CRAZY TO COME TO MY FRONT DOOR.
LET'S PUT HIM DOWN NOW.
HA!

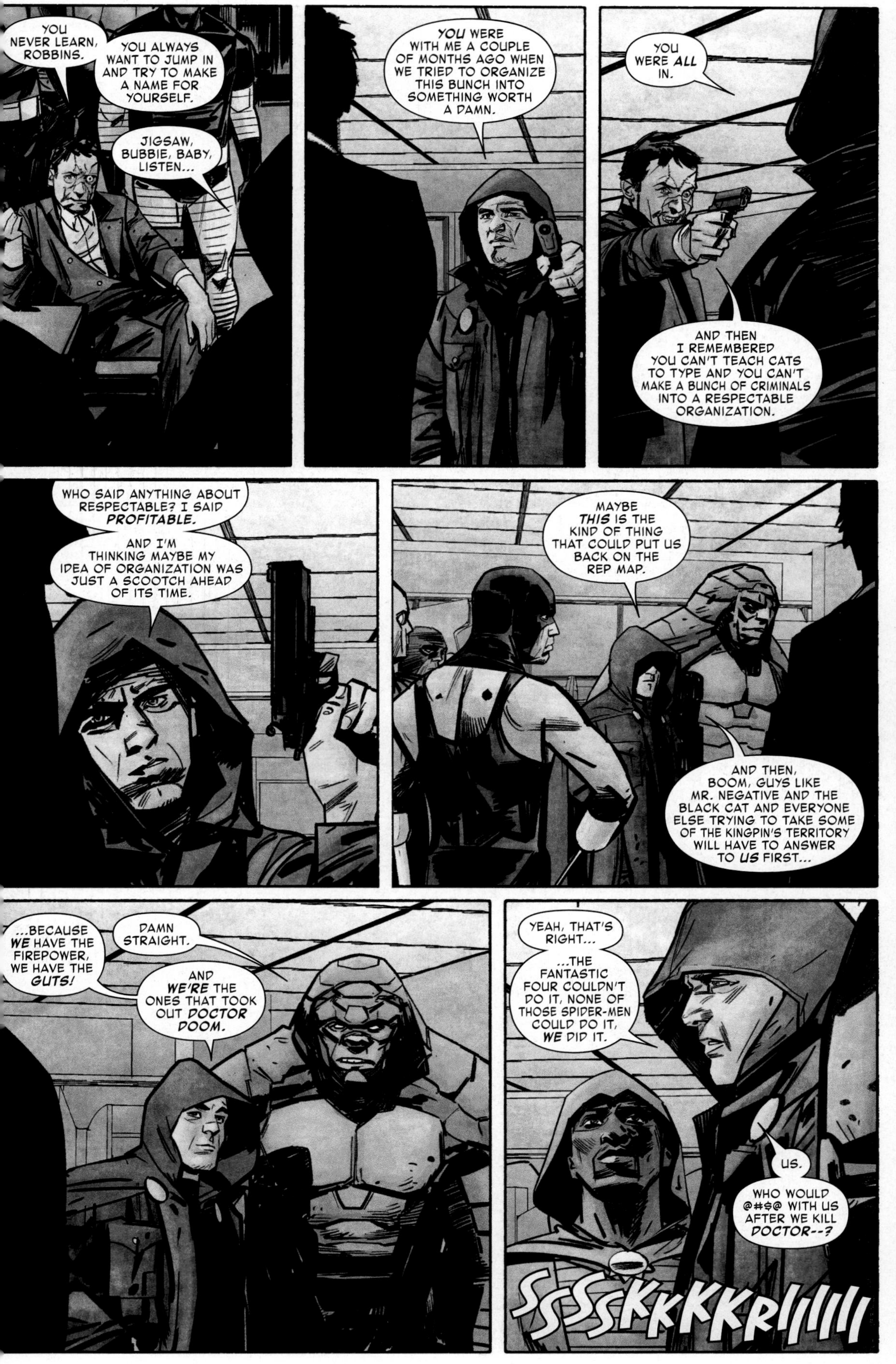
YOU NEVER LEARN, ROBBINS.
YOU ALWAYS WANT TO JUMP IN AND TRY TO MAKE A NAME FOR YOURSELF.
JIGSAW, BUBBIE, BABY, LISTEN...
YOU WERE WITH ME A COUPLE OF MONTHS AGO WHEN WE TRIED TO ORGANIZE THIS BUNCH INTO SOMETHING WORTH A DAMN.
YOU WERE ALL IN.
AND THEN I REMEMBERED YOU CAN'T TEACH CATS TO TYPE AND YOU CAN'T MAKE A BUNCH OF CRIMINALS INTO A RESPECTABLE ORGANIZATION.
WHO SAID ANYTHING ABOUT RESPECTABLE? I SAID PROFITABLE.
AND I'M THINKING MAYBE MY IDEA OF ORGANIZATION WAS JUST A SCOOTCH AHEAD OF ITS TIME.
MAYBE THIS IS THE KIND OF THING THAT COULD PUT US BACK ON THE REP MAP.
AND THEN, BOOM, GUYS LIKE MR. NEGATIVE AND THE BLACK CAT AND EVERYONE ELSE TRYING TO TAKE SOME OF THE KINGPIN'S TERRITORY WILL HAVE TO ANSWER TO US FIRST...
...BECAUSE WE HAVE THE FIREPOWER, WE HAVE THE GUTS!
DAMN STRAIGHT.
AND WE'RE THE ONES THAT TOOK OUT DOCTOR DOOM.
YEAH, THAT'S RIGHT...
...THE FANTASTIC FOUR COULDN'T DO IT, NONE OF THOSE SPIDER-MEN COULD DO IT, WE DID IT.
US.
WHO WOULD @#$@ WITH US AFTER WE KILL DOCTOR--?
SSSSKKKKRIIIIII

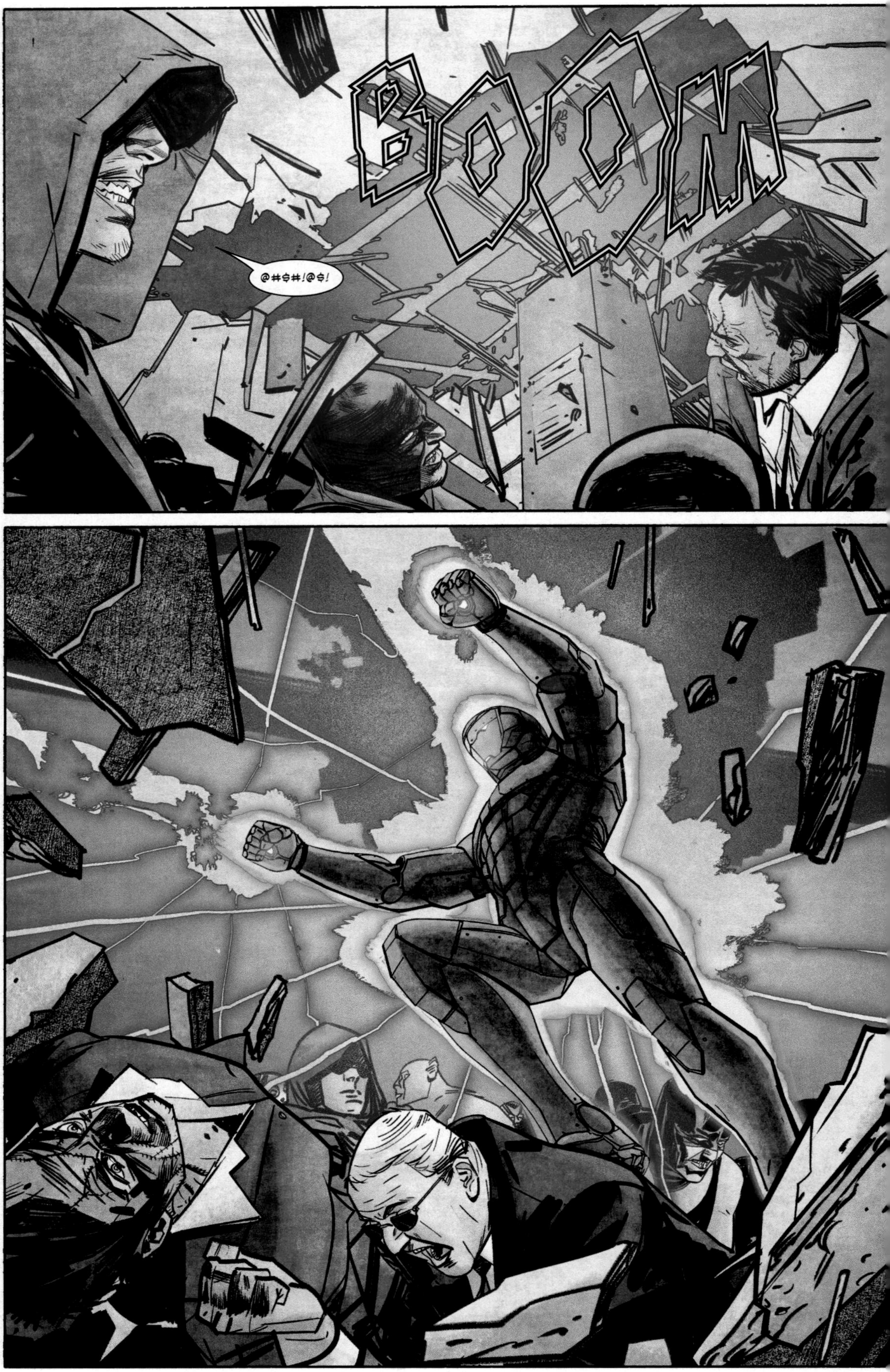
BOOM
@#$#!@$!

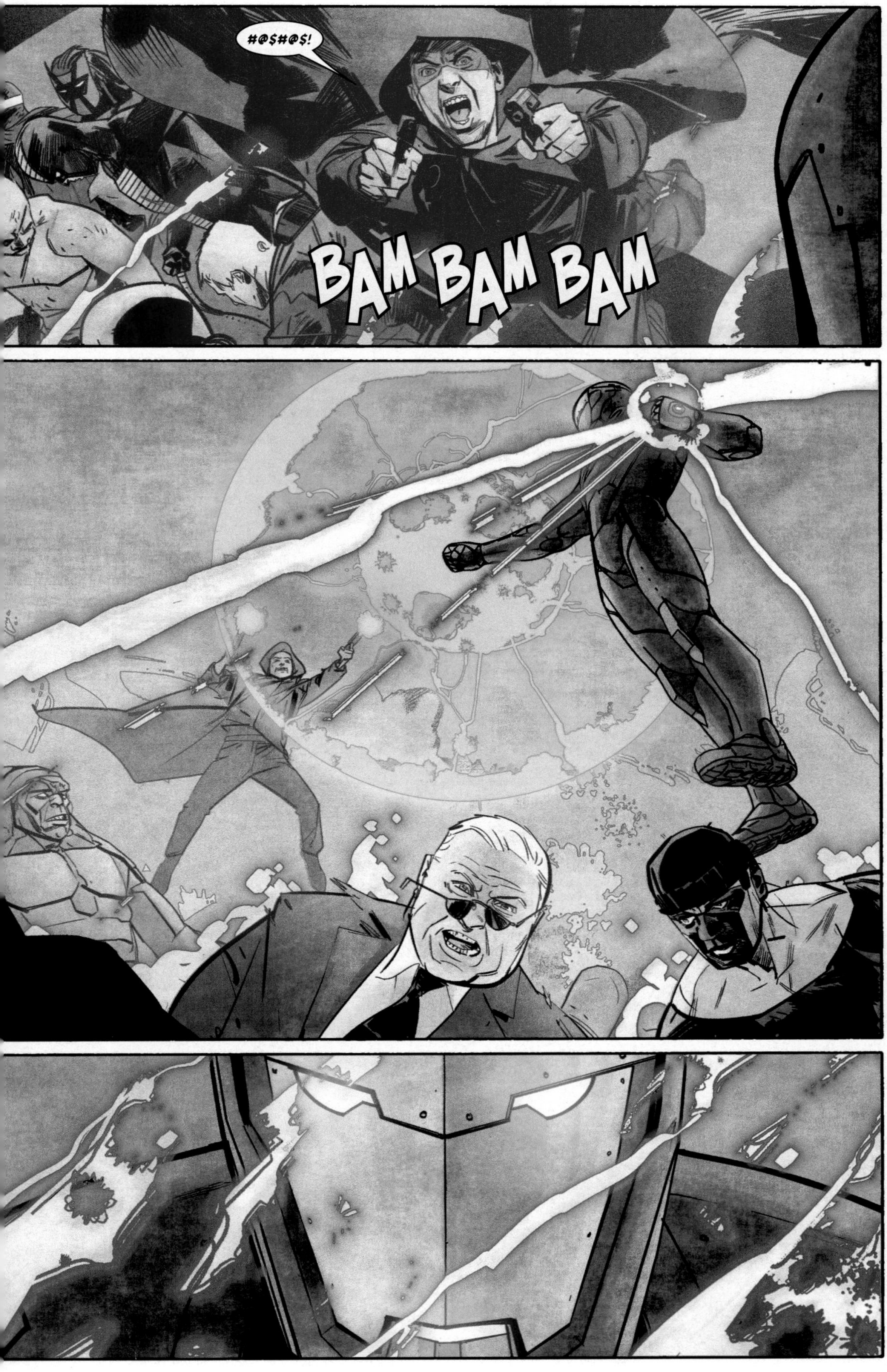
#@$#@$!
BAM BAM BAM

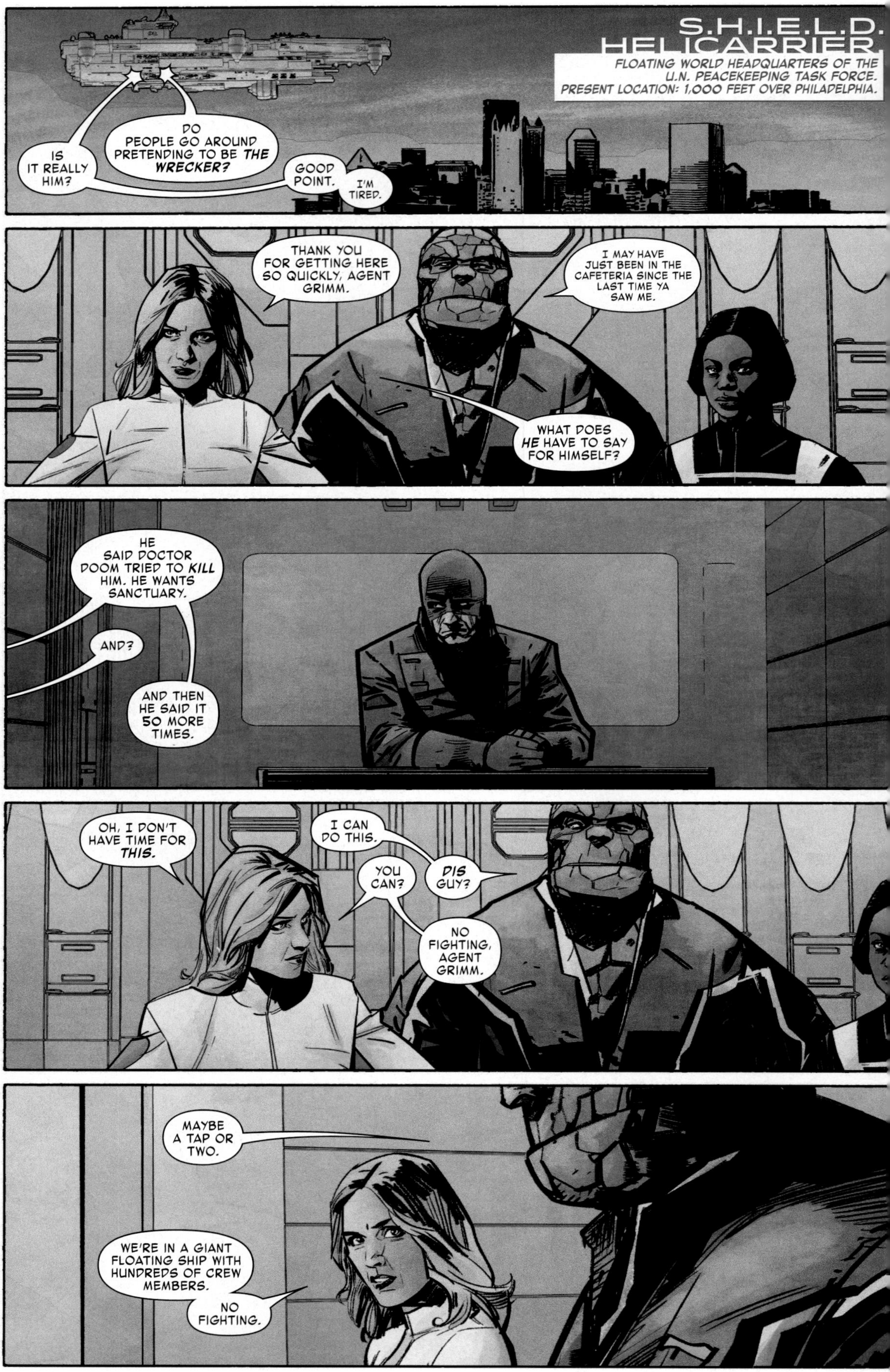
S.H.I.E.L.D. HELICARRIER.
FLOATING WORLD HEADQUARTERS OF THE U.N. PEACEKEEPING TASK FORCE. PRESENT LOCATION: 1,000 FEET OVER PHILADELPHIA.
IS IT REALLY HIM?
DO PEOPLE GO AROUND PRETENDING TO BE THE WRECKER?
GOOD POINT.
I'M TIRED.
THANK YOU FOR GETTING HERE SO QUICKLY, AGENT GRIMM.
I MAY HAVE JUST BEEN IN THE CAFETERIA SINCE THE LAST TIME YA SAW ME.
WHAT DOES HE HAVE TO SAY FOR HIMSELF?
HE SAID DOCTOR DOOM TRIED TO KILL HIM. HE WANTS SANCTUARY.
AND?
AND THEN HE SAID IT 50 MORE TIMES.
OH, I DON'T HAVE TIME FOR THIS.
I CAN DO THIS.
DIS GUY?
YOU CAN?
NO FIGHTING, AGENT GRIMM.
MAYBE A TAP OR TWO.
WE'RE IN A GIANT FLOATING SHIP WITH HUNDREDS OF CREW MEMBERS.
NO FIGHTING.

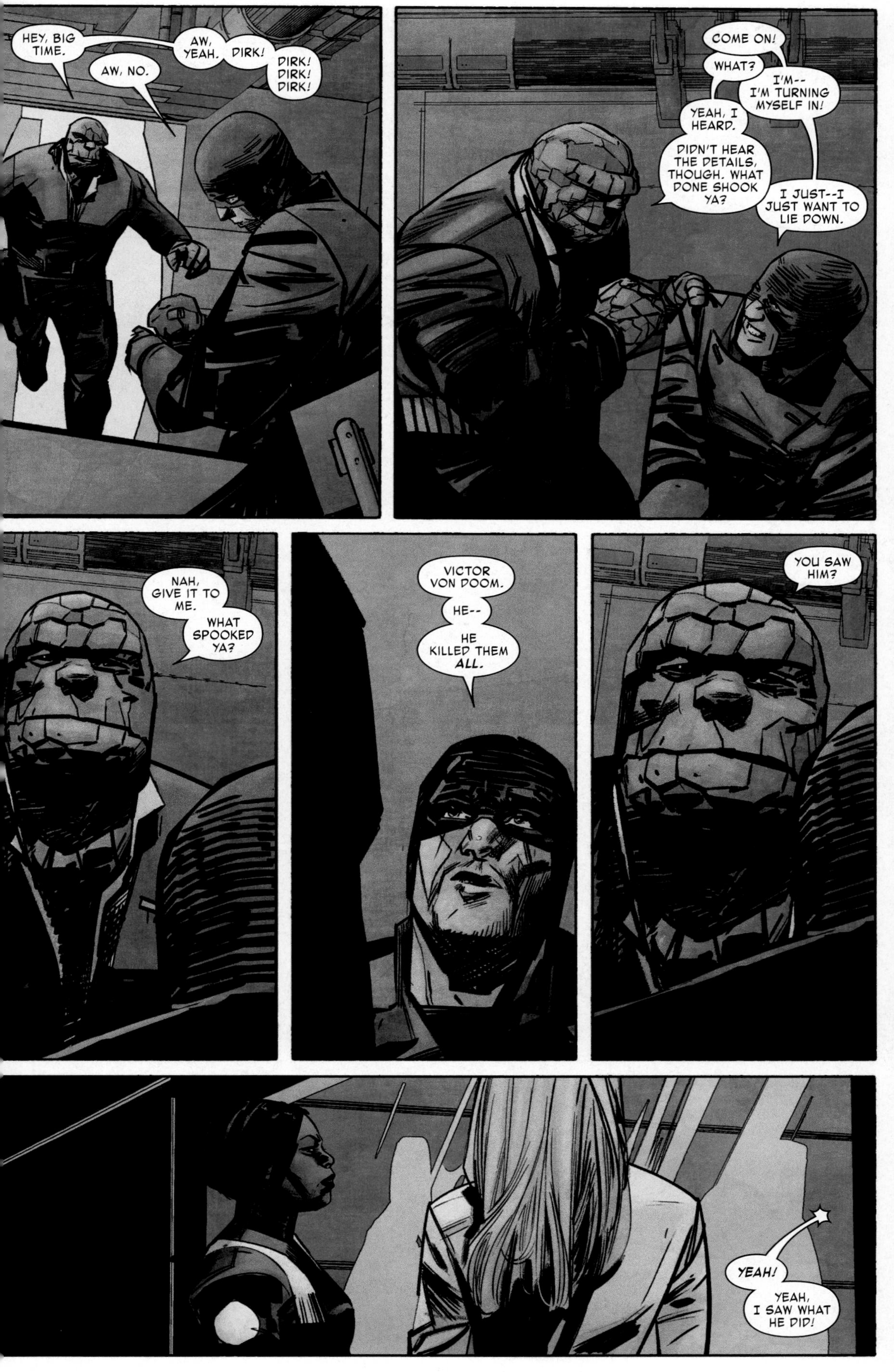
HEY, BIG TIME.
AW, YEAH.
DIRK!
DIRK! DIRK! DIRK!
AW, NO.
COME ON!
WHAT?
I'M-- I'M TURNING MYSELF IN!
YEAH, I HEARD.
DIDN'T HEAR THE DETAILS, THOUGH. WHAT DONE SHOOK YA?
I JUST--I JUST WANT TO LIE DOWN.
NAH, GIVE IT TO ME.
WHAT SPOOKED YA?
VICTOR VON DOOM.
HE--
HE KILLED THEM ALL.
YOU SAW HIM?
YEAH!
YEAH, I SAW WHAT HE DID!

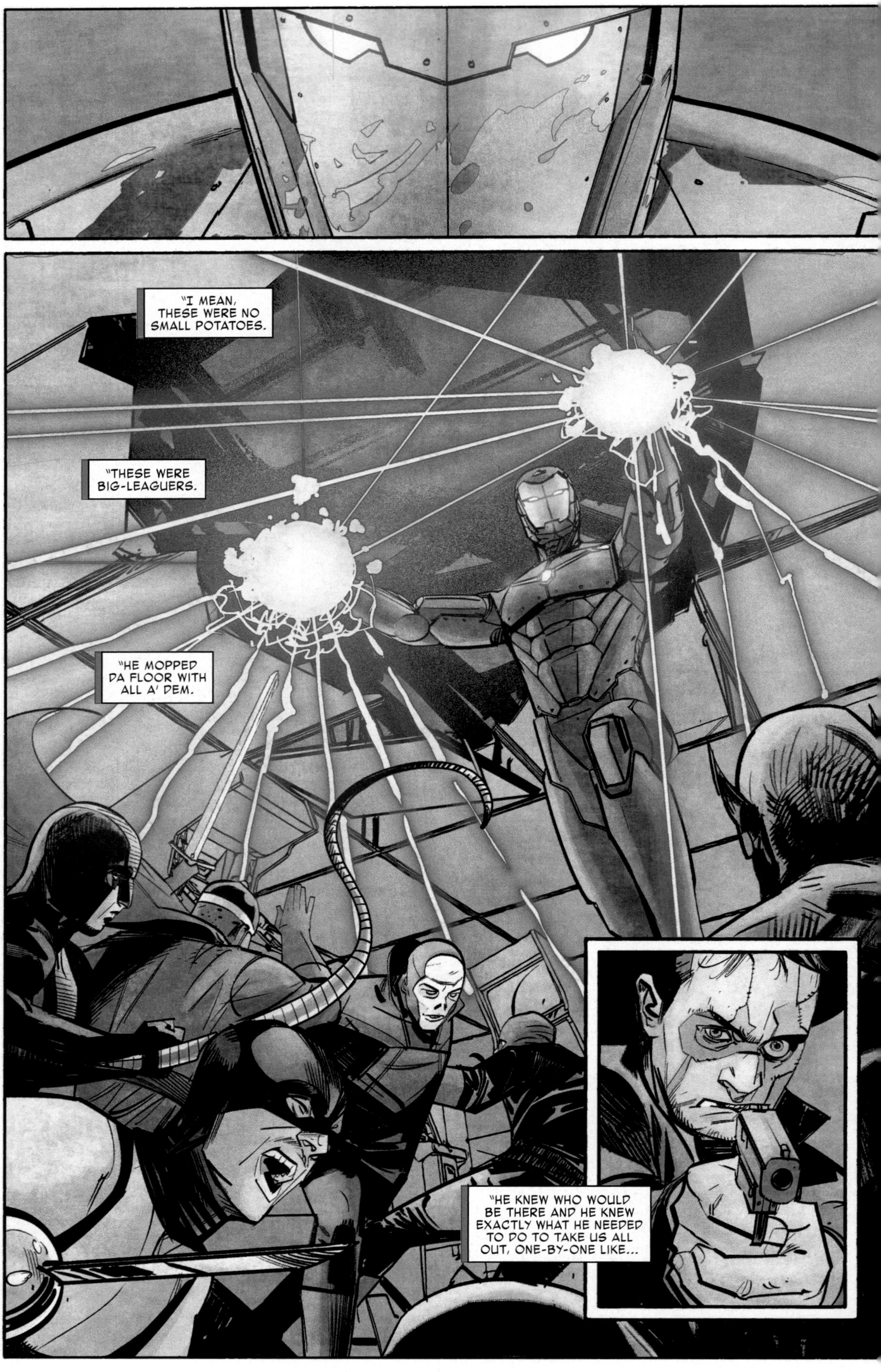
"I MEAN, THESE WERE NO SMALL POTATOES.
"THESE WERE BIG-LEAGUERS.
"HE MOPPED DA FLOOR WITH ALL A' DEM.
"HE KNEW WHO WOULD BE THERE AND HE KNEW EXACTLY WHAT HE NEEDED TO DO TO TAKE US ALL OUT, ONE-BY-ONE LIKE...

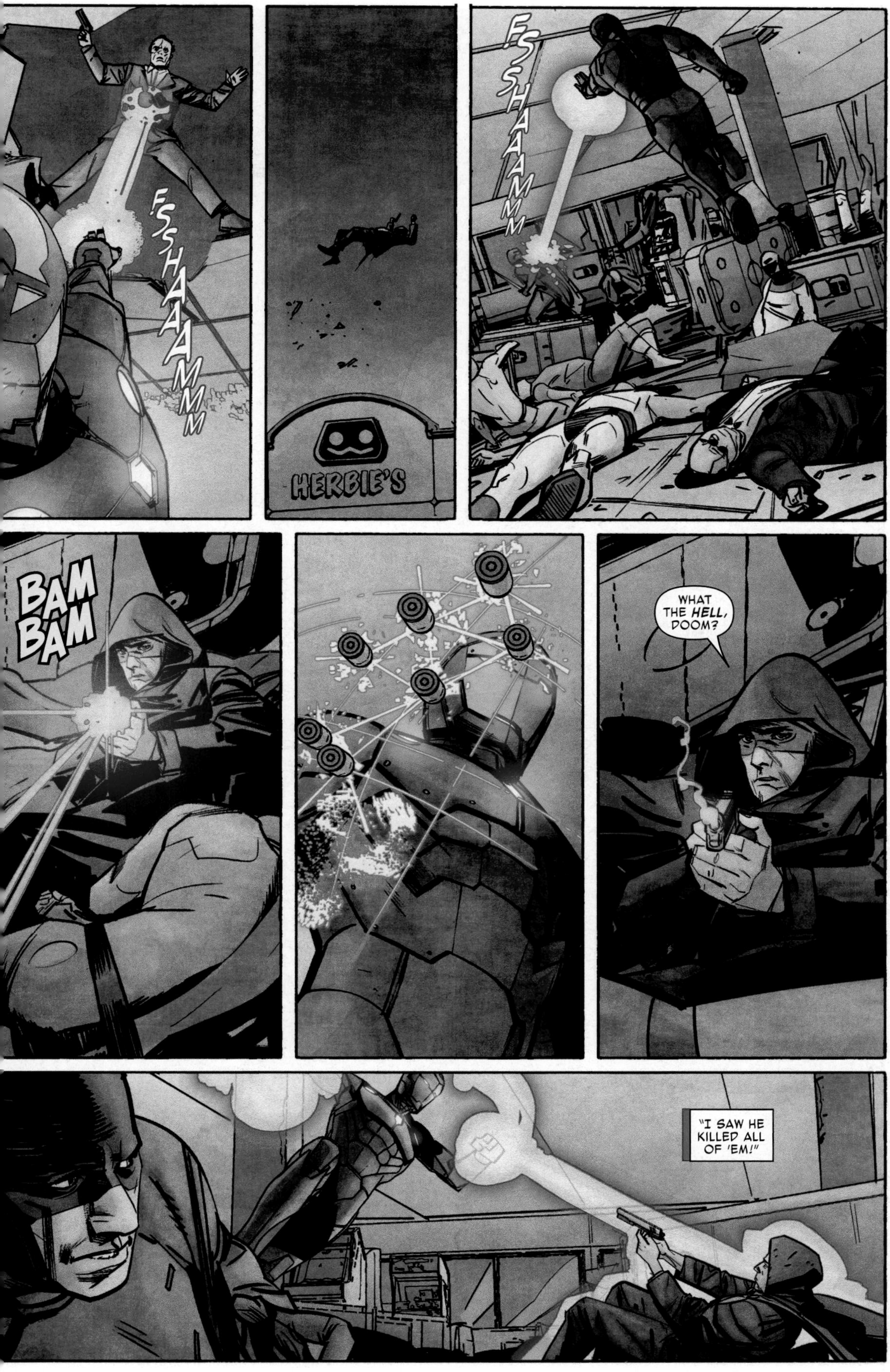
FSSHAAAAMMM
HERBIE'S
FSSHAAAAMMM
BAM BAM
WHAT THE HELL, DOOM?
"I SAW HE KILLED ALL OF 'EM!"

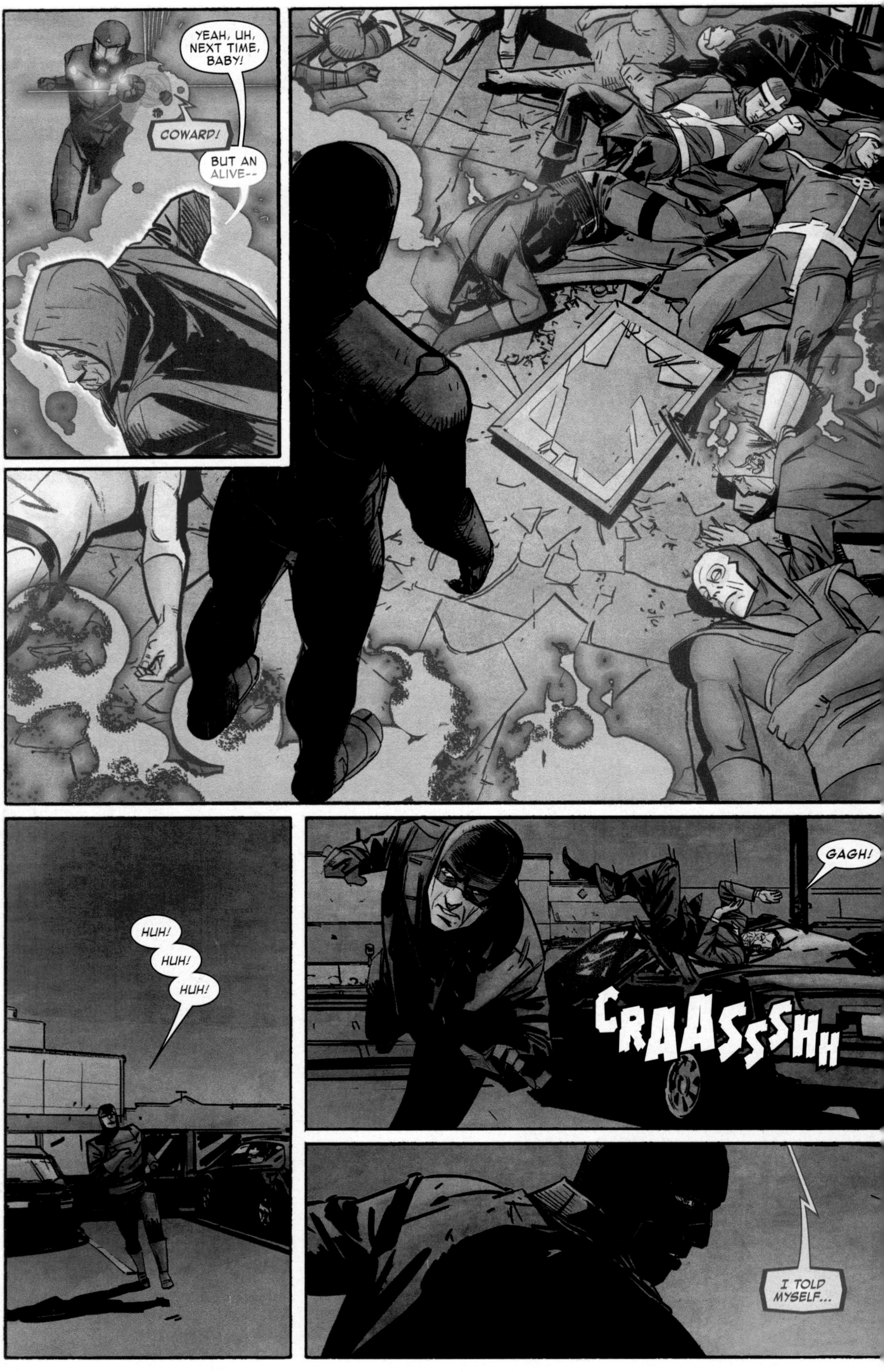
YEAH, UH, NEXT TIME, BABY!
COWARD!
BUT AN ALIVE--
HUH!
HUH!
HUH!
GAGH!
CRAASSSHH
I TOLD MYSELF...

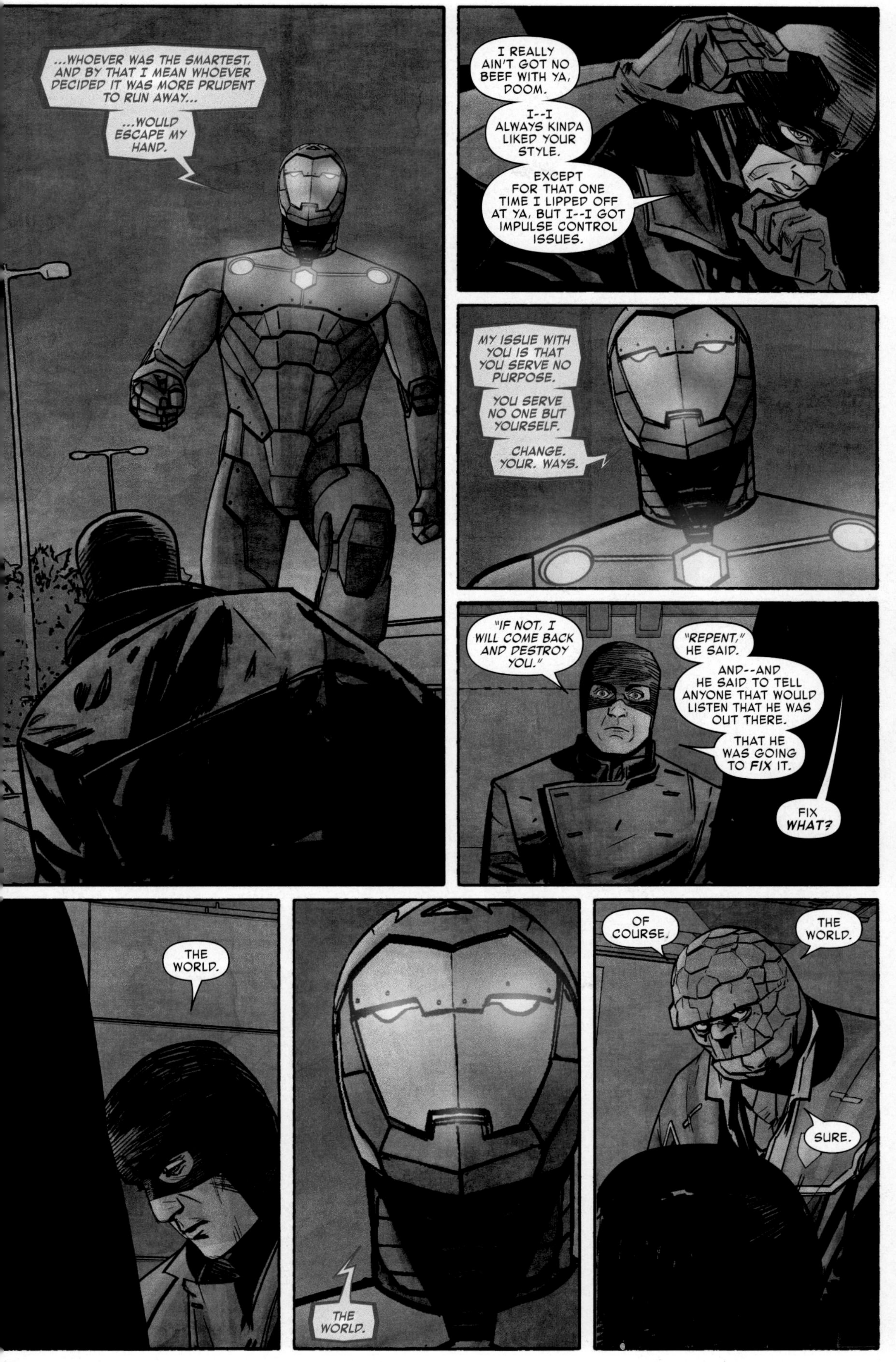
...WHOEVER WAS THE SMARTEST, AND BY THAT I MEAN WHOEVER DECIDED IT WAS MORE PRUDENT TO RUN AWAY...
...WOULD ESCAPE MY HAND.
I REALLY AIN'T GOT NO BEEF WITH YA, DOOM.
I--I ALWAYS KINDA LIKED YOUR STYLE.
EXCEPT FOR THAT ONE TIME I LIPPED OFF AT YA, BUT I--I GOT IMPULSE CONTROL ISSUES.
MY ISSUE WITH YOU IS THAT YOU SERVE NO PURPOSE.
YOU SERVE NO ONE BUT YOURSELF.
CHANGE. YOUR. WAYS.
"IF NOT, I WILL COME BACK AND DESTROY YOU."
"REPENT," HE SAID.
AND--AND HE SAID TO TELL ANYONE THAT WOULD LISTEN THAT HE WAS OUT THERE.
THAT HE WAS GOING TO FIX IT.
FIX WHAT?
THE WORLD.
THE WORLD.
OF COURSE.
THE WORLD.
SURE.

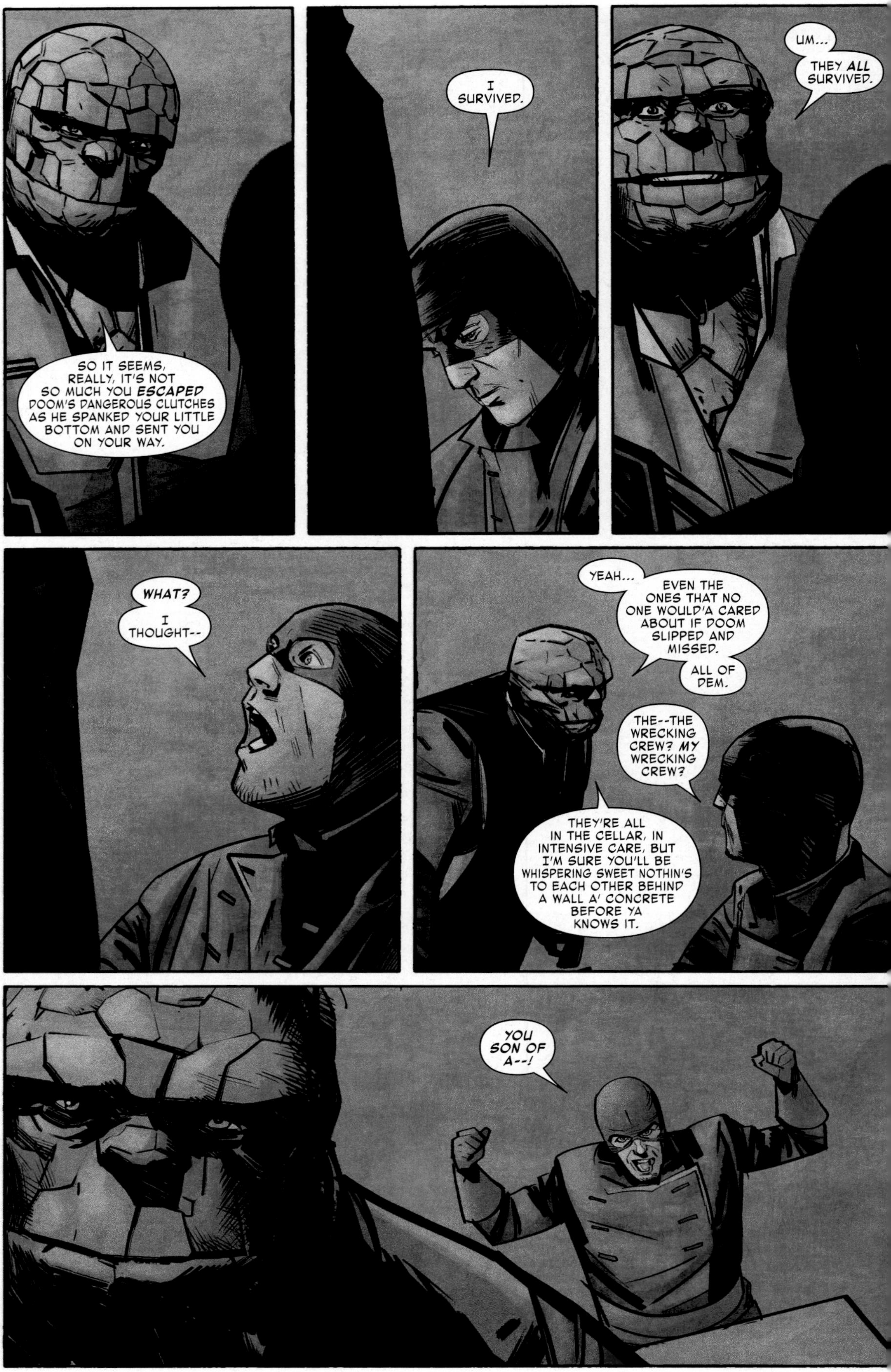

SO IT SEEMS, REALLY, IT'S NOT SO MUCH YOU *ESCAPED* DOOM'S DANGEROUS CLUTCHES AS HE SPANKED YOUR LITTLE BOTTOM AND SENT YOU ON YOUR WAY.
I SURVIVED.
UM...
THEY *ALL* SURVIVED.
WHAT?
I THOUGHT--
YEAH...
EVEN THE ONES THAT NO ONE WOULD'A CARED ABOUT IF DOOM SLIPPED AND MISSED.
ALL OF DEM.
THE--THE WRECKING CREW? *MY* WRECKING CREW?
THEY'RE ALL IN THE CELLAR, IN INTENSIVE CARE, BUT I'M SURE YOU'LL BE WHISPERING SWEET NOTHIN'S TO EACH OTHER BEHIND A WALL A' CONCRETE BEFORE YA KNOWS IT.
YOU SON OF A--!

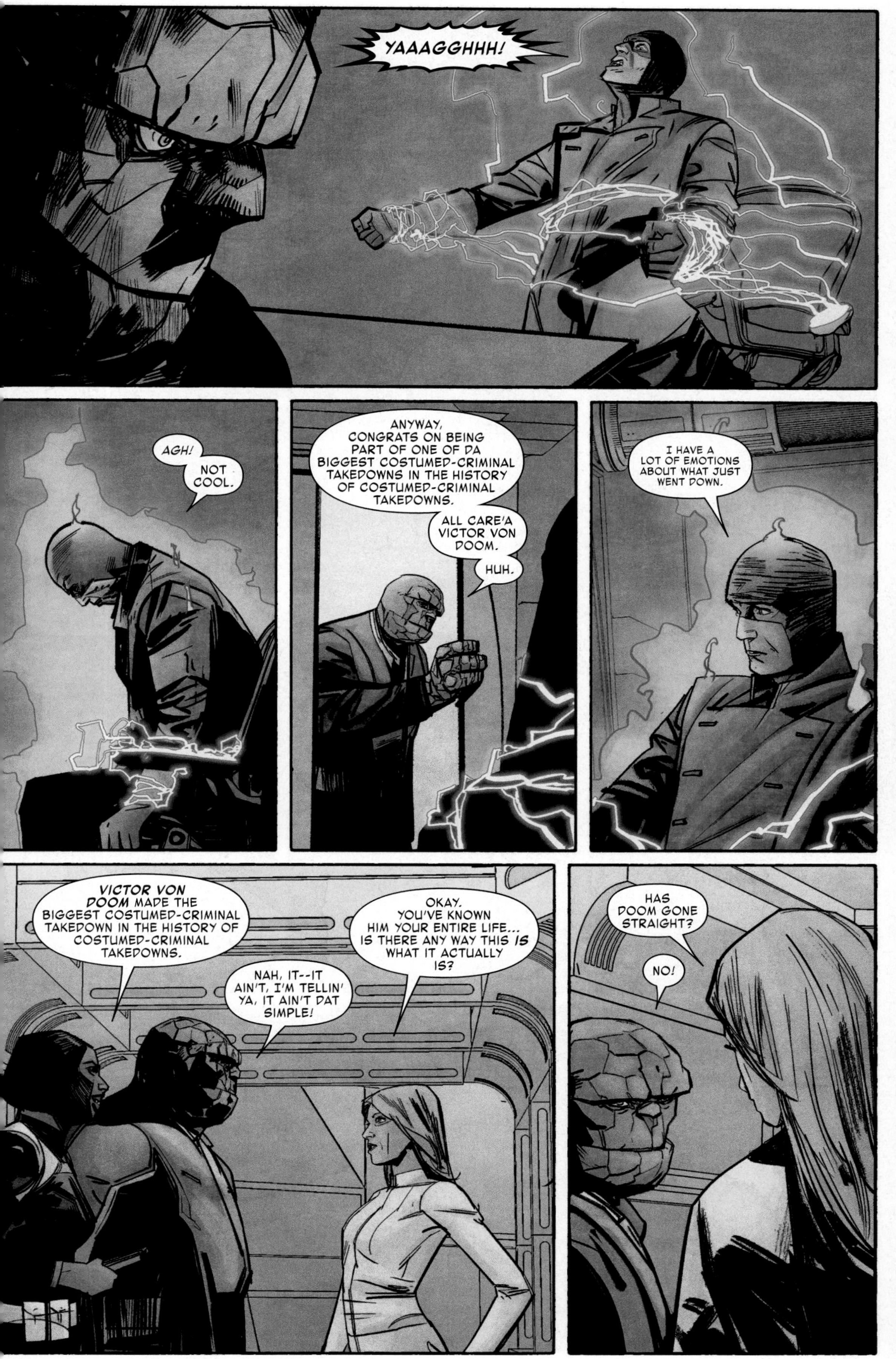
YAAAGGHHH!
AGH!
NOT COOL.
ANYWAY, CONGRATS ON BEING PART OF ONE OF DA BIGGEST COSTUMED-CRIMINAL TAKEDOWNS IN THE HISTORY OF COSTUMED-CRIMINAL TAKEDOWNS.
ALL CARE'A VICTOR VON DOOM.
HUH.
I HAVE A LOT OF EMOTIONS ABOUT WHAT JUST WENT DOWN.
VICTOR VON DOOM MADE THE BIGGEST COSTUMED-CRIMINAL TAKEDOWN IN THE HISTORY OF COSTUMED-CRIMINAL TAKEDOWNS.
NAH, IT--IT AIN'T, I'M TELLIN' YA, IT AIN'T DAT SIMPLE!
OKAY. YOU'VE KNOWN HIM YOUR ENTIRE LIFE... IS THERE ANY WAY THIS IS WHAT IT ACTUALLY IS?
HAS DOOM GONE STRAIGHT?
NO!

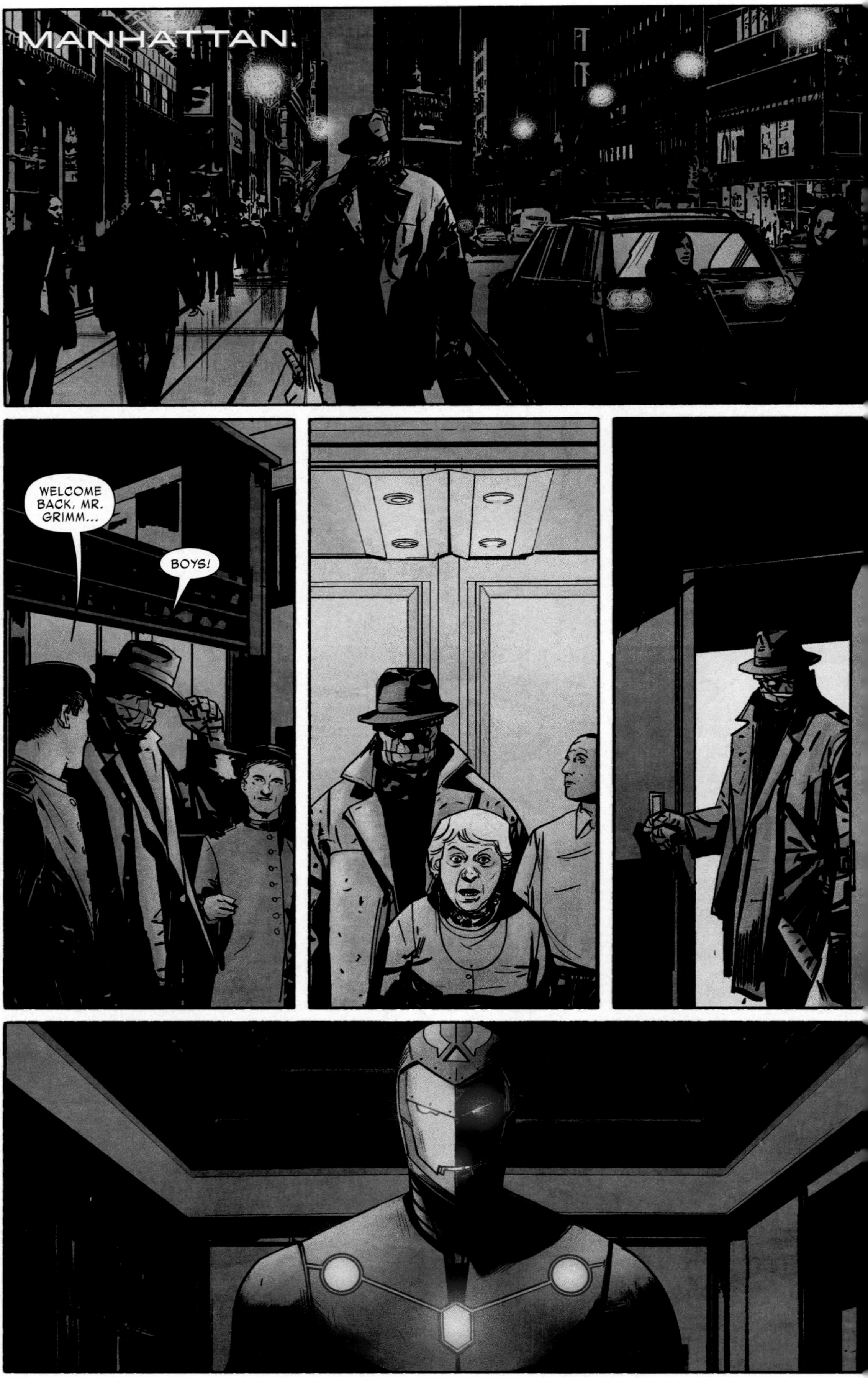
MANHATTAN.
NO STANDING ANYTIME
WELCOME BACK, MR. GRIMM...
BOYS!

OH, MY STARS AND GARTERS!

YOU ABSOLUTE PAIN IS THE TUCHAS!

FOR ONCE...KEEP YOUR TEMPER, GRIMM!

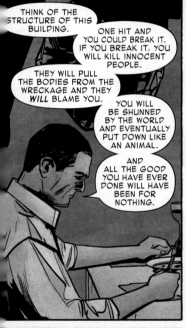

THINK OF THE STRUCTURE OF THIS BUILDING.

ONE HIT AND YOU COULD BREAK IT. IF YOU BREAK IT, YOU WILL KILL INNOCENT PEOPLE.

THEY WILL PULL THE BODIES FROM THE WRECKAGE AND THEY *WILL* BLAME YOU.

YOU WILL BE SHUNNED BY THE WORLD AND EVENTUALLY PUT DOWN LIKE AN ANIMAL.

AND ALL THE GOOD YOU HAVE EVER DONE WILL HAVE BEEN FOR NOTHING.

OKAY, GEEZ, YOU DON'T HAVE TO GET *SO* DESCRIPTIVE.

I WILL REIMBURSE YOU FOR THE ROOM SERVICE. I HAD NOT EATEN IN A WHILE.

IT SOMETIMES SLIPS MY MIND.

VIC, I KNOW YOU WEREN'T RAISED ALL NORMAL LIKE THE *REST* OF US, BUT YOU GOTTA KNOW THIS KIND OF THING, POPPIN' INTO PEOPLE'S WORLDS, ESPECIALLY PEOPLE LIKE ME WHO CAN'T STAND TA LOOK AT YA, IT'S NOT NORMAL.

I WOULD ARGUE THAT THERE IS NOTHING ABOUT THE TWO OF US THAT THE WORLD WOULD CONSIDER NORMAL.

WELL, OKAY.

BUT LISTEN-- YOU MAKE MY SKIN CRAWL, YOUR VOICE MAKES ME WANT TO PUNCH MY OWN FACE, AND EVERY TIME YOU LOOK AT ME WITH THAT SMUG STARE I REMEMBER EVERY @#$@#$ UP THING YOU EVER DID OR SAID, EVERY EVIL, SELFISH--

BENJAMIN. I'M SORRY.

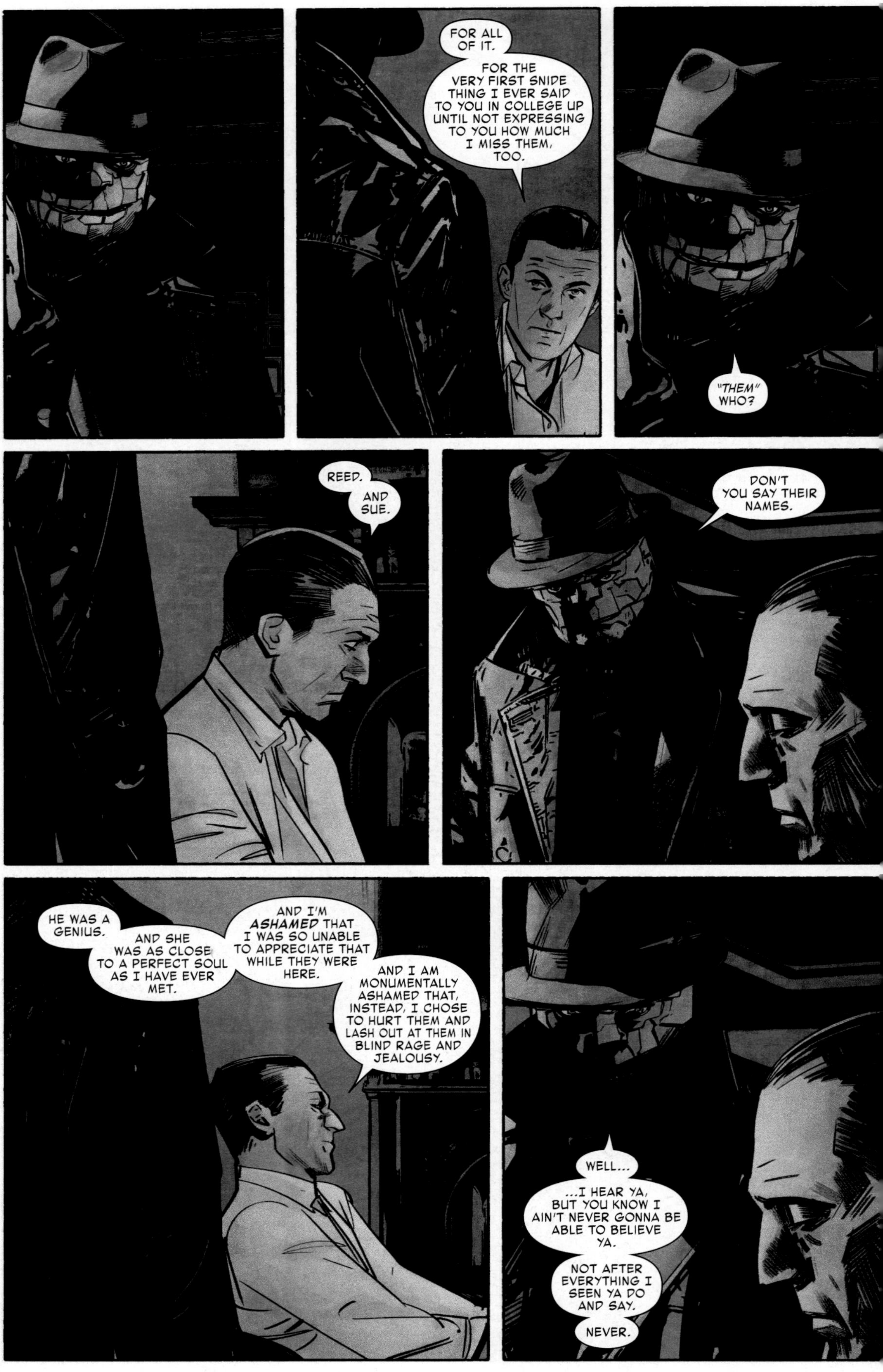
FOR ALL OF IT.
FOR THE VERY FIRST SNIDE THING I EVER SAID TO YOU IN COLLEGE UP UNTIL NOT EXPRESSING TO YOU HOW MUCH I MISS THEM, TOO.
"THEM" WHO?
REED.
AND SUE.
DON'T YOU SAY THEIR NAMES.
HE WAS A GENIUS.
AND SHE WAS AS CLOSE TO A PERFECT SOUL AS I HAVE EVER MET.
AND I'M ASHAMED THAT I WAS SO UNABLE TO APPRECIATE THAT WHILE THEY WERE HERE.
AND I AM MONUMENTALLY ASHAMED THAT, INSTEAD, I CHOSE TO HURT THEM AND LASH OUT AT THEM IN BLIND RAGE AND JEALOUSY.
WELL...
...I HEAR YA, BUT YOU KNOW I AIN'T NEVER GONNA BE ABLE TO BELIEVE YA.
NOT AFTER EVERYTHING I SEEN YA DO AND SAY.
NEVER.

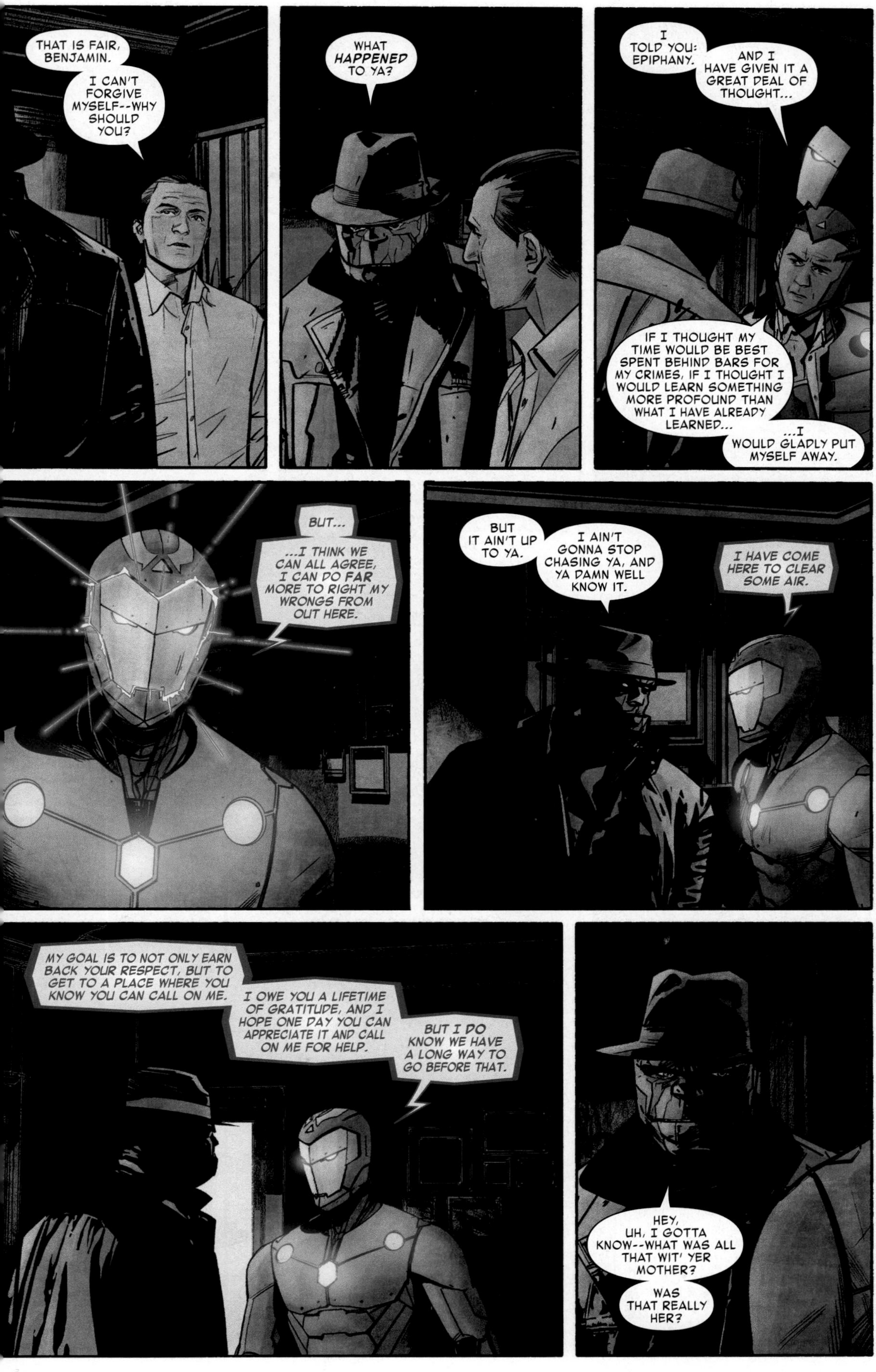
THAT IS FAIR, BENJAMIN.
I CAN'T FORGIVE MYSELF--WHY SHOULD YOU?
WHAT *HAPPENED* TO YA?
I TOLD YOU: EPIPHANY.
AND I HAVE GIVEN IT A GREAT DEAL OF THOUGHT...
IF I THOUGHT MY TIME WOULD BE BEST SPENT BEHIND BARS FOR MY CRIMES, IF I THOUGHT I WOULD LEARN SOMETHING MORE PROFOUND THAN WHAT I HAVE ALREADY LEARNED...
...I WOULD GLADLY PUT MYSELF AWAY.
BUT...
...I THINK WE CAN ALL AGREE, I CAN DO **FAR** MORE TO RIGHT MY WRONGS FROM OUT HERE.
BUT IT AIN'T UP TO YA.
I AIN'T GONNA STOP CHASING YA, AND YA DAMN WELL KNOW IT.
I HAVE COME HERE TO CLEAR SOME AIR.
MY GOAL IS TO NOT ONLY EARN BACK YOUR RESPECT, BUT TO GET TO A PLACE WHERE YOU KNOW YOU CAN CALL ON ME.
I OWE YOU A LIFETIME OF GRATITUDE, AND I HOPE ONE DAY YOU CAN APPRECIATE IT AND CALL ON ME FOR HELP.
BUT I DO KNOW WE HAVE A LONG WAY TO GO BEFORE THAT.
HEY, UH, I GOTTA KNOW--WHAT WAS ALL THAT WIT' YER MOTHER?
WAS THAT REALLY HER?

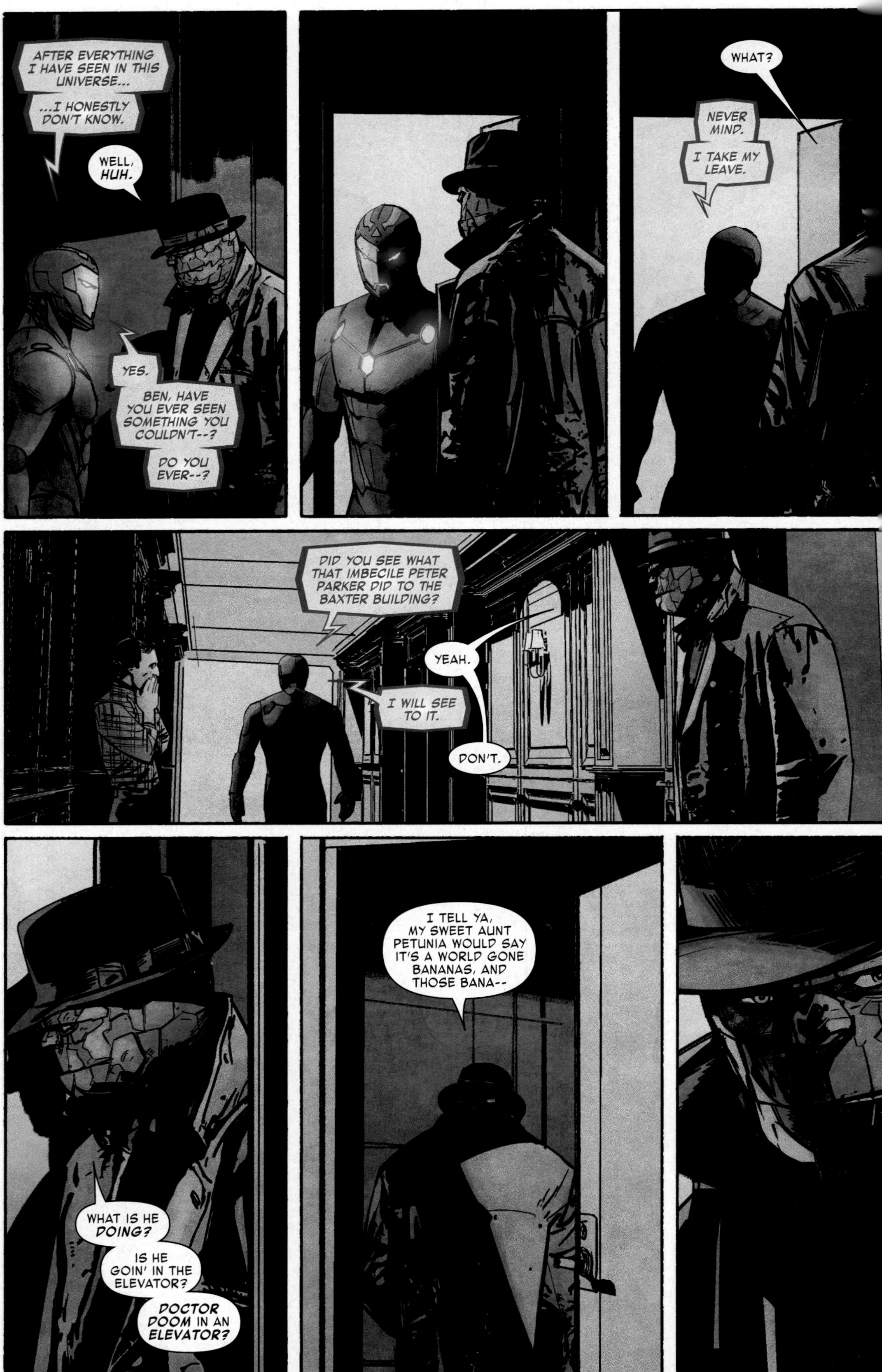
AFTER EVERYTHING I HAVE SEEN IN THIS UNIVERSE...
...I HONESTLY DON'T KNOW.
WELL, HUH.
YES.
BEN, HAVE YOU EVER SEEN SOMETHING YOU COULDN'T--?
DO YOU EVER--?
WHAT?
NEVER MIND.
I TAKE MY LEAVE.
DID YOU SEE WHAT THAT IMBECILE PETER PARKER DID TO THE BAXTER BUILDING?
YEAH.
I WILL SEE TO IT.
DON'T.
WHAT IS HE DOING?
IS HE GOIN' IN THE ELEVATOR?
DOCTOR DOOM IN AN ELEVATOR?
I TELL YA, MY SWEET AUNT PETUNIA WOULD SAY IT'S A WORLD GONE BANANAS, AND THOSE BANA--

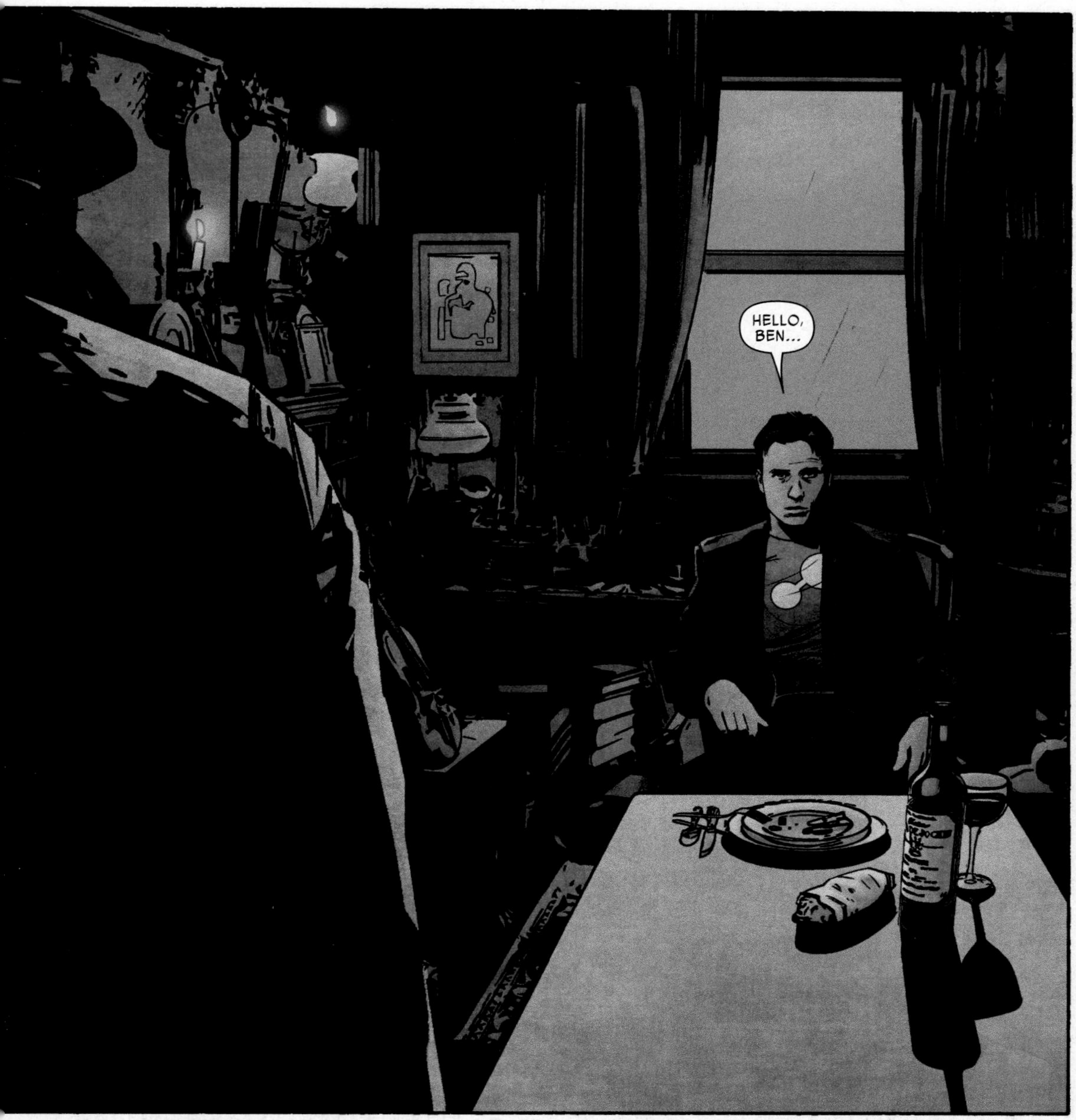
HELLO, BEN...

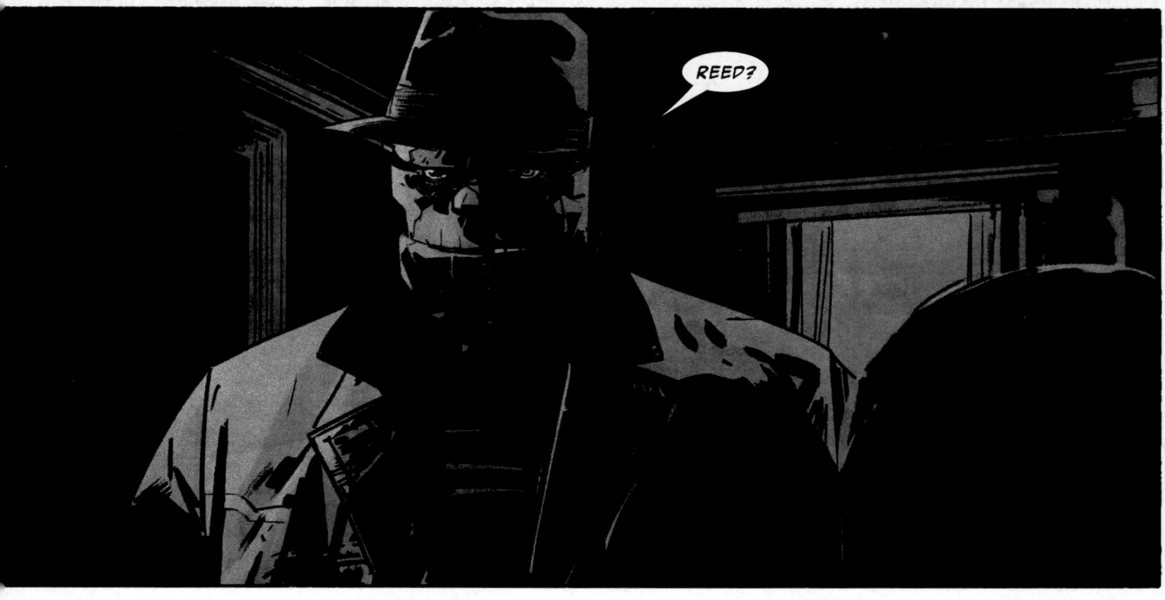
REED?

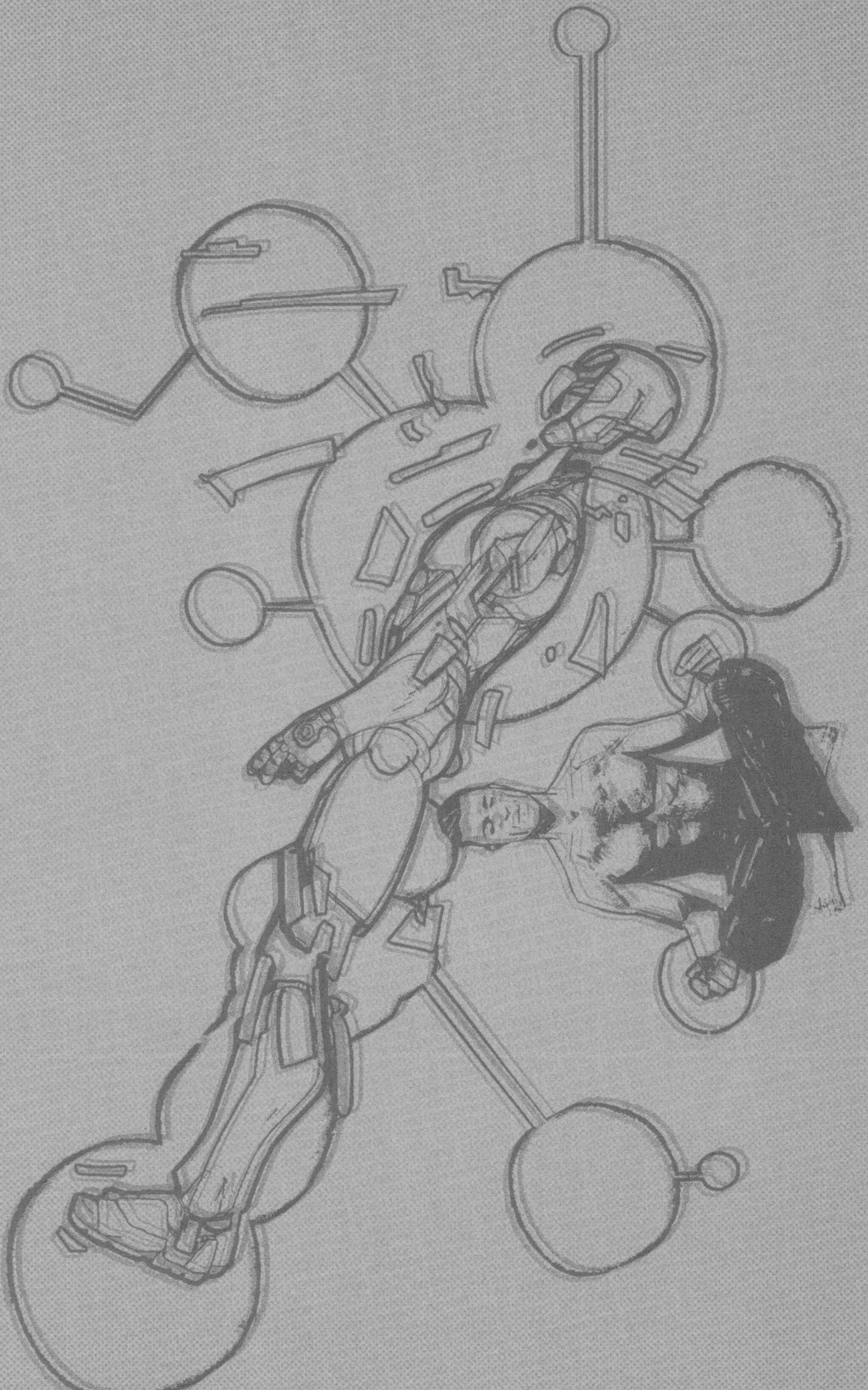

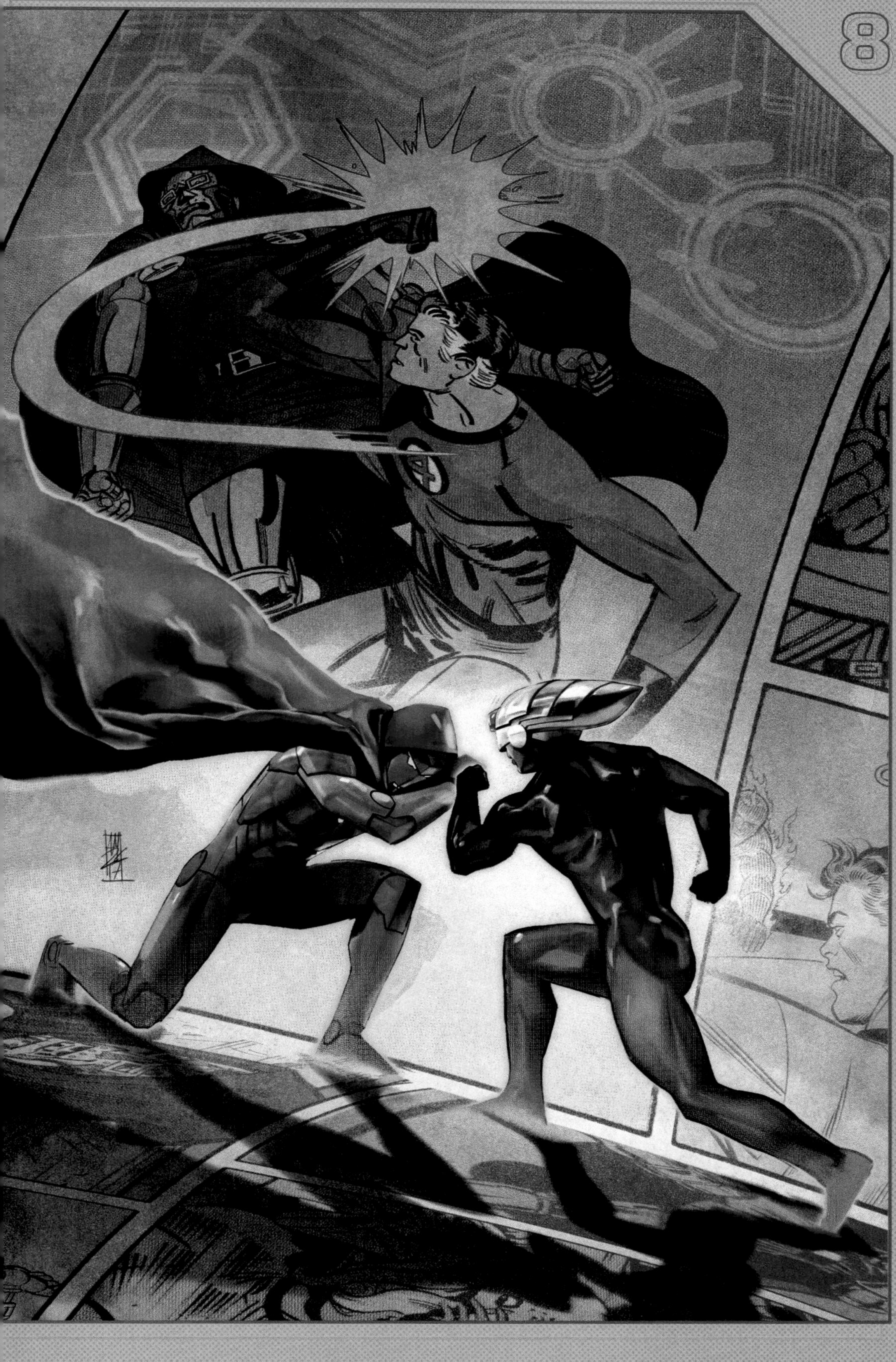
8

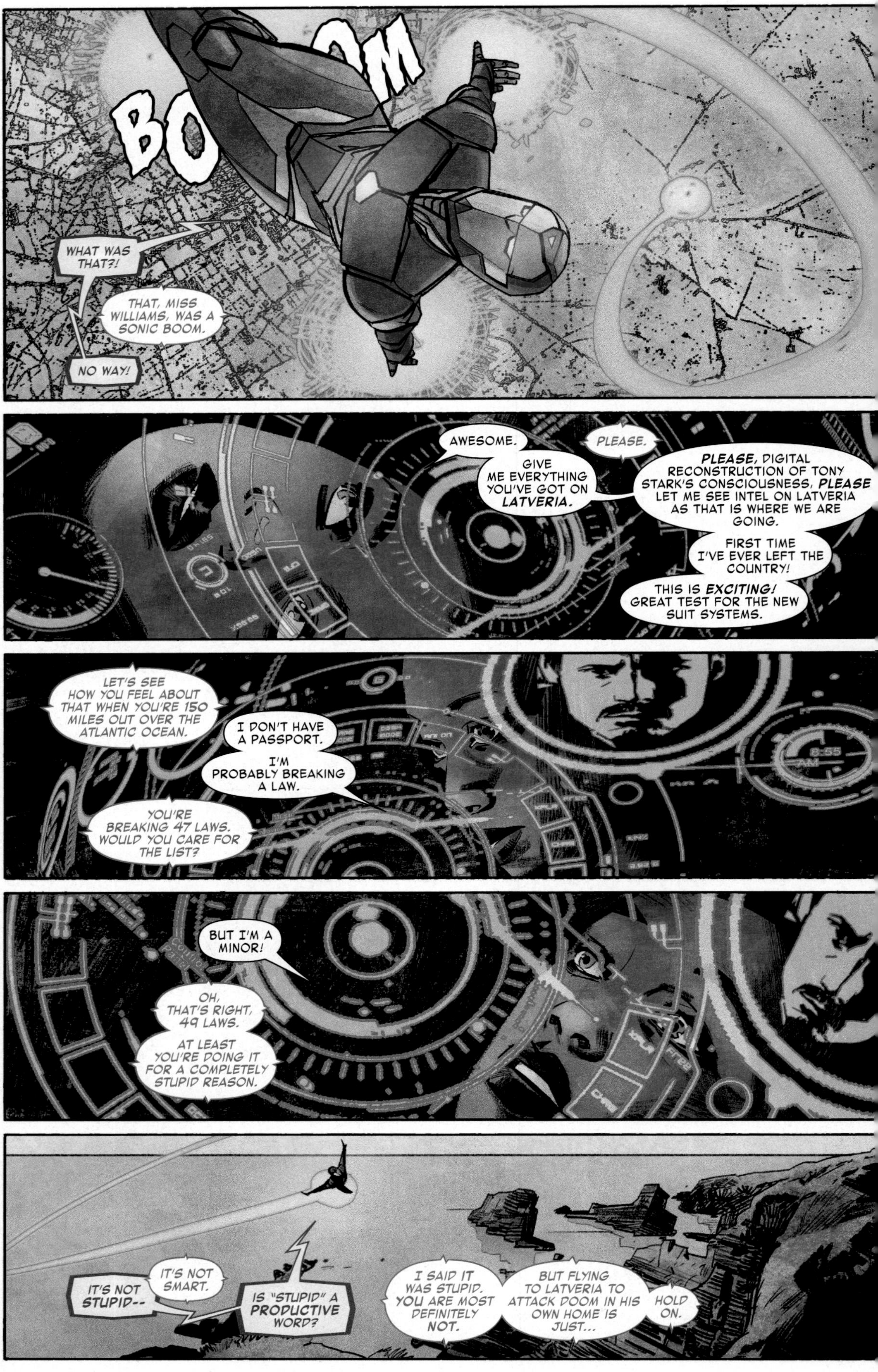
BOOM
WHAT WAS THAT?!
THAT, MISS WILLIAMS, WAS A SONIC BOOM.
NO WAY!
AWESOME.
GIVE ME EVERYTHING YOU'VE GOT ON LATVERIA.
PLEASE.
PLEASE, DIGITAL RECONSTRUCTION OF TONY STARK'S CONSCIOUSNESS, PLEASE LET ME SEE INTEL ON LATVERIA AS THAT IS WHERE WE ARE GOING.
FIRST TIME I'VE EVER LEFT THE COUNTRY!
THIS IS EXCITING! GREAT TEST FOR THE NEW SUIT SYSTEMS.
LET'S SEE HOW YOU FEEL ABOUT THAT WHEN YOU'RE 150 MILES OUT OVER THE ATLANTIC OCEAN.
I DON'T HAVE A PASSPORT.
I'M PROBABLY BREAKING A LAW.
YOU'RE BREAKING 47 LAWS. WOULD YOU CARE FOR THE LIST?
BUT I'M A MINOR!
OH, THAT'S RIGHT, 49 LAWS.
AT LEAST YOU'RE DOING IT FOR A COMPLETELY STUPID REASON.
IT'S NOT STUPID--
IT'S NOT SMART.
IS "STUPID" A PRODUCTIVE WORD?
I SAID IT WAS STUPID. YOU ARE MOST DEFINITELY NOT.
BUT FLYING TO LATVERIA TO ATTACK DOOM IN HIS OWN HOME IS JUST...
HOLD ON.

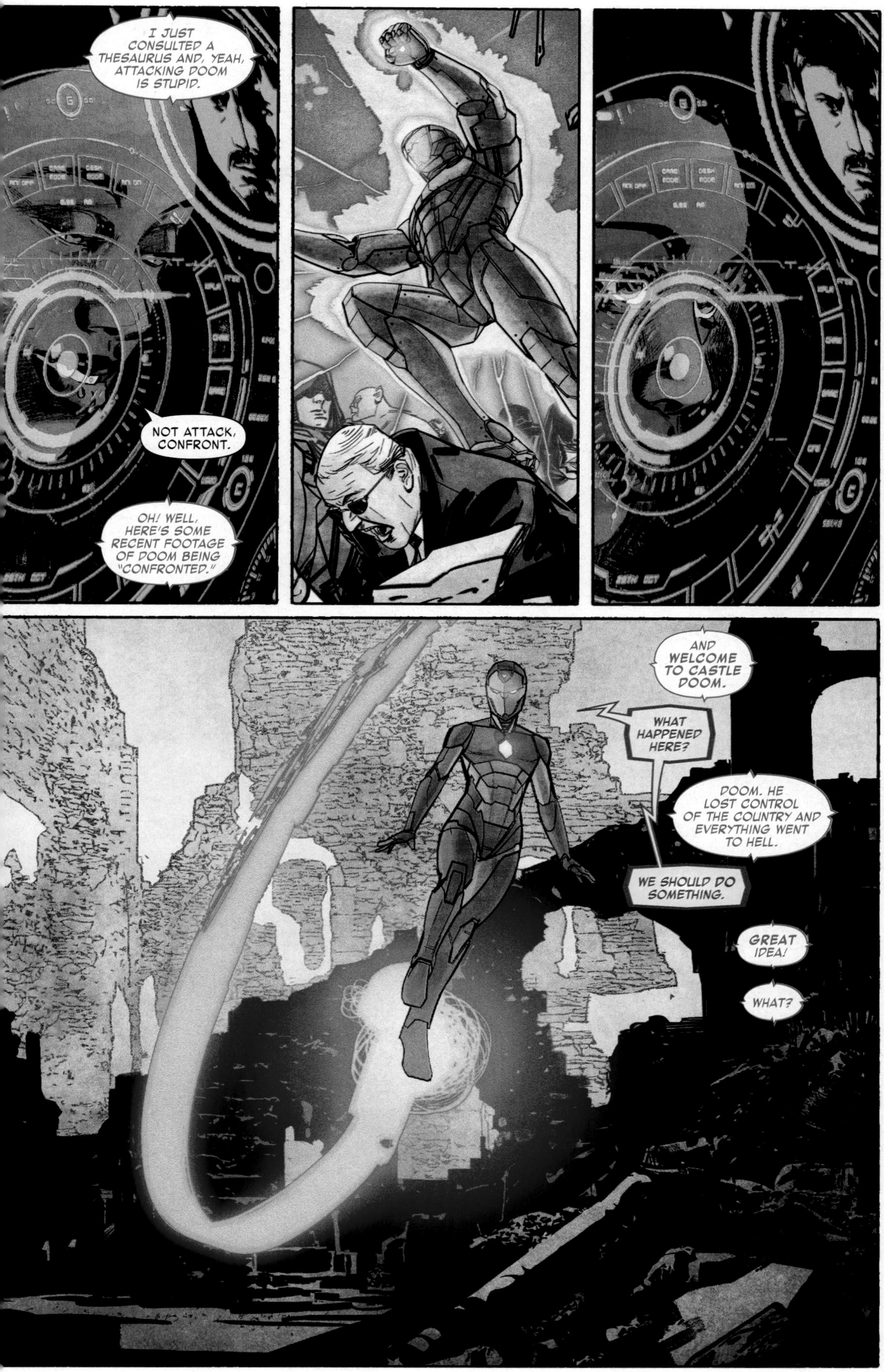
I JUST CONSULTED A THESAURUS AND, YEAH, ATTACKING DOOM IS STUPID.
NOT ATTACK, CONFRONT.
OH! WELL, HERE'S SOME RECENT FOOTAGE OF DOOM BEING "CONFRONTED."
AND WELCOME TO CASTLE DOOM.
WHAT HAPPENED HERE?
DOOM. HE LOST CONTROL OF THE COUNTRY AND EVERYTHING WENT TO HELL.
WE SHOULD DO SOMETHING.
GREAT IDEA!
WHAT?

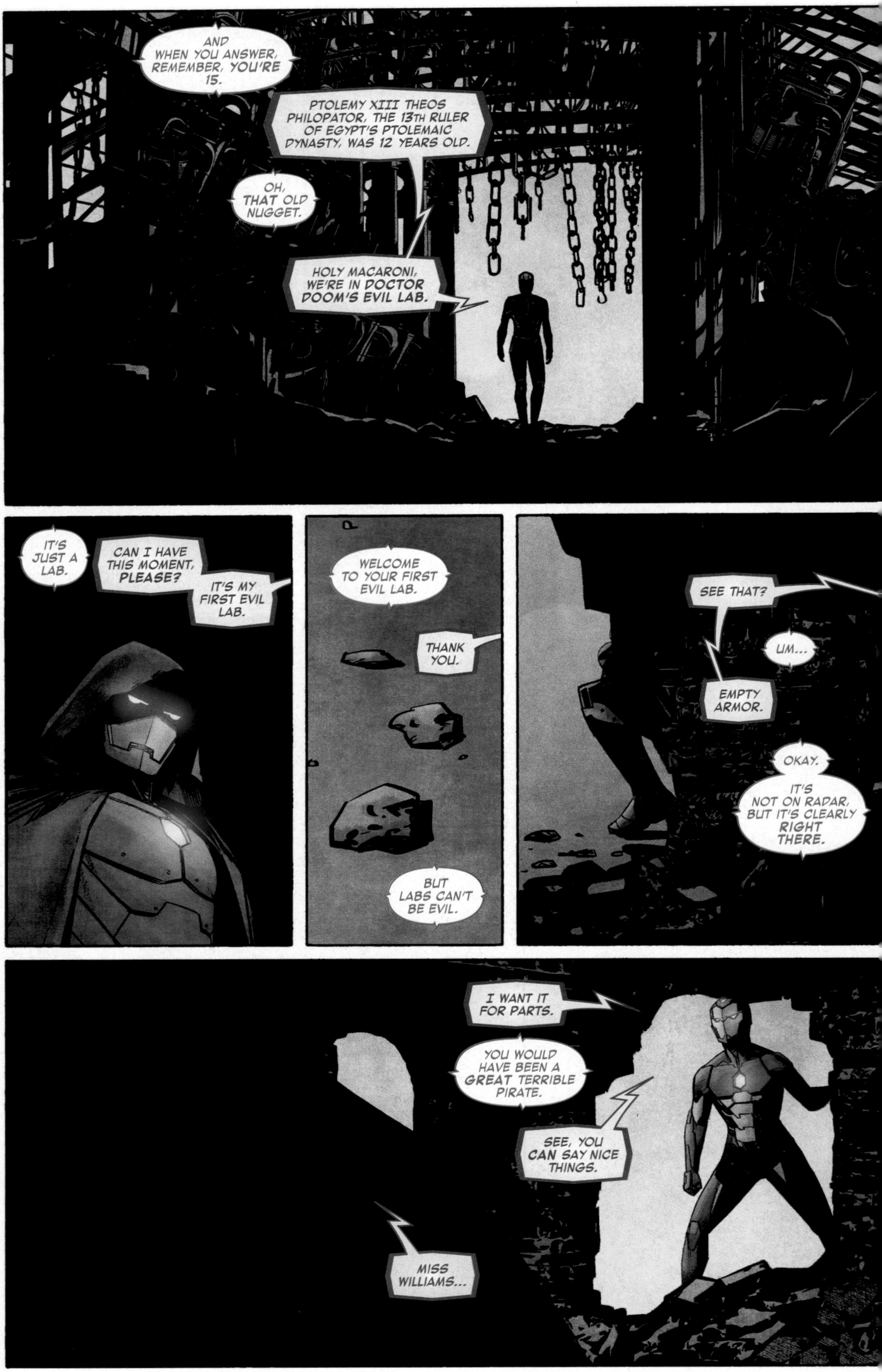
AND WHEN YOU ANSWER, REMEMBER, YOU'RE 15.
PTOLEMY XIII THEOS PHILOPATOR, THE 13TH RULER OF EGYPT'S PTOLEMAIC DYNASTY, WAS 12 YEARS OLD.
OH, THAT OLD NUGGET.
HOLY MACARONI, WE'RE IN DOCTOR DOOM'S EVIL LAB.
IT'S JUST A LAB.
CAN I HAVE THIS MOMENT, PLEASE?
IT'S MY FIRST EVIL LAB.
WELCOME TO YOUR FIRST EVIL LAB.
THANK YOU.
BUT LABS CAN'T BE EVIL.
SEE THAT?
UM...
EMPTY ARMOR.
OKAY.
IT'S NOT ON RADAR, BUT IT'S CLEARLY RIGHT THERE.
I WANT IT FOR PARTS.
YOU WOULD HAVE BEEN A GREAT TERRIBLE PIRATE.
SEE, YOU CAN SAY NICE THINGS.
MISS WILLIAMS...

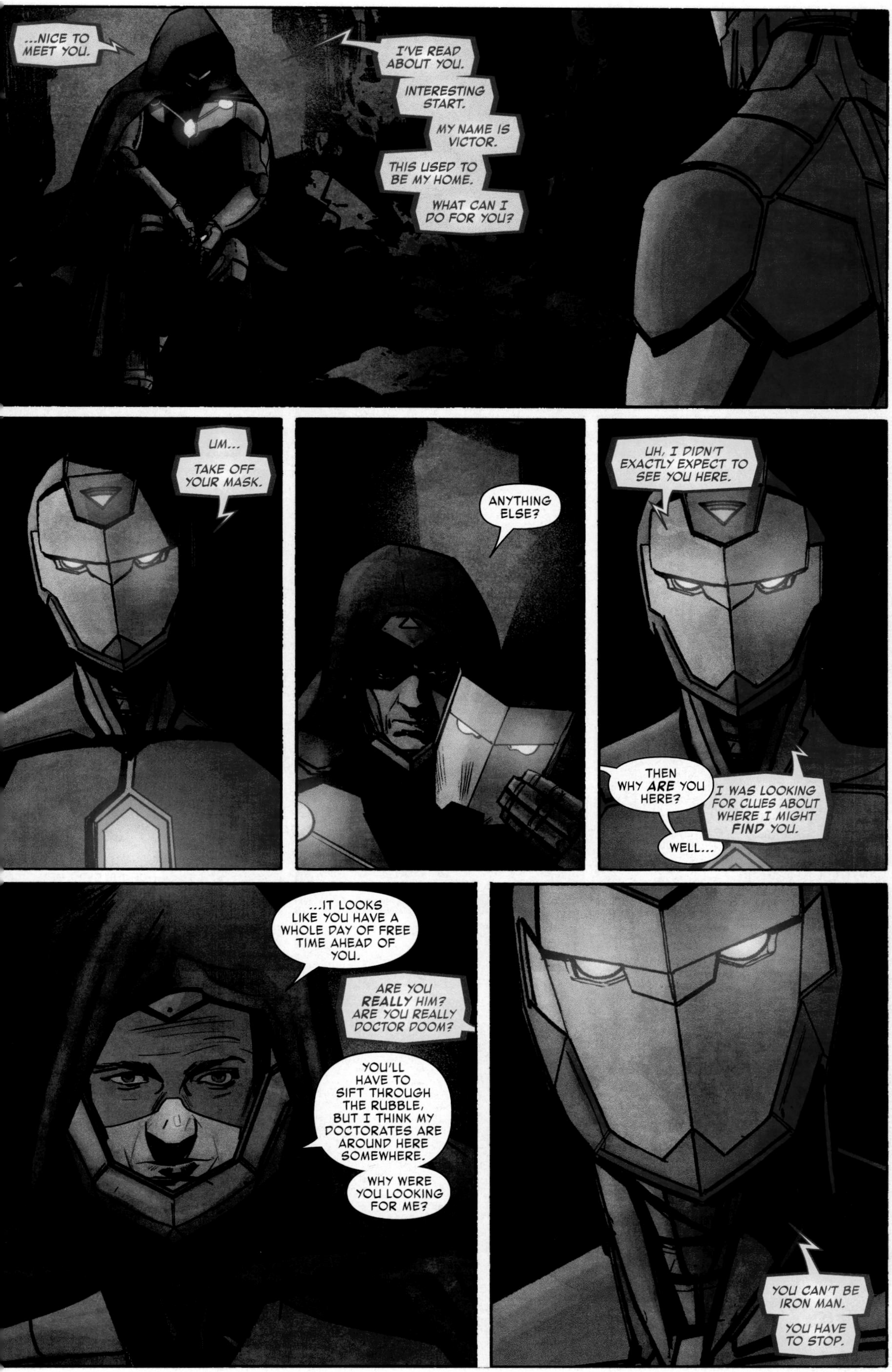

...NICE TO MEET YOU.
I'VE READ ABOUT YOU.
INTERESTING START.
MY NAME IS VICTOR.
THIS USED TO BE MY HOME.
WHAT CAN I DO FOR YOU?
UM...
TAKE OFF YOUR MASK.
ANYTHING ELSE?
UH, I DIDN'T EXACTLY EXPECT TO SEE YOU HERE.
THEN WHY ARE YOU HERE?
I WAS LOOKING FOR CLUES ABOUT WHERE I MIGHT FIND YOU.
WELL...
...IT LOOKS LIKE YOU HAVE A WHOLE DAY OF FREE TIME AHEAD OF YOU.
ARE YOU REALLY HIM? ARE YOU REALLY DOCTOR DOOM?
YOU'LL HAVE TO SIFT THROUGH THE RUBBLE, BUT I THINK MY DOCTORATES ARE AROUND HERE SOMEWHERE.
WHY WERE YOU LOOKING FOR ME?
YOU CAN'T BE IRON MAN.
YOU HAVE TO STOP.

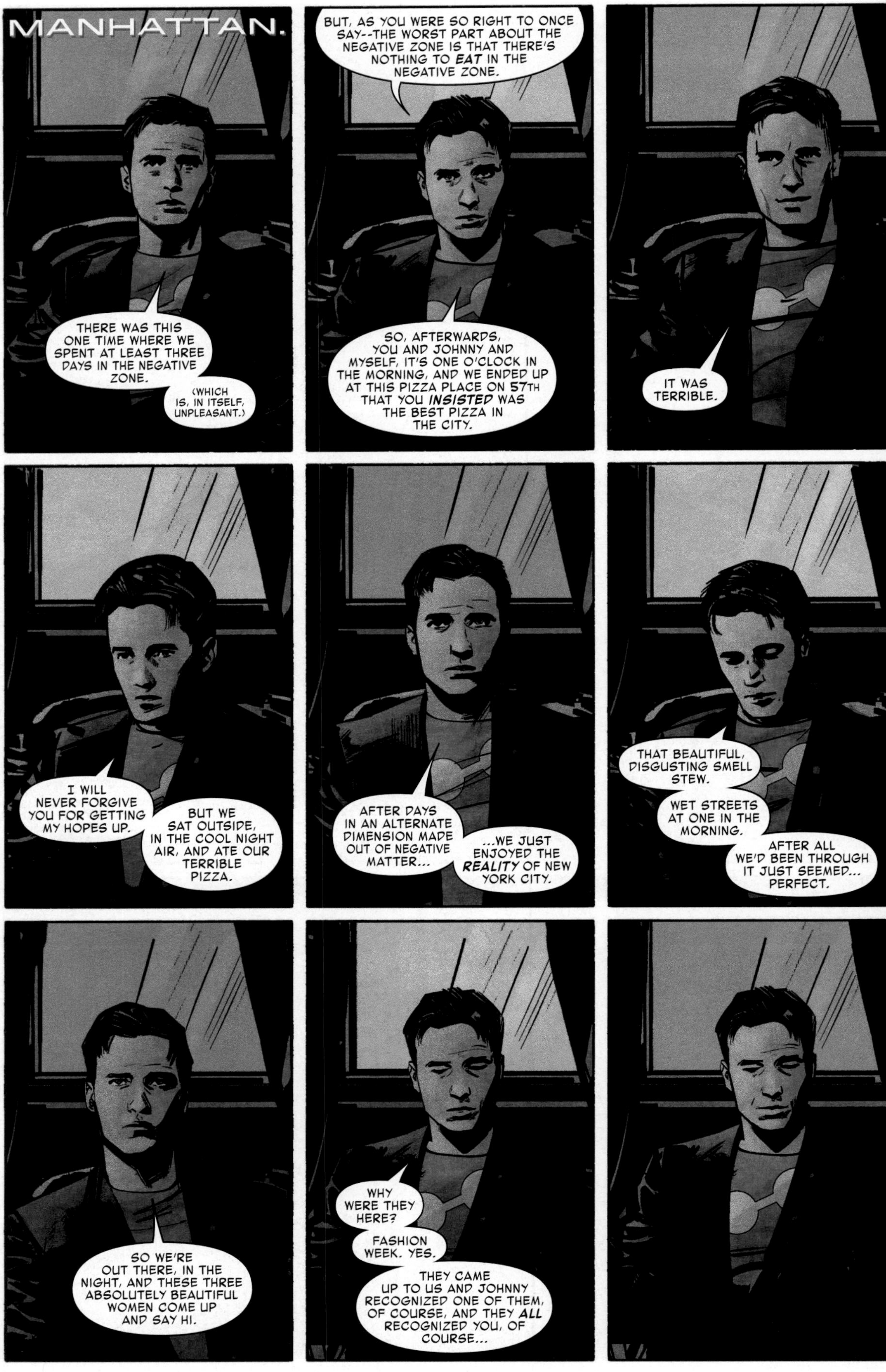
MANHATTAN.
THERE WAS THIS ONE TIME WHERE WE SPENT AT LEAST THREE DAYS IN THE NEGATIVE ZONE.
(WHICH IS, IN ITSELF, UNPLEASANT.)
BUT, AS YOU WERE SO RIGHT TO ONCE SAY--THE WORST PART ABOUT THE NEGATIVE ZONE IS THAT THERE'S NOTHING TO EAT IN THE NEGATIVE ZONE.
SO, AFTERWARDS, YOU AND JOHNNY AND MYSELF, IT'S ONE O'CLOCK IN THE MORNING, AND WE ENDED UP AT THIS PIZZA PLACE ON 57TH THAT YOU INSISTED WAS THE BEST PIZZA IN THE CITY.
IT WAS TERRIBLE.
I WILL NEVER FORGIVE YOU FOR GETTING MY HOPES UP.
BUT WE SAT OUTSIDE, IN THE COOL NIGHT AIR, AND ATE OUR TERRIBLE PIZZA.
AFTER DAYS IN AN ALTERNATE DIMENSION MADE OUT OF NEGATIVE MATTER...
...WE JUST ENJOYED THE REALITY OF NEW YORK CITY.
THAT BEAUTIFUL, DISGUSTING SMELL STEW.
WET STREETS AT ONE IN THE MORNING.
AFTER ALL WE'D BEEN THROUGH IT JUST SEEMED... PERFECT.
SO WE'RE OUT THERE, IN THE NIGHT, AND THESE THREE ABSOLUTELY BEAUTIFUL WOMEN COME UP AND SAY HI.
WHY WERE THEY HERE?
FASHION WEEK. YES.
THEY CAME UP TO US AND JOHNNY RECOGNIZED ONE OF THEM, OF COURSE, AND THEY ALL RECOGNIZED YOU, OF COURSE...

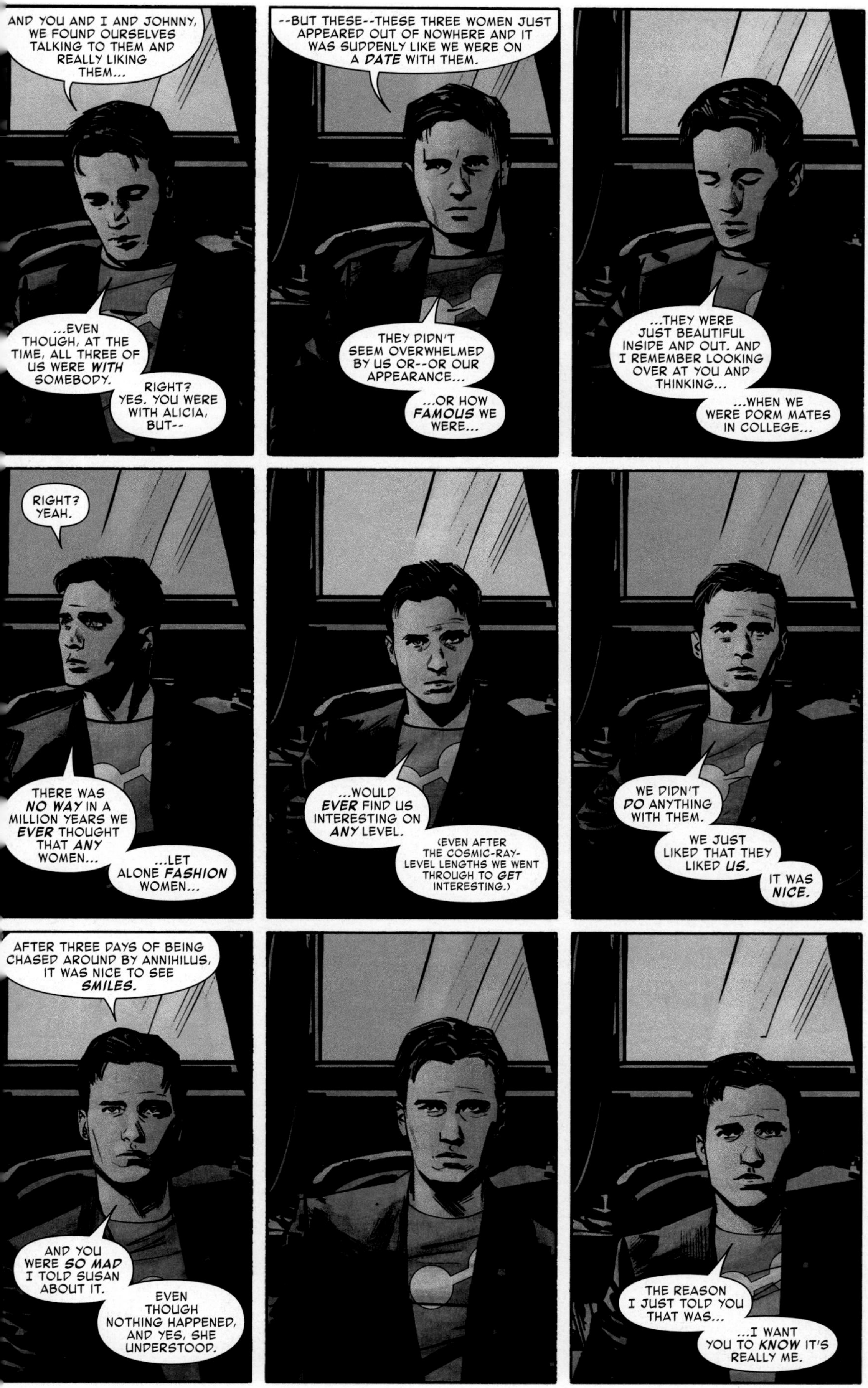
AND YOU AND I AND JOHNNY, WE FOUND OURSELVES TALKING TO THEM AND REALLY LIKING THEM...
...EVEN THOUGH, AT THE TIME, ALL THREE OF US WERE *WITH* SOMEBODY.
RIGHT? YES. YOU WERE WITH ALICIA, BUT--
--BUT THESE--THESE THREE WOMEN JUST APPEARED OUT OF NOWHERE AND IT WAS SUDDENLY LIKE WE WERE ON A *DATE* WITH THEM.
THEY DIDN'T SEEM OVERWHELMED BY US OR--OR OUR APPEARANCE...
...OR HOW *FAMOUS* WE WERE...
...THEY WERE JUST BEAUTIFUL INSIDE AND OUT. AND I REMEMBER LOOKING OVER AT YOU AND THINKING...
...WHEN WE WERE DORM MATES IN COLLEGE...
RIGHT? YEAH.
THERE WAS *NO WAY* IN A MILLION YEARS WE *EVER* THOUGHT THAT *ANY* WOMEN...
...LET ALONE *FASHION* WOMEN...
...WOULD *EVER* FIND US INTERESTING ON *ANY* LEVEL.
(EVEN AFTER THE COSMIC-RAY-LEVEL LENGTHS WE WENT THROUGH TO *GET* INTERESTING.)
WE DIDN'T *DO* ANYTHING WITH THEM.
WE JUST LIKED THAT THEY LIKED *US.*
IT WAS *NICE.*
AFTER THREE DAYS OF BEING CHASED AROUND BY ANNIHILUS, IT WAS NICE TO SEE *SMILES.*
AND YOU WERE *SO MAD* I TOLD SUSAN ABOUT IT.
EVEN THOUGH NOTHING HAPPENED, AND YES, SHE UNDERSTOOD.
THE REASON I JUST TOLD YOU THAT WAS...
...I WANT YOU TO *KNOW* IT'S REALLY ME.

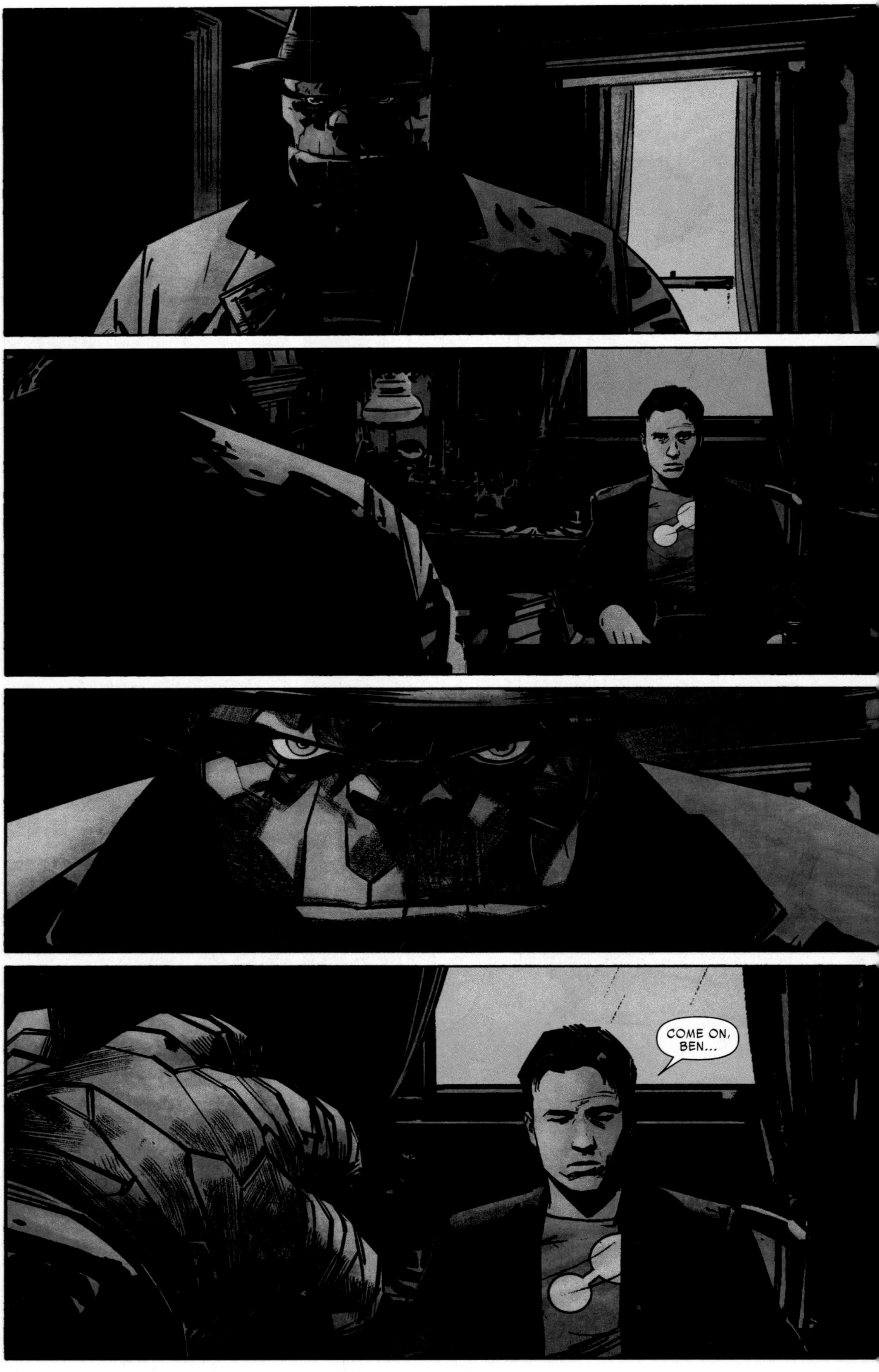
COME ON, BEN...

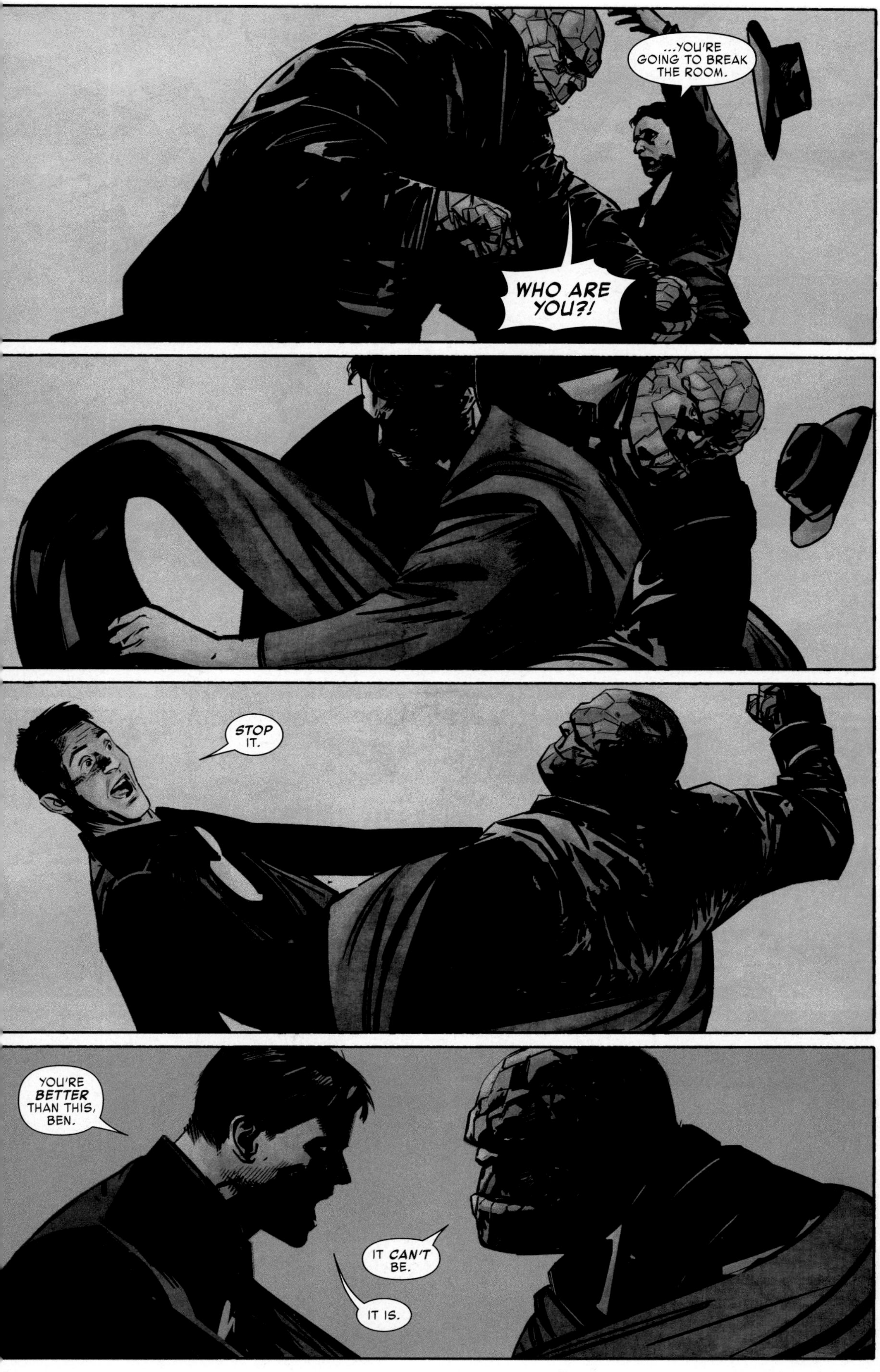
...YOU'RE GOING TO BREAK THE ROOM.
WHO ARE YOU?!
STOP IT.
YOU'RE BETTER THAN THIS, BEN.
IT CAN'T BE.
IT IS.

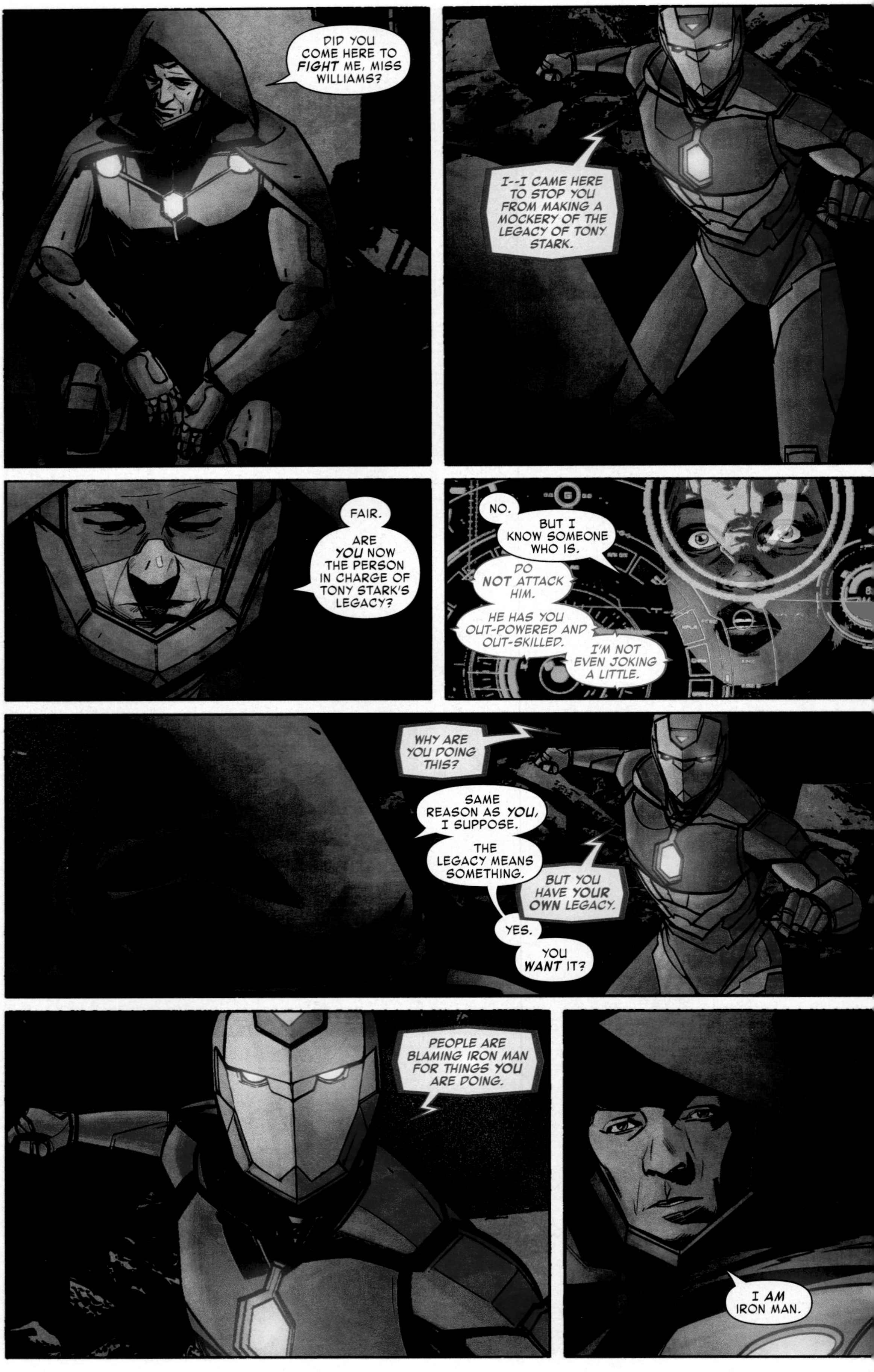

DID YOU COME HERE TO FIGHT ME, MISS WILLIAMS?
I--I CAME HERE TO STOP YOU FROM MAKING A MOCKERY OF THE LEGACY OF TONY STARK.
FAIR.
ARE YOU NOW THE PERSON IN CHARGE OF TONY STARK'S LEGACY?
NO.
BUT I KNOW SOMEONE WHO IS.
DO NOT ATTACK HIM.
HE HAS YOU OUT-POWERED AND OUT-SKILLED.
I'M NOT EVEN JOKING A LITTLE.
WHY ARE YOU DOING THIS?
SAME REASON AS YOU, I SUPPOSE.
THE LEGACY MEANS SOMETHING.
BUT YOU HAVE YOUR OWN LEGACY.
YES.
YOU WANT IT?
PEOPLE ARE BLAMING IRON MAN FOR THINGS YOU ARE DOING.
I AM IRON MAN.

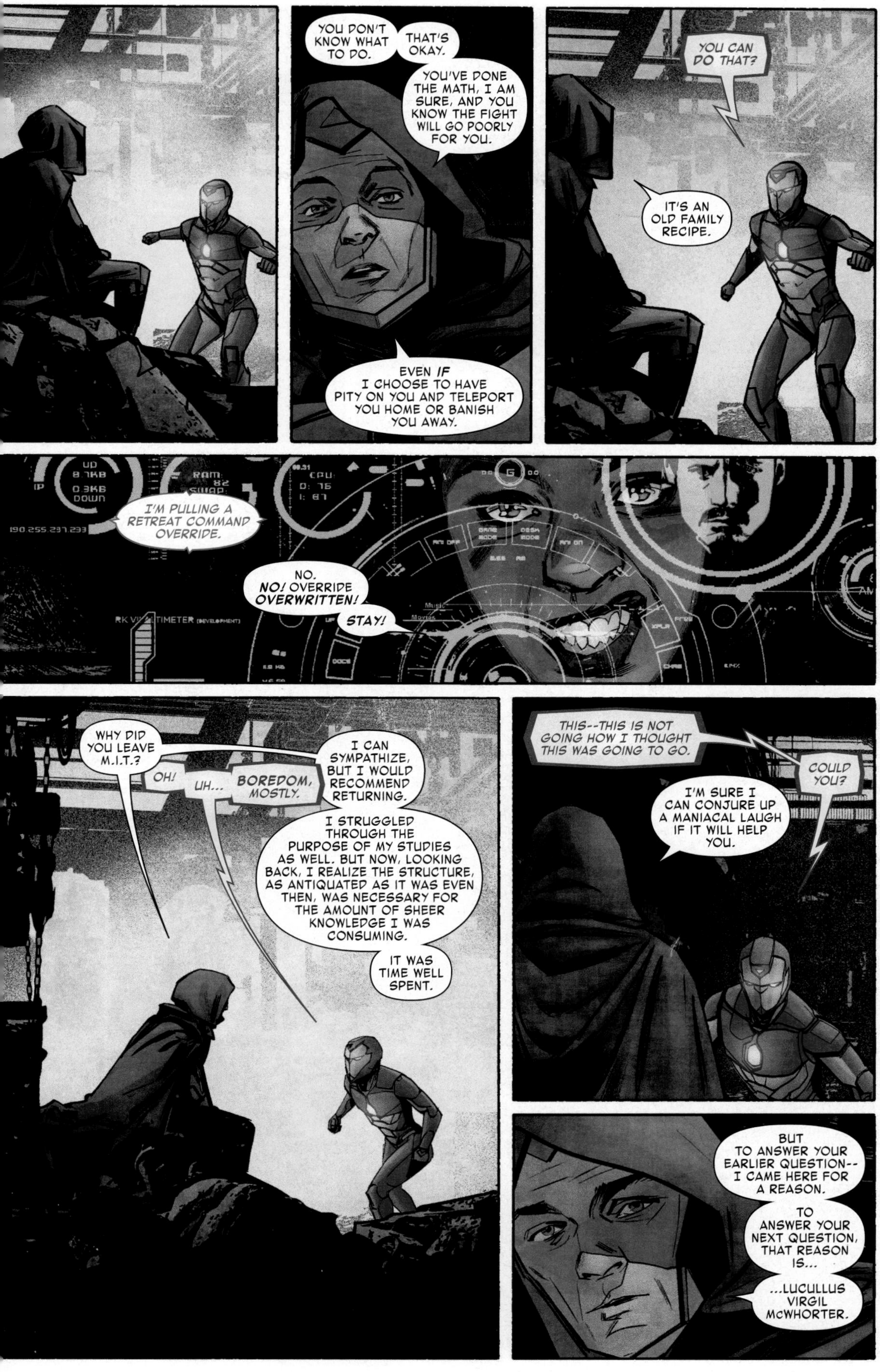
YOU DON'T KNOW WHAT TO DO.
THAT'S OKAY.
YOU'VE DONE THE MATH, I AM SURE, AND YOU KNOW THE FIGHT WILL GO POORLY FOR YOU.
EVEN *IF* I CHOOSE TO HAVE PITY ON YOU AND TELEPORT YOU HOME OR BANISH YOU AWAY.
YOU CAN DO THAT?
IT'S AN OLD FAMILY RECIPE.
I'M PULLING A RETREAT COMMAND OVERRIDE.
NO. **NO!** OVERRIDE **OVERWRITTEN!**
STAY!
WHY DID YOU LEAVE M.I.T.?
OH!
UH...
BOREDOM, MOSTLY.
I CAN SYMPATHIZE, BUT I WOULD RECOMMEND RETURNING.
I STRUGGLED THROUGH THE PURPOSE OF MY STUDIES AS WELL. BUT NOW, LOOKING BACK, I REALIZE THE STRUCTURE, AS ANTIQUATED AS IT WAS EVEN THEN, WAS NECESSARY FOR THE AMOUNT OF SHEER KNOWLEDGE I WAS CONSUMING.
IT WAS TIME WELL SPENT.
THIS--THIS IS NOT GOING HOW I THOUGHT THIS WAS GOING TO GO.
COULD YOU?
I'M SURE I CAN CONJURE UP A MANIACAL LAUGH IF IT WILL HELP YOU.
BUT TO ANSWER YOUR EARLIER QUESTION-- I CAME HERE FOR A REASON.
TO ANSWER YOUR NEXT QUESTION, THAT REASON IS...
...LUCULLUS VIRGIL McWHORTER.

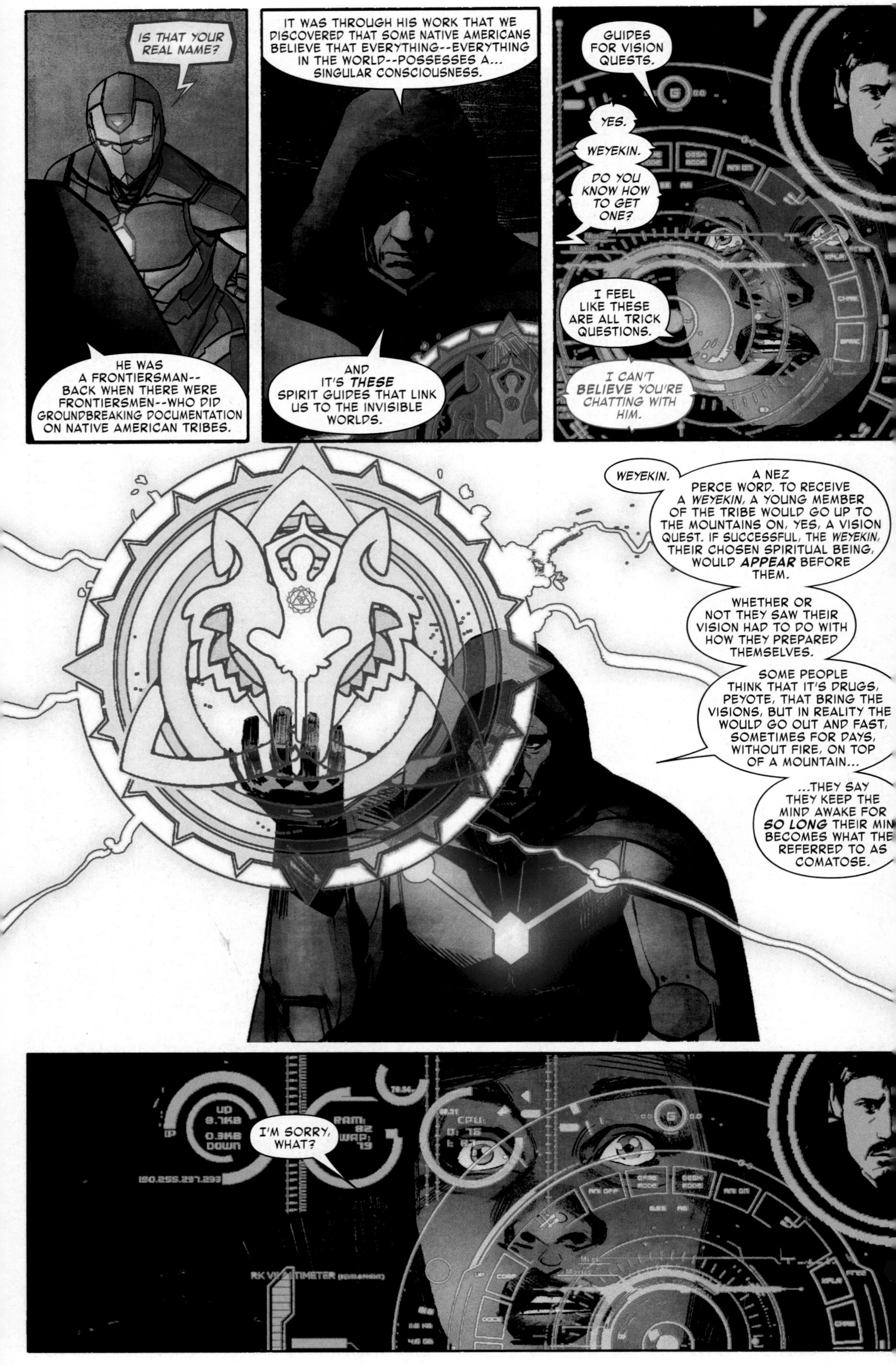
IS THAT YOUR REAL NAME?
HE WAS A FRONTIERSMAN--BACK WHEN THERE WERE FRONTIERSMEN--WHO DID GROUNDBREAKING DOCUMENTATION ON NATIVE AMERICAN TRIBES.
IT WAS THROUGH HIS WORK THAT WE DISCOVERED THAT SOME NATIVE AMERICANS BELIEVE THAT EVERYTHING--EVERYTHING IN THE WORLD--POSSESSES A... SINGULAR CONSCIOUSNESS.
AND IT'S THESE SPIRIT GUIDES THAT LINK US TO THE INVISIBLE WORLDS.
GUIDES FOR VISION QUESTS.
YES.
WEYEKIN.
DO YOU KNOW HOW TO GET ONE?
I FEEL LIKE THESE ARE ALL TRICK QUESTIONS.
I CAN'T BELIEVE YOU'RE CHATTING WITH HIM.
WEYEKIN.
A NEZ PERCE WORD. TO RECEIVE A WEYEKIN, A YOUNG MEMBER OF THE TRIBE WOULD GO UP TO THE MOUNTAINS ON, YES, A VISION QUEST. IF SUCCESSFUL, THE WEYEKIN, THEIR CHOSEN SPIRITUAL BEING, WOULD APPEAR BEFORE THEM.
WHETHER OR NOT THEY SAW THEIR VISION HAD TO DO WITH HOW THEY PREPARED THEMSELVES.
SOME PEOPLE THINK THAT IT'S DRUGS, PEYOTE, THAT BRING THE VISIONS, BUT IN REALITY THE WOULD GO OUT AND FAST, SOMETIMES FOR DAYS, WITHOUT FIRE, ON TOP OF A MOUNTAIN...
...THEY SAY THEY KEEP THE MIND AWAKE FOR SO LONG THEIR MIN BECOMES WHAT THE REFERRED TO AS COMATOSE.
UP
8.7KB
0.3KB
DOWN
RAM: 82
WAP: 79
190.255.297.293
I'M SORRY, WHAT?
CPU:
RK VIP TIMETER

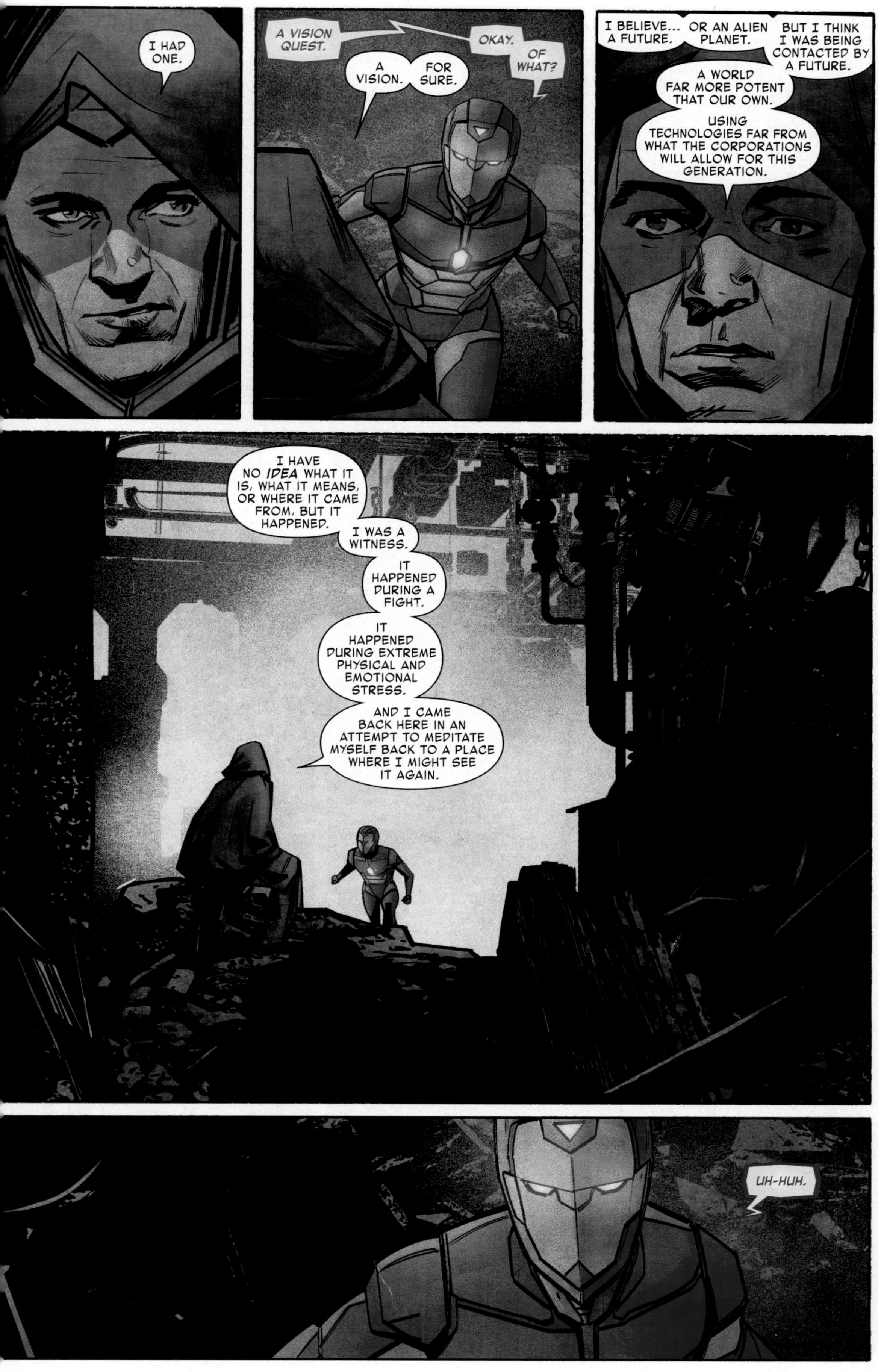
I HAD ONE.
A VISION QUEST.
OKAY.
OF WHAT?
A VISION.
FOR SURE.
I BELIEVE... A FUTURE.
OR AN ALIEN PLANET.
BUT I THINK I WAS BEING CONTACTED BY A FUTURE.
A WORLD FAR MORE POTENT THAT OUR OWN.
USING TECHNOLOGIES FAR FROM WHAT THE CORPORATIONS WILL ALLOW FOR THIS GENERATION.
I HAVE NO IDEA WHAT IT IS, WHAT IT MEANS, OR WHERE IT CAME FROM, BUT IT HAPPENED.
I WAS A WITNESS.
IT HAPPENED DURING A FIGHT.
IT HAPPENED DURING EXTREME PHYSICAL AND EMOTIONAL STRESS.
AND I CAME BACK HERE IN AN ATTEMPT TO MEDITATE MYSELF BACK TO A PLACE WHERE I MIGHT SEE IT AGAIN.
UH-HUH.

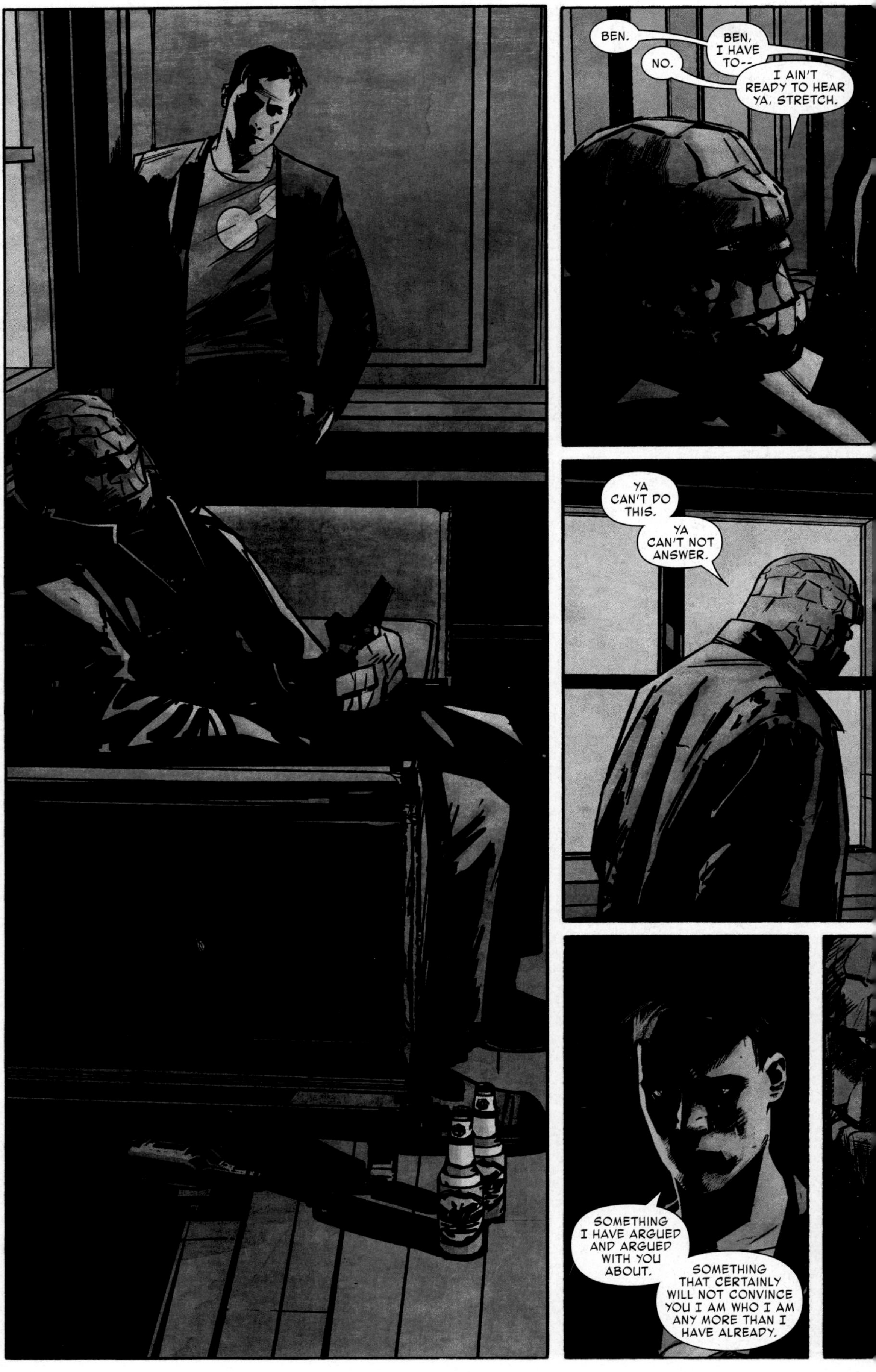
BEN.
BEN, I HAVE TO--
NO.
I AIN'T READY TO HEAR YA, STRETCH.
YA CAN'T DO THIS.
YA CAN'T NOT ANSWER.
SOMETHING I HAVE ARGUED AND ARGUED WITH YOU ABOUT.
SOMETHING THAT CERTAINLY WILL NOT CONVINCE YOU I AM WHO I AM ANY MORE THAN I HAVE ALREADY.

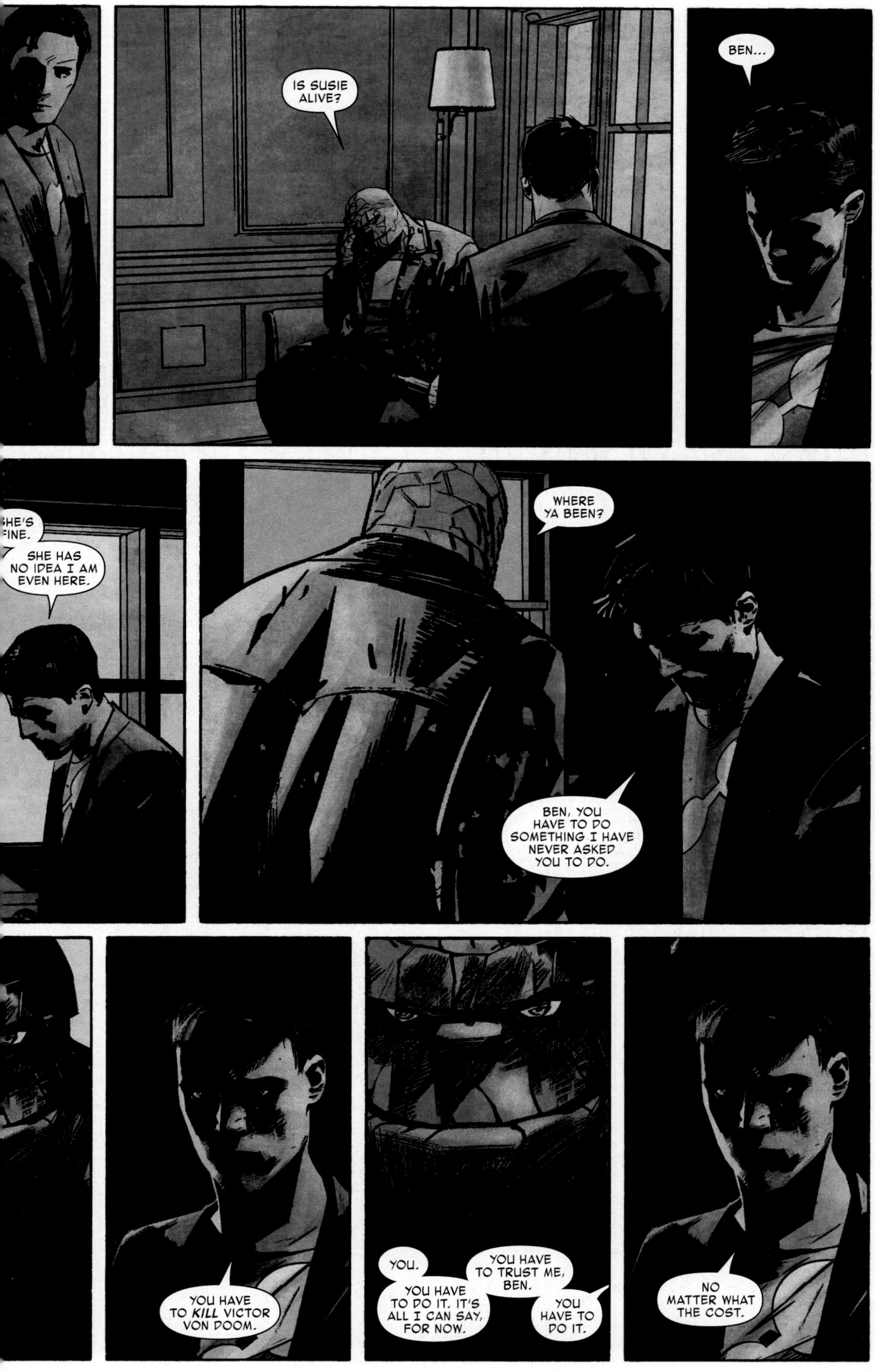
IS SUSIE ALIVE?
BEN...
SHE'S FINE.
SHE HAS NO IDEA I AM EVEN HERE.
WHERE YA BEEN?
BEN, YOU HAVE TO DO SOMETHING I HAVE NEVER ASKED YOU TO DO.
YOU HAVE TO KILL VICTOR VON DOOM.
YOU.
YOU HAVE TO TRUST ME, BEN.
YOU HAVE TO DO IT. IT'S ALL I CAN SAY, FOR NOW.
YOU HAVE TO DO IT.
NO MATTER WHAT THE COST.

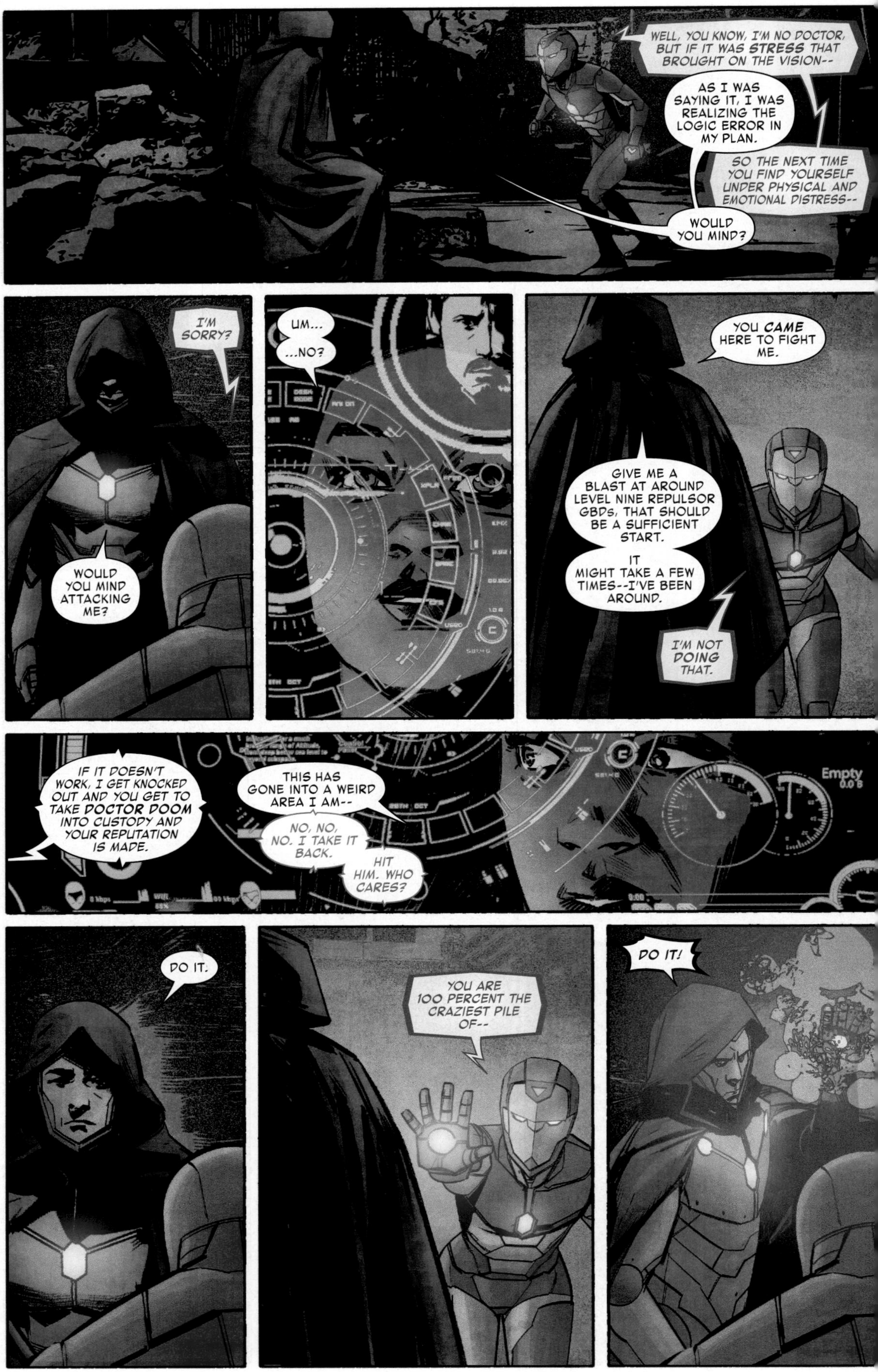
WELL, YOU KNOW, I'M NO DOCTOR, BUT IF IT WAS STRESS THAT BROUGHT ON THE VISION--
AS I WAS SAYING IT, I WAS REALIZING THE LOGIC ERROR IN MY PLAN.
SO THE NEXT TIME YOU FIND YOURSELF UNDER PHYSICAL AND EMOTIONAL DISTRESS--
WOULD YOU MIND?
I'M SORRY?
WOULD YOU MIND ATTACKING ME?
UM...
...NO?
YOU CAME HERE TO FIGHT ME.
GIVE ME A BLAST AT AROUND LEVEL NINE REPULSOR GBDs, THAT SHOULD BE A SUFFICIENT START.
IT MIGHT TAKE A FEW TIMES--I'VE BEEN AROUND.
I'M NOT DOING THAT.
IF IT DOESN'T WORK, I GET KNOCKED OUT AND YOU GET TO TAKE DOCTOR DOOM INTO CUSTODY AND YOUR REPUTATION IS MADE.
THIS HAS GONE INTO A WEIRD AREA I AM--
NO, NO, NO. I TAKE IT BACK.
HIT HIM. WHO CARES?
Empty
DO IT.
YOU ARE 100 PERCENT THE CRAZIEST PILE OF--
DO IT!

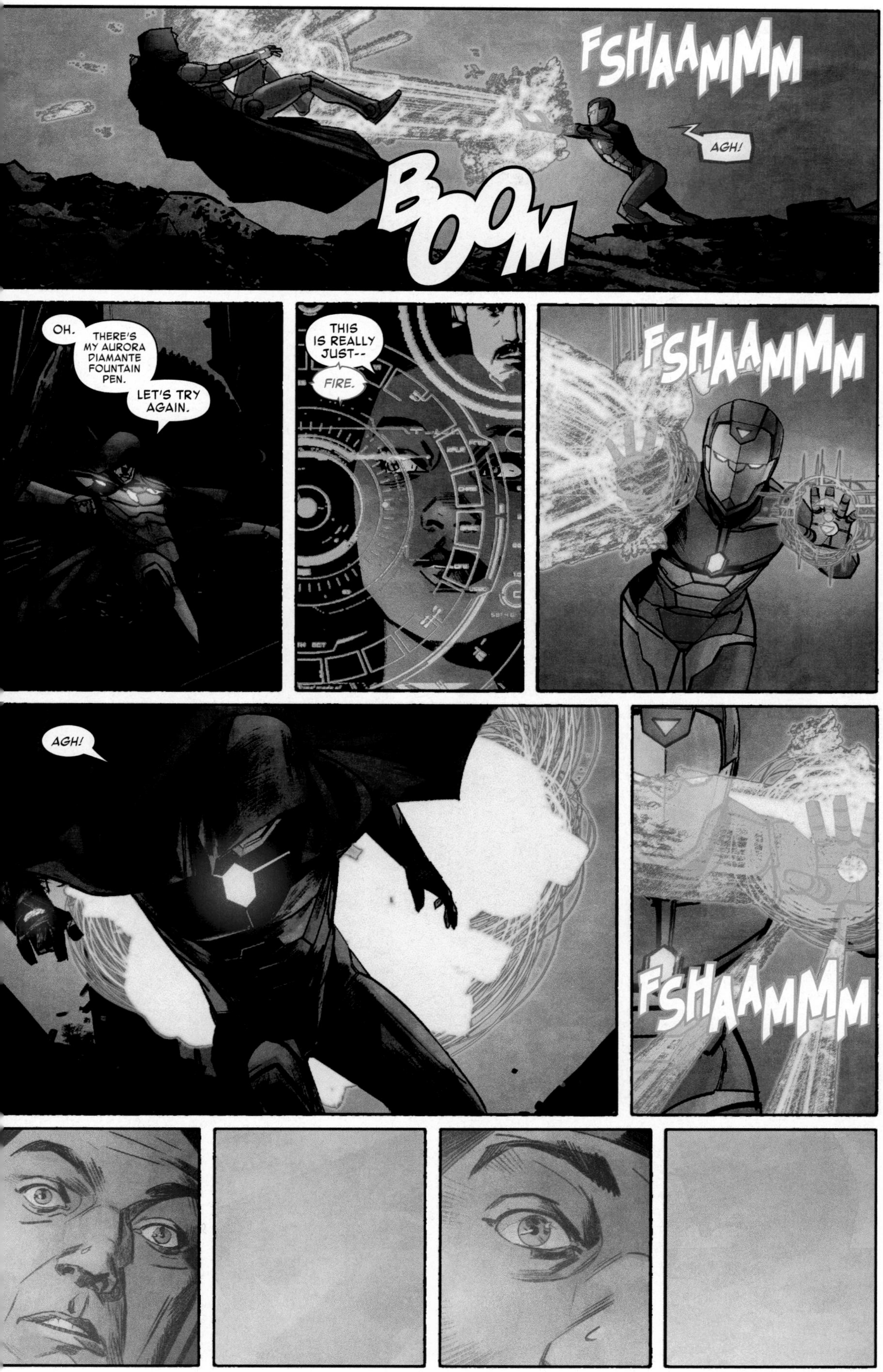
FSHAAMMM
AGH!
BOOM
OH.
THERE'S MY AURORA DIAMANTE FOUNTAIN PEN.
LET'S TRY AGAIN.
THIS IS REALLY JUST--
FIRE.
FSHAAMMM
AGH!
FSHAAMMM

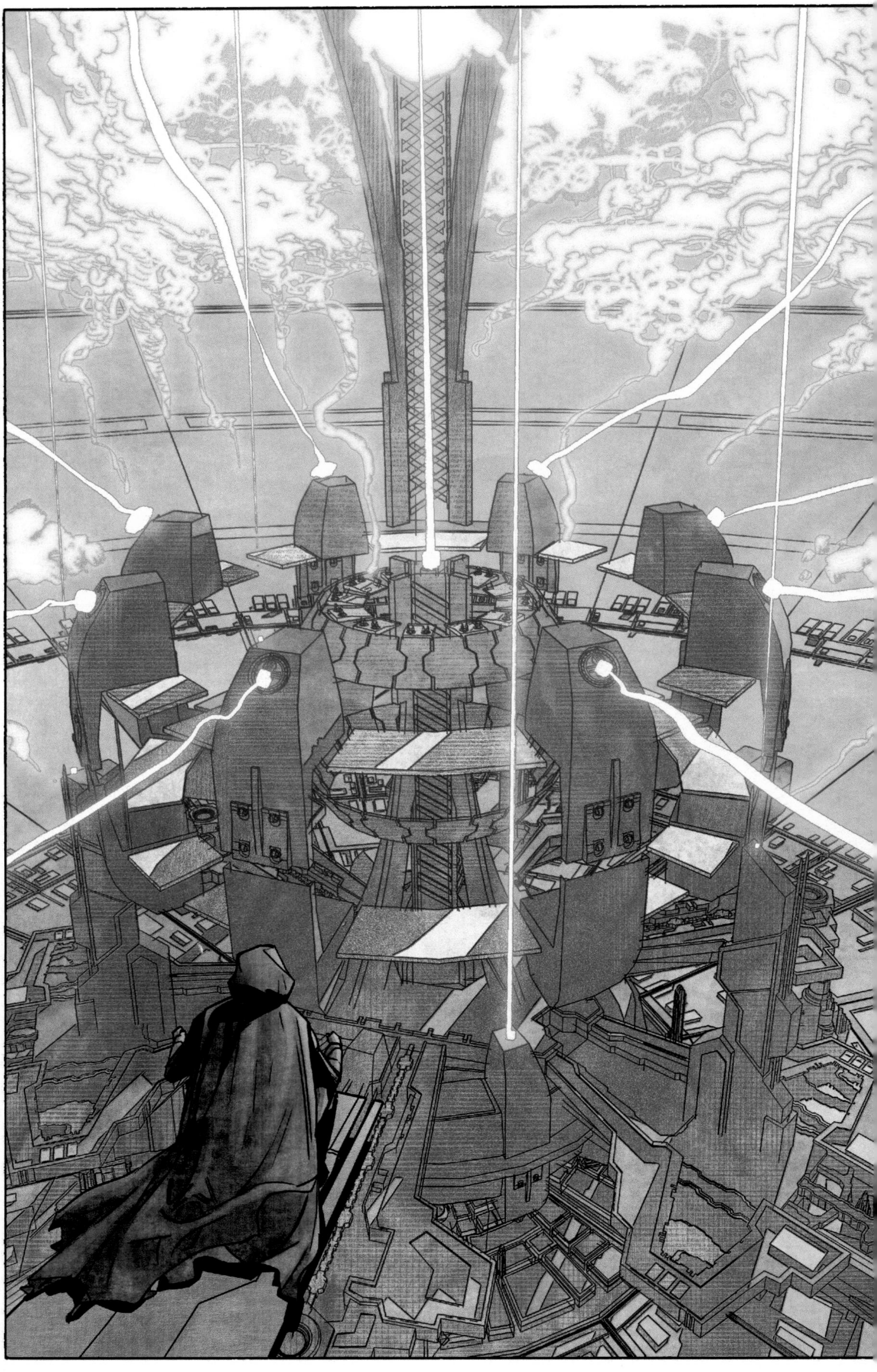

AGH.

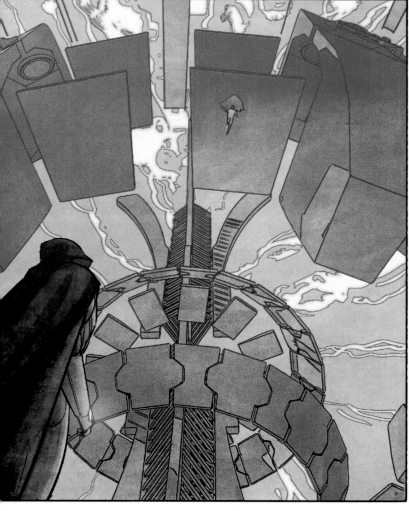

HELLO?

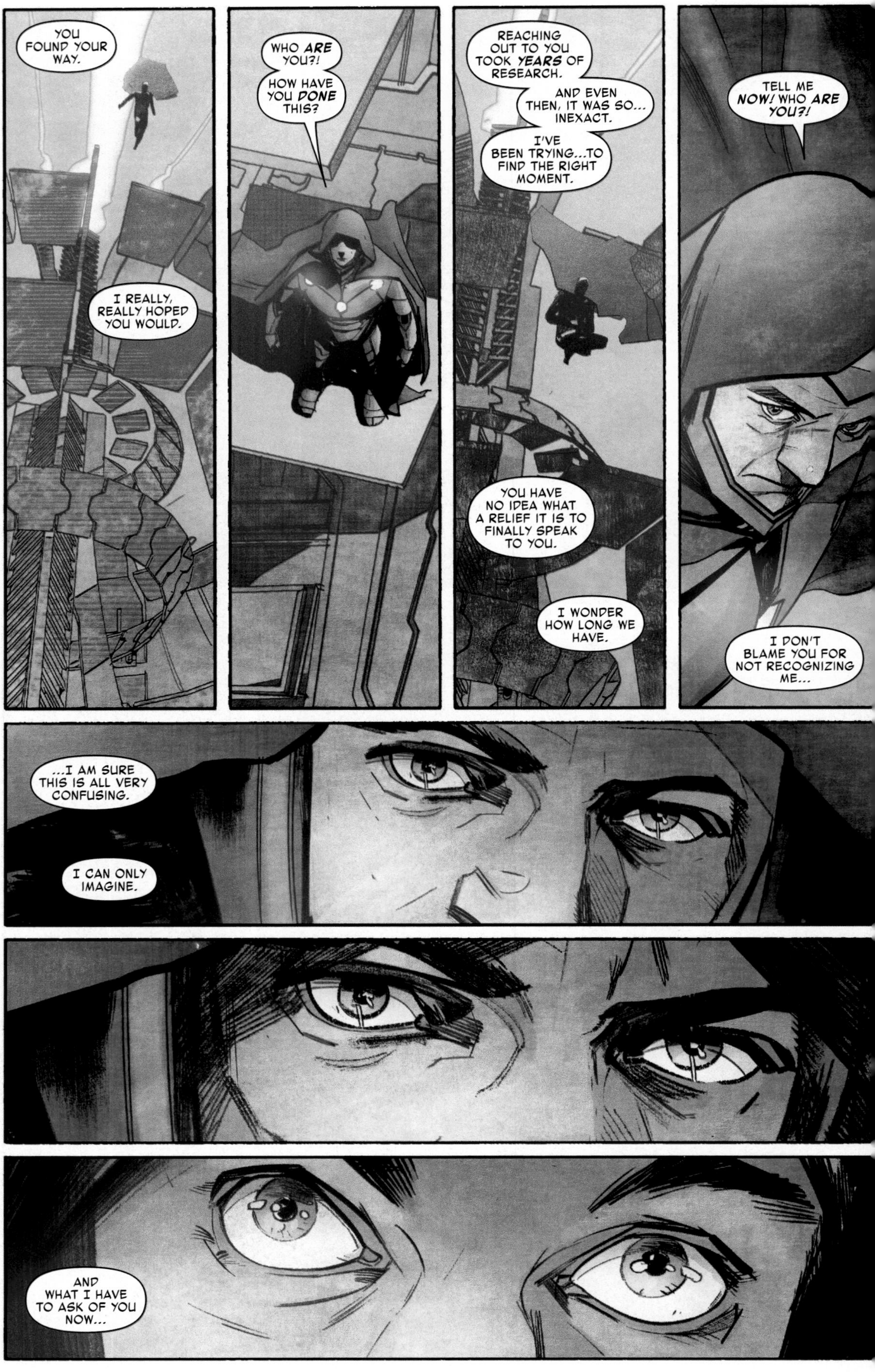
YOU FOUND YOUR WAY.
I REALLY, REALLY HOPED YOU WOULD.
WHO *ARE* YOU?!
HOW HAVE YOU *DONE* THIS?
REACHING OUT TO YOU TOOK *YEARS* OF RESEARCH.
AND EVEN THEN, IT WAS SO... INEXACT.
I'VE BEEN TRYING...TO FIND THE RIGHT MOMENT.
YOU HAVE NO IDEA WHAT A RELIEF IT IS TO FINALLY SPEAK TO YOU.
I WONDER HOW LONG WE HAVE.
TELL ME *NOW!* WHO *ARE YOU?!*
I DON'T BLAME YOU FOR NOT RECOGNIZING ME...
...I AM SURE THIS IS ALL VERY CONFUSING.
I CAN ONLY IMAGINE.
AND WHAT I HAVE TO ASK OF YOU NOW...

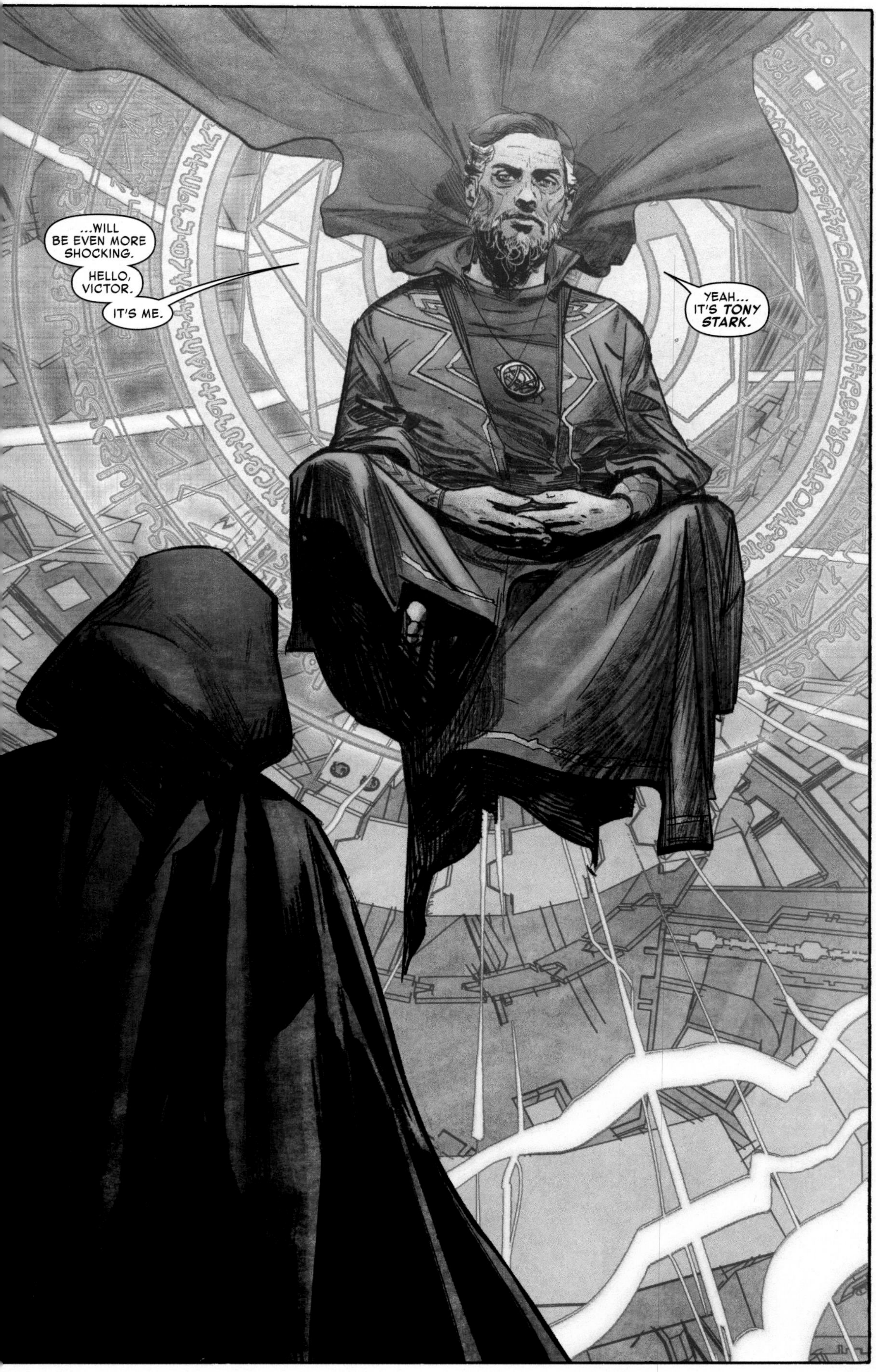
...WILL BE EVEN MORE SHOCKING.
HELLO, VICTOR.
IT'S ME.
YEAH... IT'S *TONY STARK.*

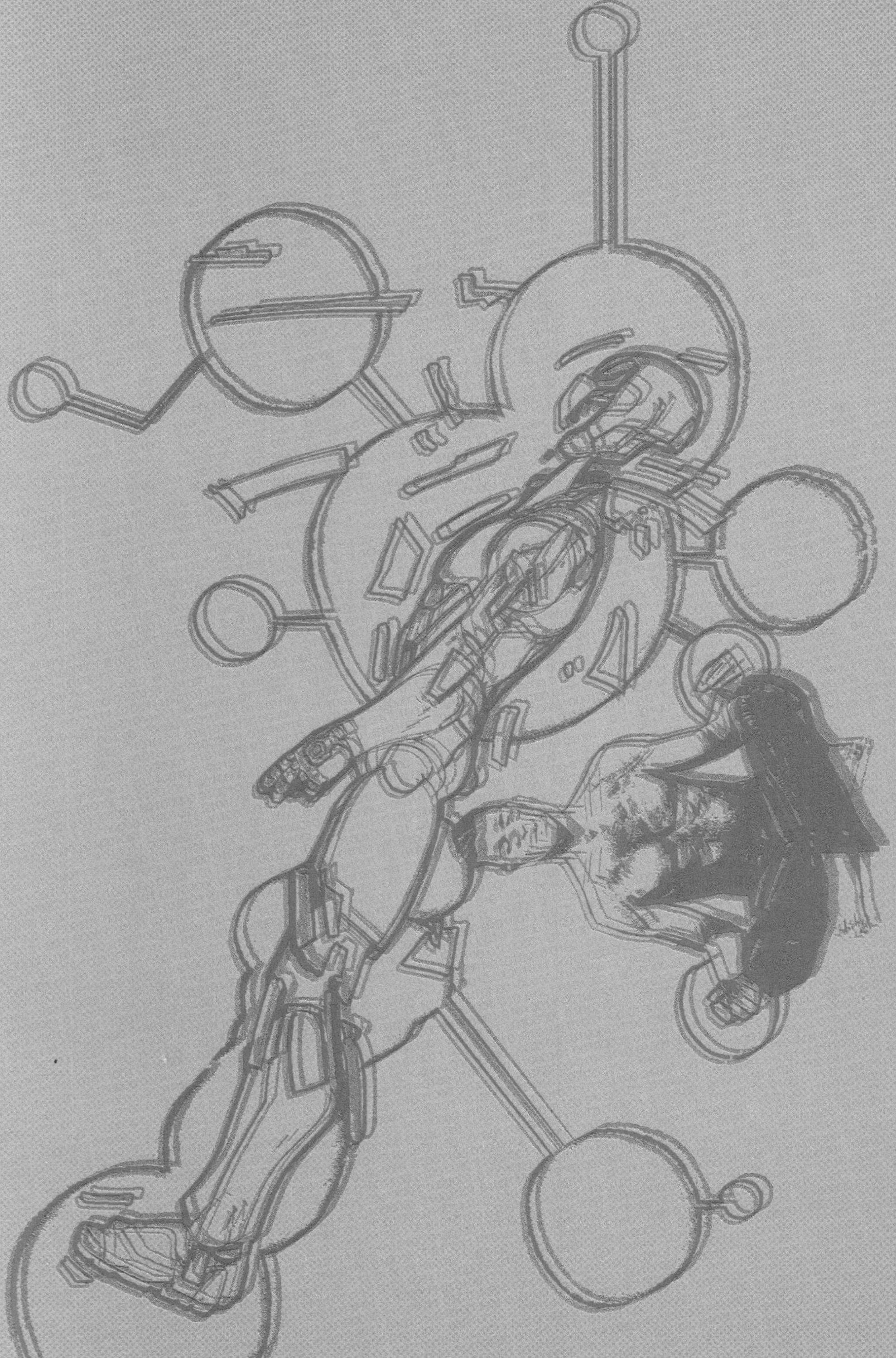

9

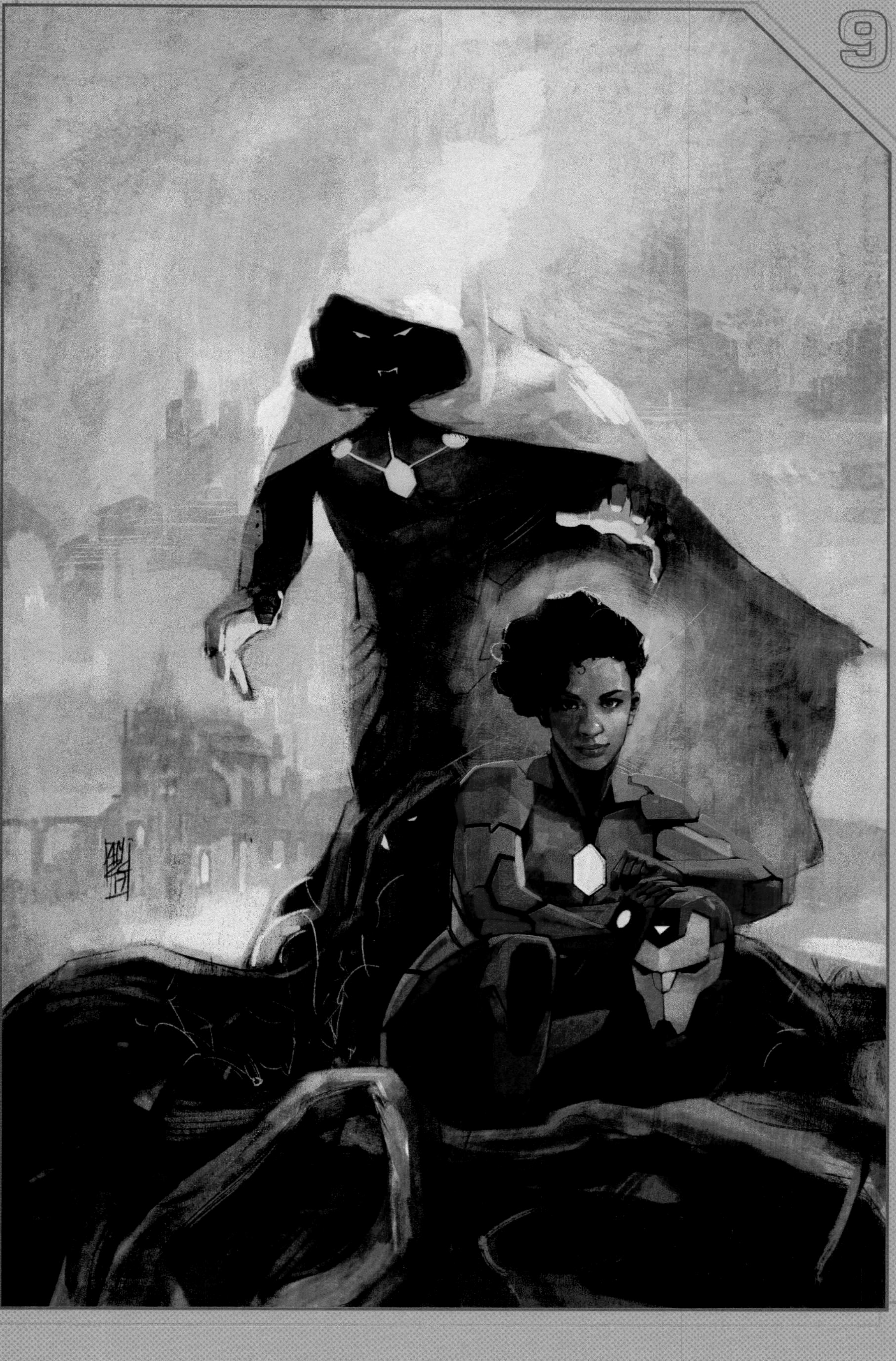

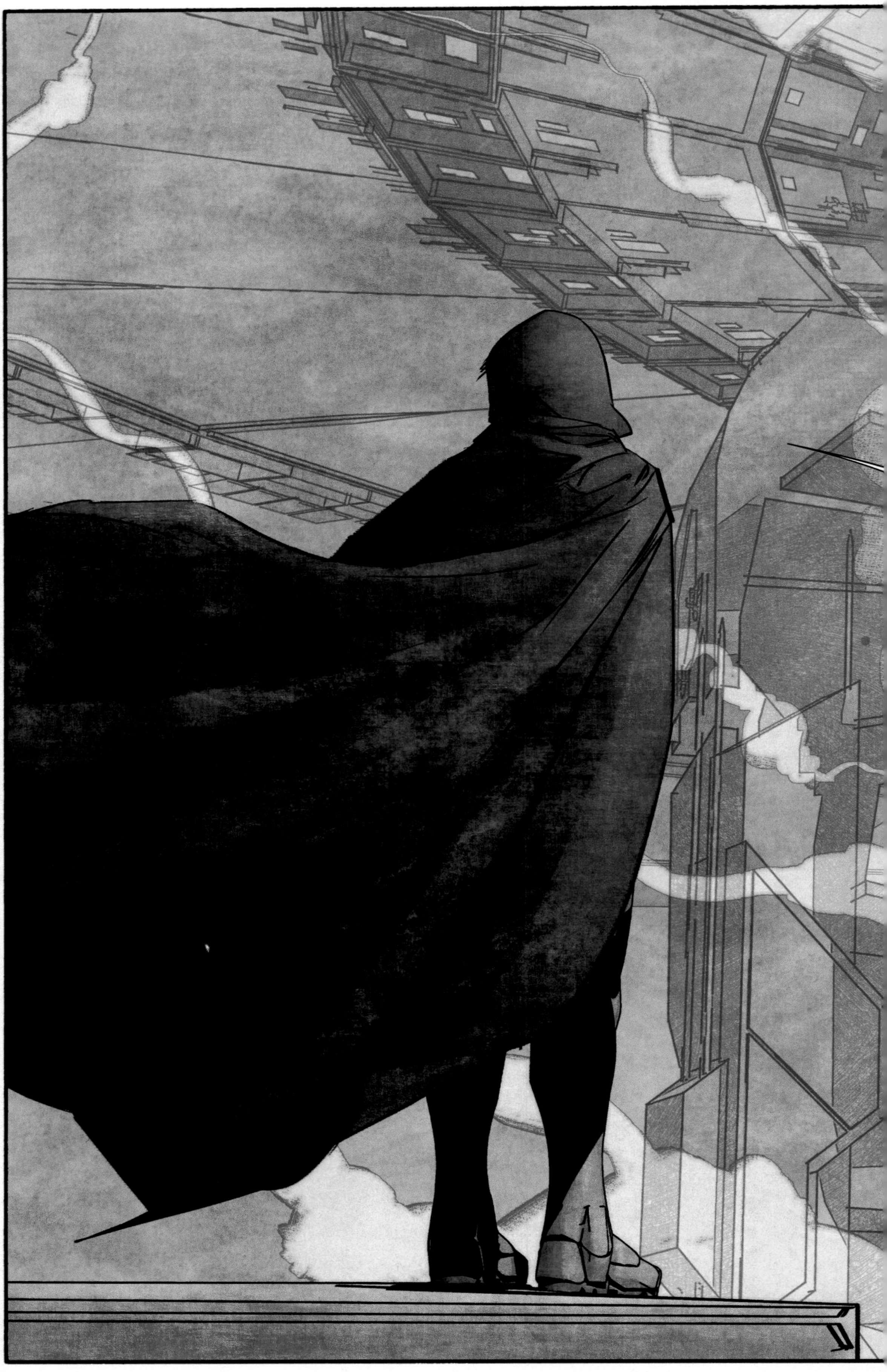

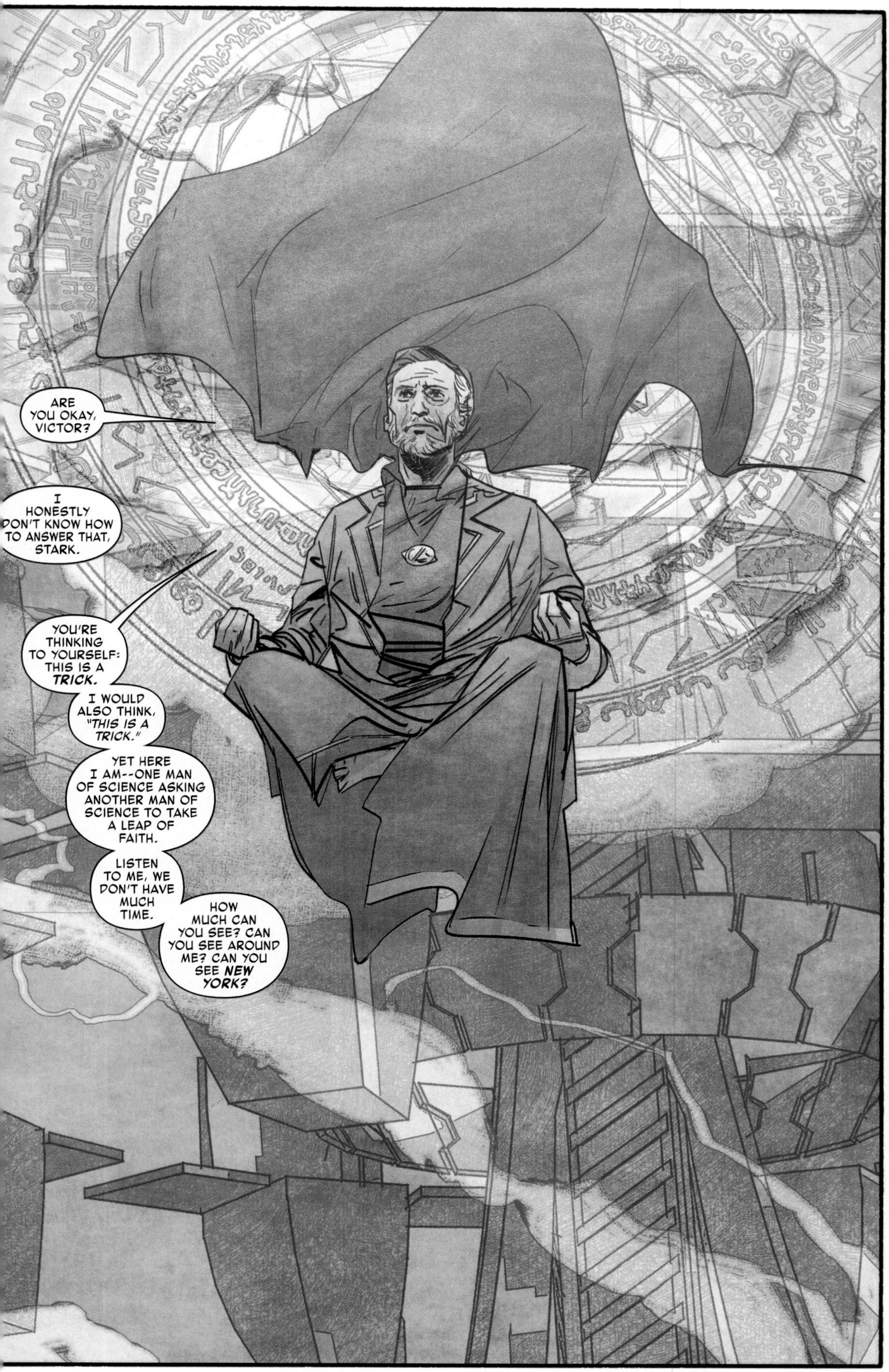
ARE YOU OKAY, VICTOR?
I HONESTLY DON'T KNOW HOW TO ANSWER THAT, STARK.
YOU'RE THINKING TO YOURSELF: THIS IS A *TRICK.*
I WOULD ALSO THINK, *"THIS IS A TRICK."*
YET HERE I AM--ONE MAN OF SCIENCE ASKING ANOTHER MAN OF SCIENCE TO TAKE A LEAP OF FAITH.
LISTEN TO ME, WE DON'T HAVE MUCH TIME.
HOW MUCH CAN YOU SEE? CAN YOU SEE AROUND ME? CAN YOU SEE *NEW YORK?*

THIS... IS *NEW YORK?*

VICTOR, YOU CAN'T-- WHAT YEAR IS THIS?

VICTOR, YOU CAN'T BE IRON MAN.

YOU HAVE TO STOP.

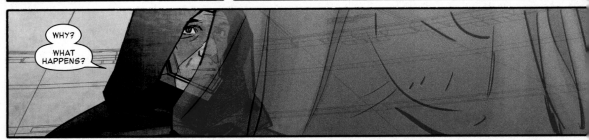

WHY? WHAT HAPPENS?

WHEN THEY COME FOR YOU, VICTOR, IT'S IMPORTANT THAT YOU ARE NOT IRON MAN, BUT--

WHO? *THEY* WHO?

IUFEARU.

WHO?

WHO?! *WHO* IS COMING FOR ME?

ERUKG!

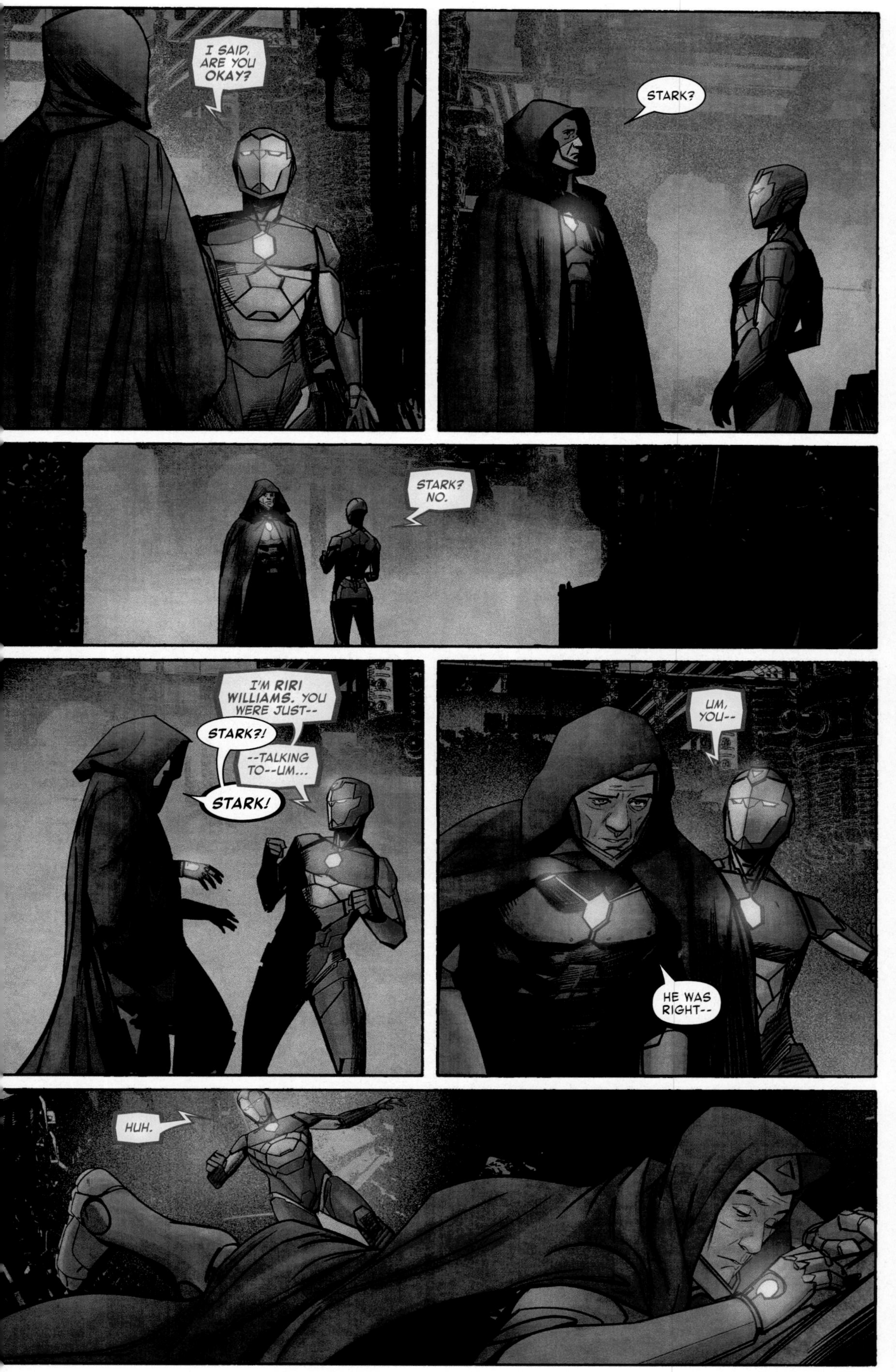
I SAID, ARE YOU OKAY?
STARK?
STARK? NO.
I'M RIRI WILLIAMS. YOU WERE JUST--
STARK?!
--TALKING TO--UM...
STARK!
UM, YOU--
HE WAS RIGHT--
HUH.

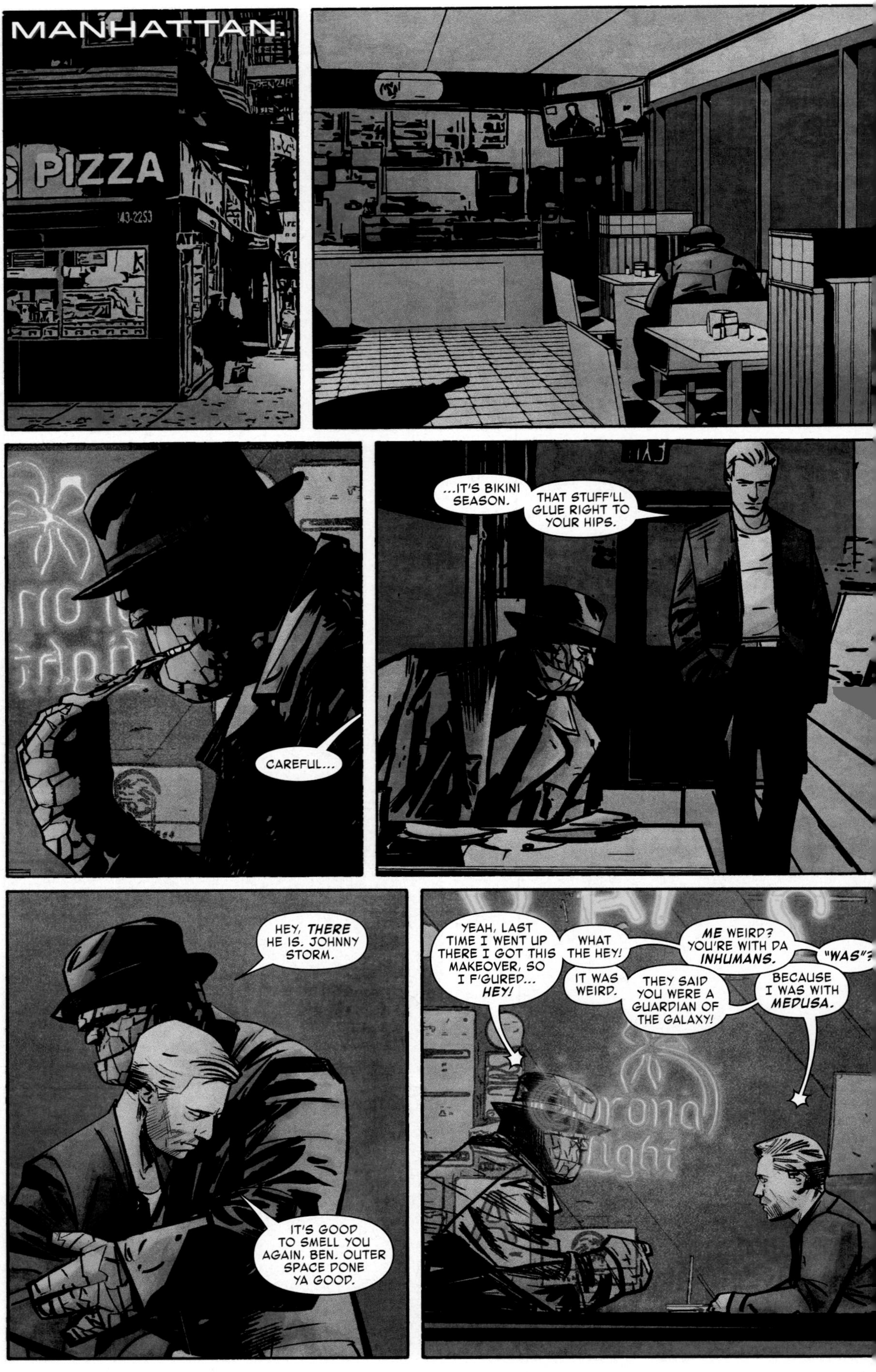
MANHATTAN.
PIZZA
CAREFUL...
...IT'S BIKINI SEASON.
THAT STUFF'LL GLUE RIGHT TO YOUR HIPS.
HEY, THERE HE IS. JOHNNY STORM.
IT'S GOOD TO SMELL YOU AGAIN, BEN. OUTER SPACE DONE YA GOOD.
YEAH, LAST TIME I WENT UP THERE I GOT THIS MAKEOVER, SO I F'GURED... HEY!
WHAT THE HEY!
IT WAS WEIRD.
ME WEIRD? YOU'RE WITH DA INHUMANS.
THEY SAID YOU WERE A GUARDIAN OF THE GALAXY!
"WAS"?
BECAUSE I WAS WITH MEDUSA.

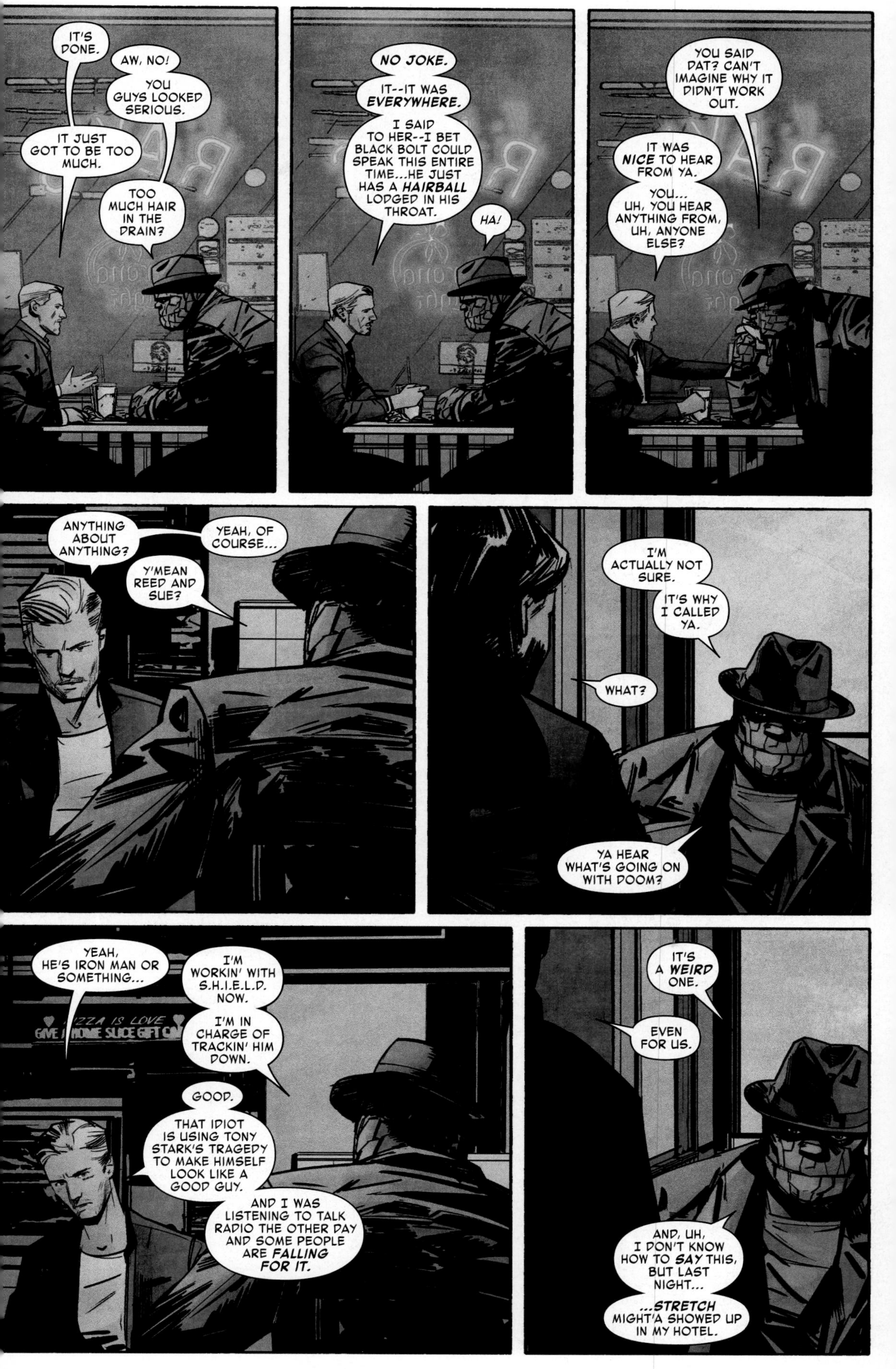
IT'S DONE.
AW, NO!
YOU GUYS LOOKED SERIOUS.
IT JUST GOT TO BE TOO MUCH.
TOO MUCH HAIR IN THE DRAIN?
NO JOKE.
IT--IT WAS *EVERYWHERE.*
I SAID TO HER--I BET BLACK BOLT COULD SPEAK THIS ENTIRE TIME...HE JUST HAS A *HAIRBALL* LODGED IN HIS THROAT.
HA!
YOU SAID DAT? CAN'T IMAGINE WHY IT DIDN'T WORK OUT.
IT WAS *NICE* TO HEAR FROM YA.
YOU... UH, YOU HEAR ANYTHING FROM, UH, ANYONE ELSE?
ANYTHING ABOUT ANYTHING?
YEAH, OF COURSE...
Y'MEAN REED AND SUE?
I'M ACTUALLY NOT SURE.
IT'S WHY I CALLED YA.
WHAT?
YA HEAR WHAT'S GOING ON WITH DOOM?
YEAH, HE'S IRON MAN OR SOMETHING...
I'M WORKIN' WITH S.H.I.E.L.D. NOW.
I'M IN CHARGE OF TRACKIN' HIM DOWN.
GOOD.
THAT IDIOT IS USING TONY STARK'S TRAGEDY TO MAKE HIMSELF LOOK LIKE A GOOD GUY.
AND I WAS LISTENING TO TALK RADIO THE OTHER DAY AND SOME PEOPLE ARE *FALLING FOR IT.*
IT'S A *WEIRD* ONE.
EVEN FOR US.
AND, UH, I DON'T KNOW HOW TO *SAY* THIS, BUT LAST NIGHT...
...*STRETCH* MIGHT'A SHOWED UP IN MY HOTEL.

...ZA IS LOVE
...ME SLICE GIFT CARD
YOU SAW REED?!
I'M NOT ONE HUNDRED PERCENT SURE.
REED RICHARDS?! YOU TALKED TO HIM?
I'M NOT--
WHAT DOES THAT MEAN?
IT MEANS I TURNED AROUND AND THERE HE WAS.
IT LOOKED LIKE HIM. HE KNEW STUFF. HE KNEW STUFF ABOUT ME.
BUT HE WOULDN'T EVEN TALK ABOUT YOUR SISTER.
SUSAN...
WOULDN'T TALK ABOUT YOUR SISTER AND TOLD ME HE WANTS ME TO KILL VICTOR.
PIZZA IS LOVE
A HOME SLICE GIFT CA...
WHAT?
I KNOW, I SAID--
NO WAY REED SAYS THAT.
THAT'S WHAT I SAY.
YOU THINK IT WAS A SHAPE-SHIFTER OR ONE OF THOSE MENTAL MENTALLOS?
I DUNNO.
I WANTED TO KNOW IF YOU TALKED TO HIM OR ANYBODY, BUT CLEARLY YOU AIN'T.
YOU FIND THE CREEP WHO IS USING MY FAMILY TO GET TO YOU AND YOU LET ME KNOW WHERE HE IS.
YEAH, I JUST NEEDED TO HEAR YOU SAY HOW CRAZY THAT WAS.
YOU'RE RIGHT.
NO WAY REED EVER TELLS ME TO KILL SOMEONE. EVEN HIM.
HOW MANY TIMES HAS REED PHYSICALLY RESTRAINED YOU FROM KILLING DOOM?
YEAH.
MAN, IT REALLY LOOKED LIKE REED. IT REALLY FELT REAL. AS REAL AS THIS.
HE KNEW THINGS ABOUT ME.
IF IT WASN'T REED, WHO WAS IT?

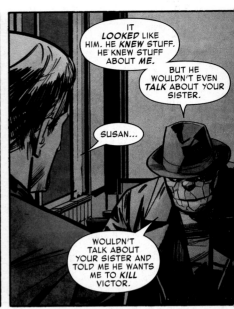

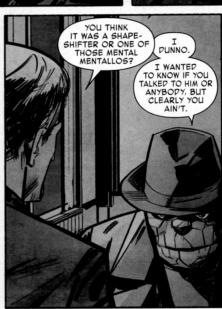

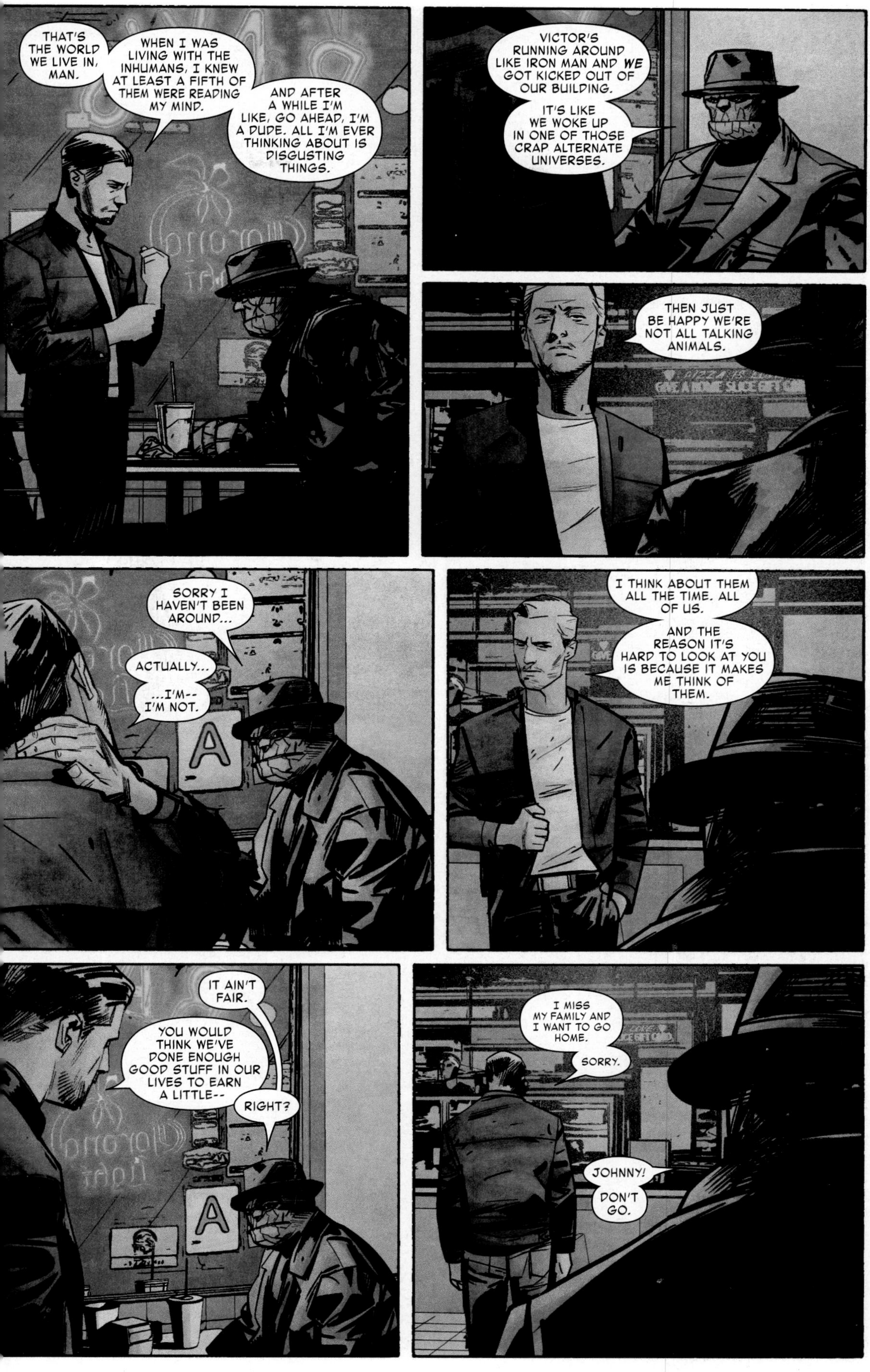
THAT'S THE WORLD WE LIVE IN, MAN.
WHEN I WAS LIVING WITH THE INHUMANS, I KNEW AT LEAST A FIFTH OF THEM WERE READING MY MIND.
AND AFTER A WHILE I'M LIKE, GO AHEAD, I'M A DUDE. ALL I'M EVER THINKING ABOUT IS DISGUSTING THINGS.
VICTOR'S RUNNING AROUND LIKE IRON MAN AND WE GOT KICKED OUT OF OUR BUILDING.
IT'S LIKE WE WOKE UP IN ONE OF THOSE CRAP ALTERNATE UNIVERSES.
THEN JUST BE HAPPY WE'RE NOT ALL TALKING ANIMALS.
GIVE A HOME SLICE GIFT CARD
SORRY I HAVEN'T BEEN AROUND...
ACTUALLY...
...I'M-- I'M NOT.
A
I THINK ABOUT THEM ALL THE TIME. ALL OF US.
AND THE REASON IT'S HARD TO LOOK AT YOU IS BECAUSE IT MAKES ME THINK OF THEM.
IT AIN'T FAIR.
YOU WOULD THINK WE'VE DONE ENOUGH GOOD STUFF IN OUR LIVES TO EARN A LITTLE--
RIGHT?
A
I MISS MY FAMILY AND I WANT TO GO HOME.
SORRY.
JOHNNY!
DON'T GO.

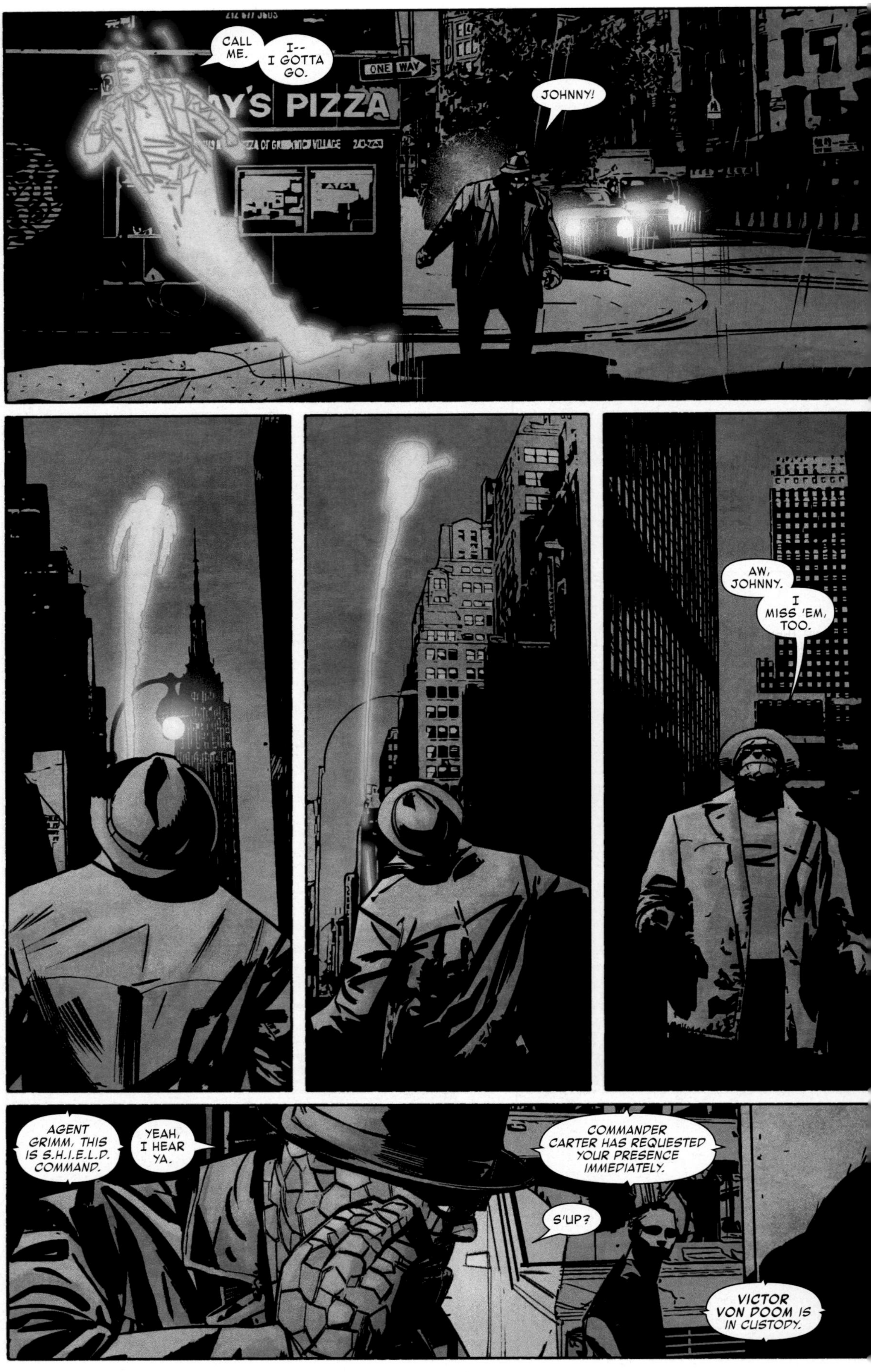
ONE WAY
AY'S PIZZA
CALL ME.
I-- I GOTTA GO.
JOHNNY!
AW, JOHNNY.
I MISS 'EM, TOO.
AGENT GRIMM, THIS IS S.H.I.E.L.D. COMMAND.
YEAH, I HEAR YA.
COMMANDER CARTER HAS REQUESTED YOUR PRESENCE IMMEDIATELY.
S'UP?
VICTOR VON DOOM IS IN CUSTODY.

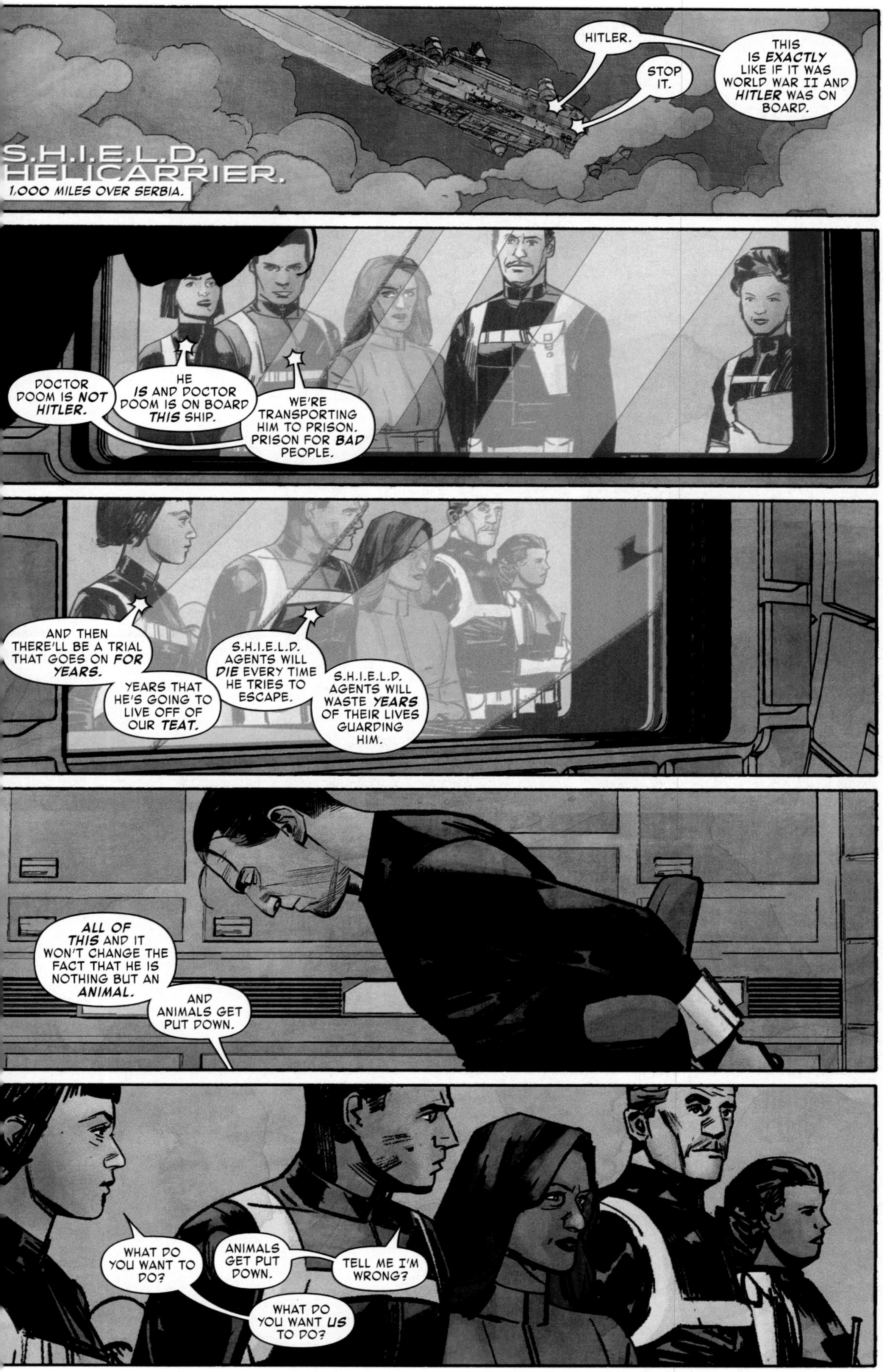
S.H.I.E.L.D. HELICARRIER.
1,000 MILES OVER SERBIA.
HITLER.
THIS IS EXACTLY LIKE IF IT WAS WORLD WAR II AND HITLER WAS ON BOARD.
STOP IT.
DOCTOR DOOM IS NOT HITLER.
HE IS AND DOCTOR DOOM IS ON BOARD THIS SHIP.
WE'RE TRANSPORTING HIM TO PRISON. PRISON FOR BAD PEOPLE.
AND THEN THERE'LL BE A TRIAL THAT GOES ON FOR YEARS.
YEARS THAT HE'S GOING TO LIVE OFF OF OUR TEAT.
S.H.I.E.L.D. AGENTS WILL DIE EVERY TIME HE TRIES TO ESCAPE.
S.H.I.E.L.D. AGENTS WILL WASTE YEARS OF THEIR LIVES GUARDING HIM.
ALL OF THIS AND IT WON'T CHANGE THE FACT THAT HE IS NOTHING BUT AN ANIMAL.
AND ANIMALS GET PUT DOWN.
WHAT DO YOU WANT TO DO?
ANIMALS GET PUT DOWN.
TELL ME I'M WRONG?
WHAT DO YOU WANT US TO DO?

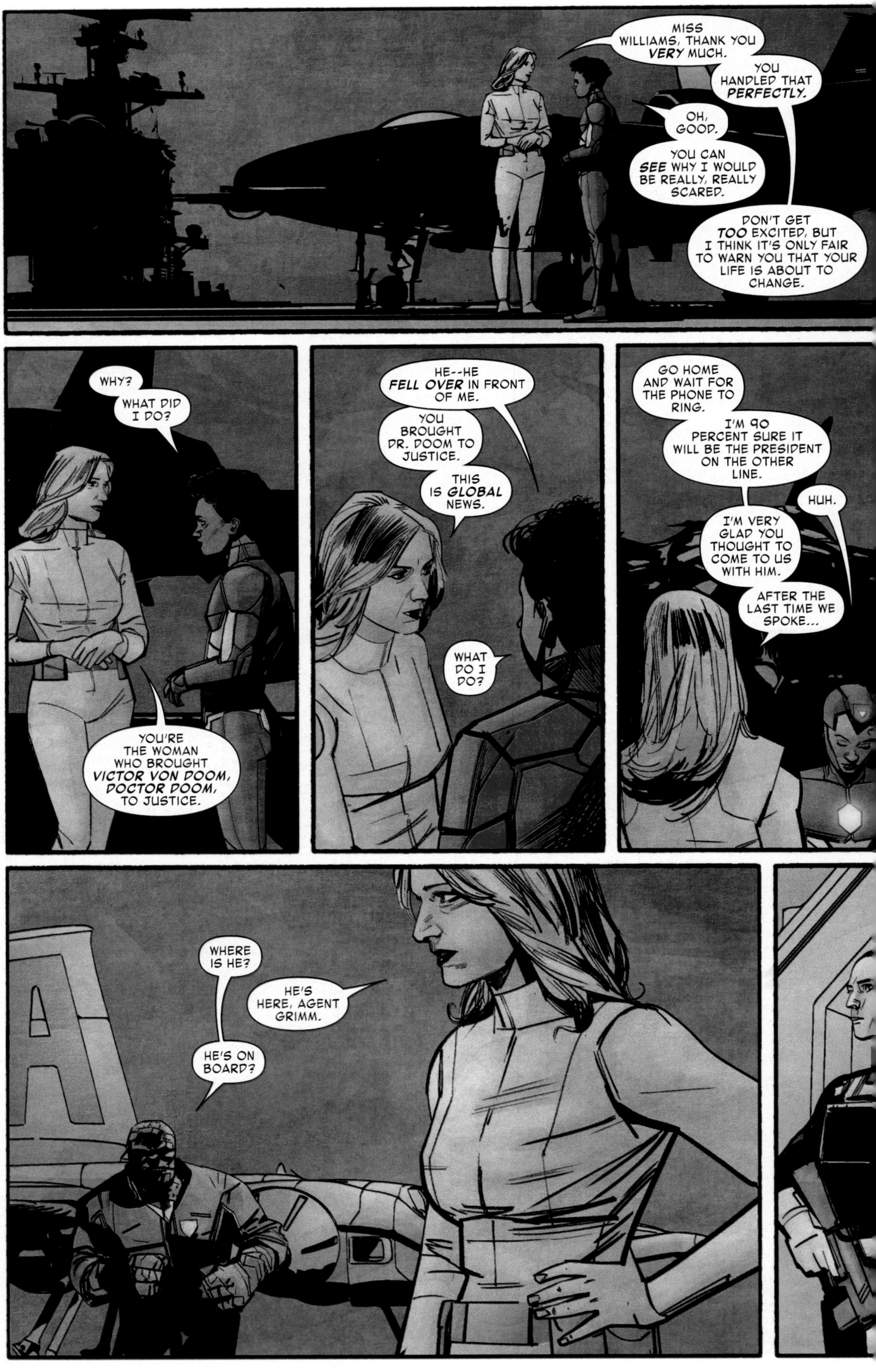
MISS WILLIAMS, THANK YOU VERY MUCH.
YOU HANDLED THAT PERFECTLY.
OH, GOOD.
YOU CAN SEE WHY I WOULD BE REALLY, REALLY SCARED.
DON'T GET TOO EXCITED, BUT I THINK IT'S ONLY FAIR TO WARN YOU THAT YOUR LIFE IS ABOUT TO CHANGE.
WHY?
WHAT DID I DO?
YOU'RE THE WOMAN WHO BROUGHT VICTOR VON DOOM, DOCTOR DOOM, TO JUSTICE.
HE--HE FELL OVER IN FRONT OF ME.
YOU BROUGHT DR. DOOM TO JUSTICE.
THIS IS GLOBAL NEWS.
WHAT DO I DO?
GO HOME AND WAIT FOR THE PHONE TO RING.
I'M 90 PERCENT SURE IT WILL BE THE PRESIDENT ON THE OTHER LINE.
HUH.
I'M VERY GLAD YOU THOUGHT TO COME TO US WITH HIM.
AFTER THE LAST TIME WE SPOKE...
WHERE IS HE?
HE'S HERE, AGENT GRIMM.
HE'S ON BOARD?

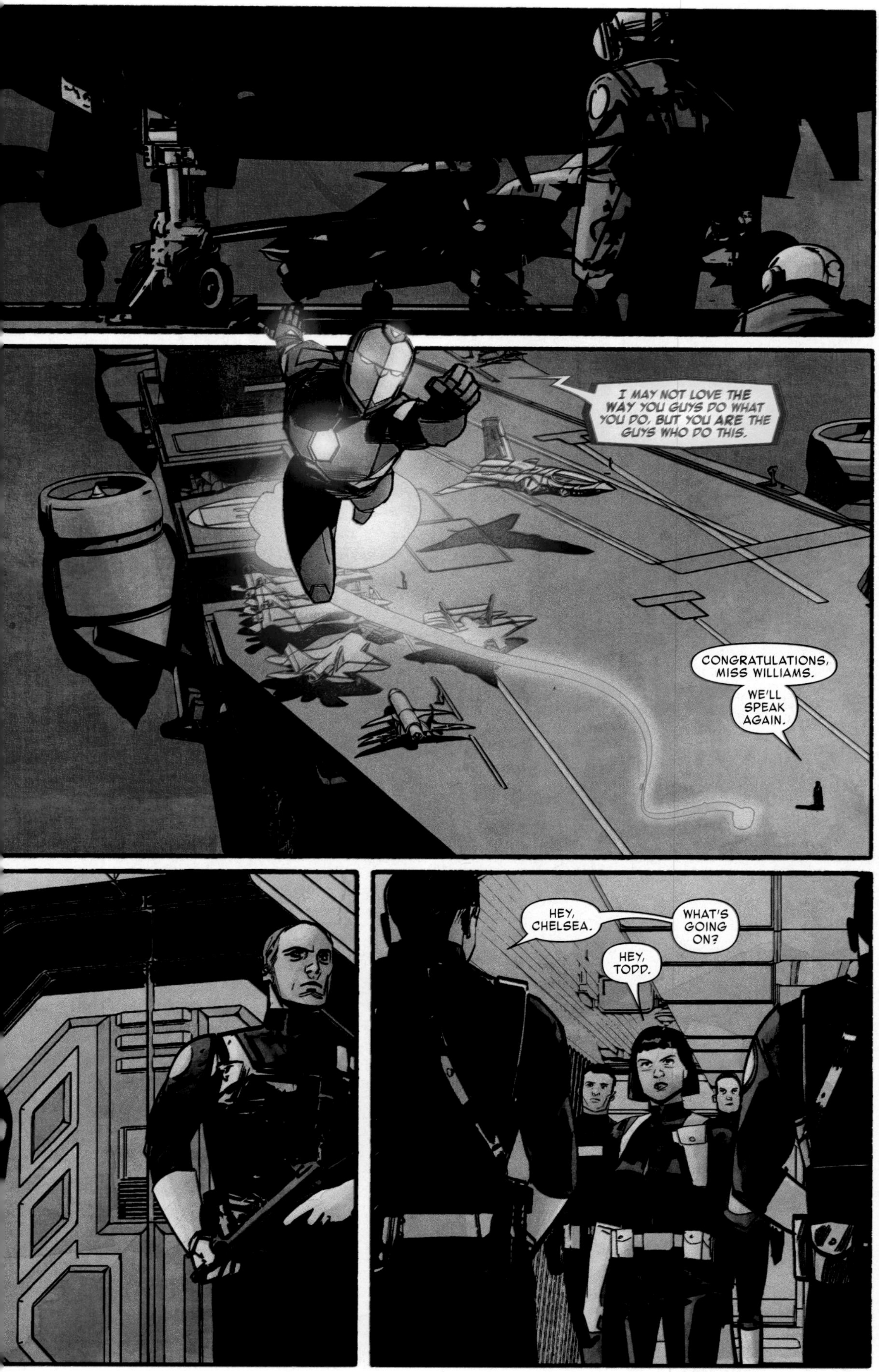
I MAY NOT LOVE THE WAY YOU GUYS DO WHAT YOU DO, BUT YOU ARE THE GUYS WHO DO THIS.
CONGRATULATIONS, MISS WILLIAMS.
WE'LL SPEAK AGAIN.
HEY, CHELSEA.
WHAT'S GOING ON?
HEY, TODD.

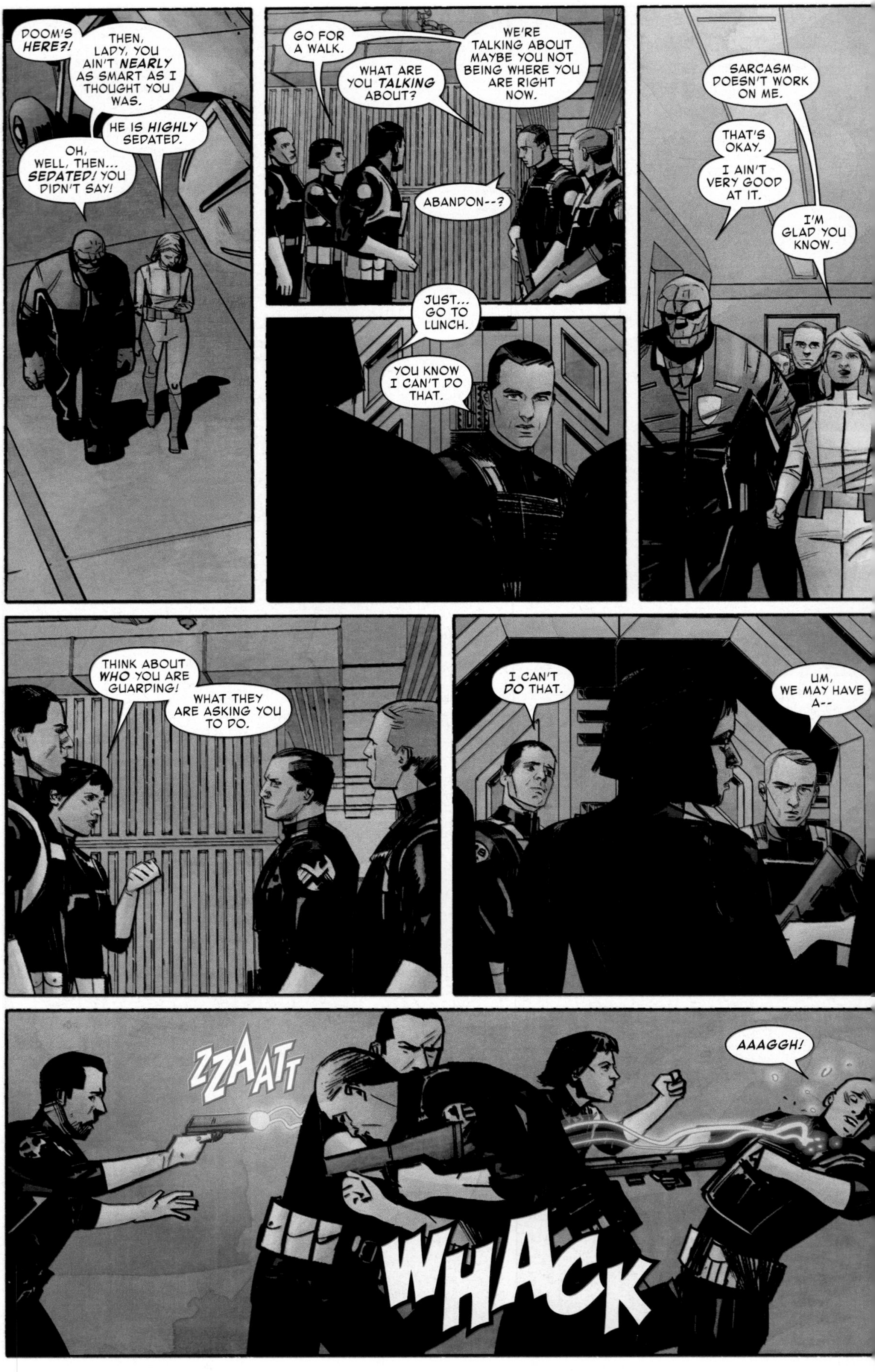
DOOM'S HERE?!
THEN, LADY, YOU AIN'T NEARLY AS SMART AS I THOUGHT YOU WAS.
HE IS HIGHLY SEDATED.
OH, WELL, THEN... SEDATED! YOU DIDN'T SAY!
GO FOR A WALK.
WHAT ARE YOU TALKING ABOUT?
WE'RE TALKING ABOUT MAYBE YOU NOT BEING WHERE YOU ARE RIGHT NOW.
ABANDON--?
JUST... GO TO LUNCH.
YOU KNOW I CAN'T DO THAT.
SARCASM DOESN'T WORK ON ME.
THAT'S OKAY.
I AIN'T VERY GOOD AT IT.
I'M GLAD YOU KNOW.
THINK ABOUT WHO YOU ARE GUARDING!
WHAT THEY ARE ASKING YOU TO DO.
I CAN'T DO THAT.
UM, WE MAY HAVE A--
ZZAATT
AAAGGH!
WHACK

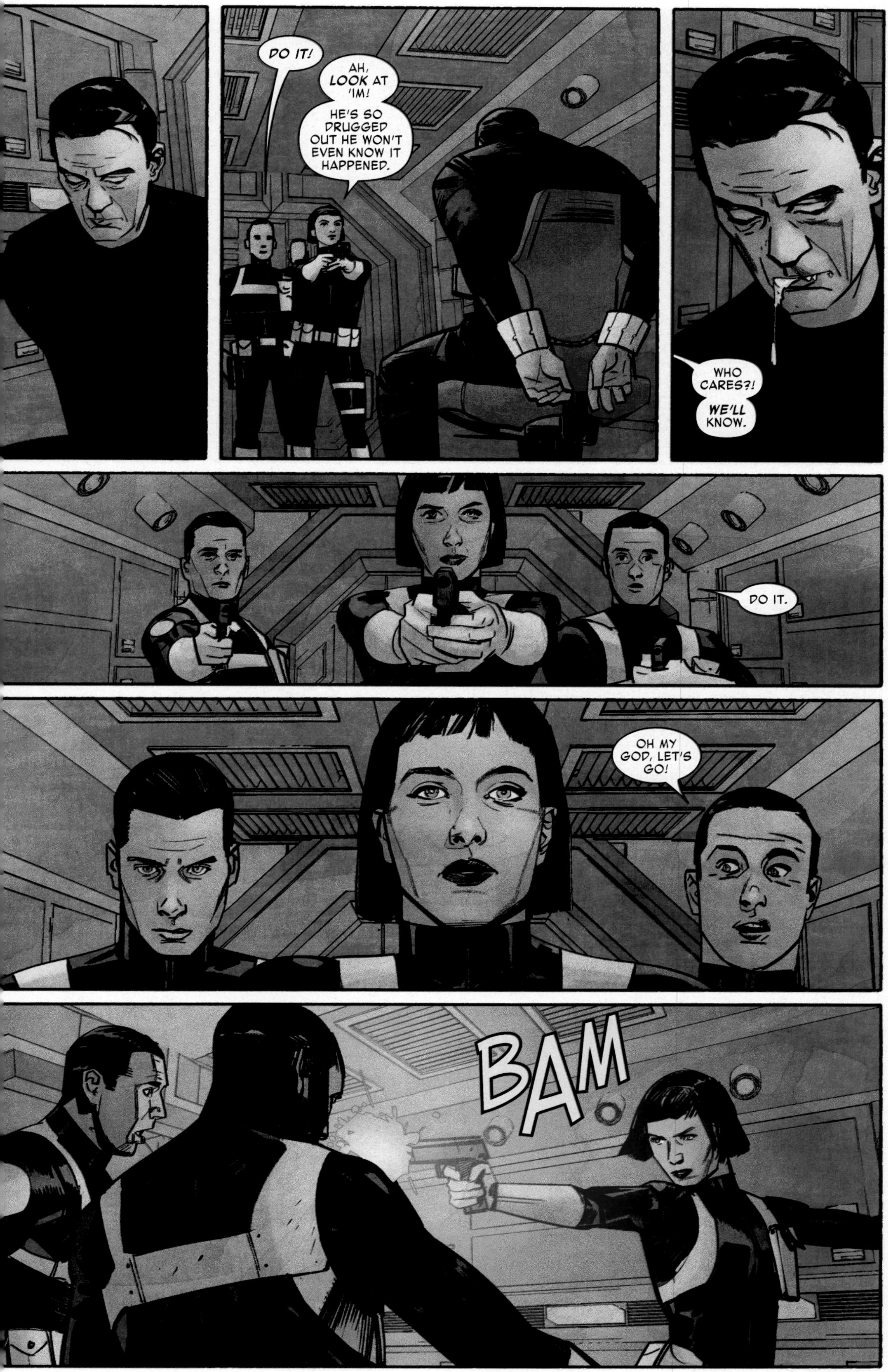
DO IT!
AH, LOOK AT 'IM!
HE'S SO DRUGGED OUT HE WON'T EVEN KNOW IT HAPPENED.
WHO CARES?! WE'LL KNOW.
DO IT.
OH MY GOD, LET'S GO!
BAM

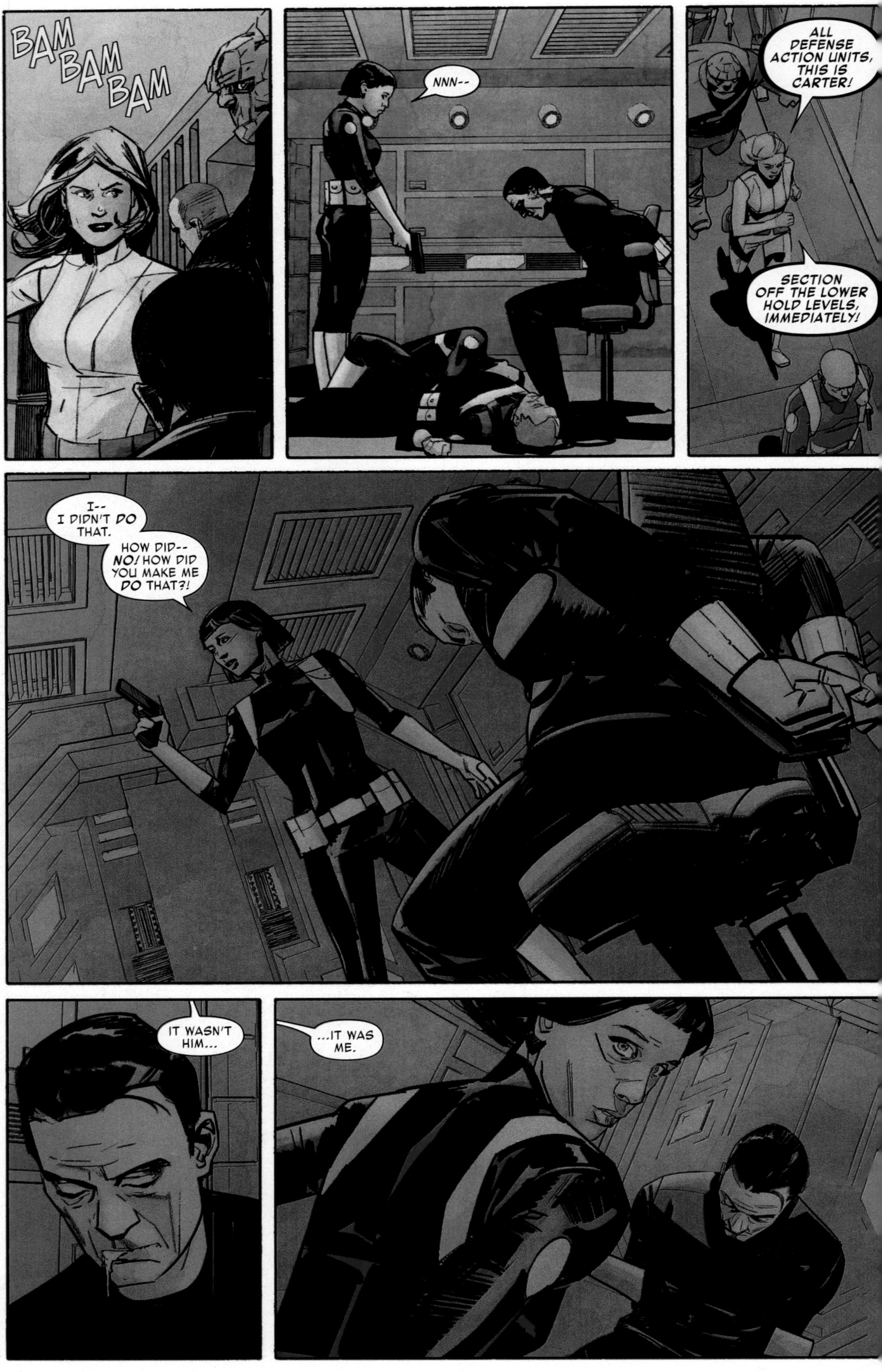
BAM BAM BAM BAM
NNN--
ALL DEFENSE ACTION UNITS, THIS IS CARTER!
SECTION OFF THE LOWER HOLD LEVELS, IMMEDIATELY!
I-- I DIDN'T DO THAT.
HOW DID-- NO! HOW DID YOU MAKE ME DO THAT?!
IT WASN'T HIM...
...IT WAS ME.

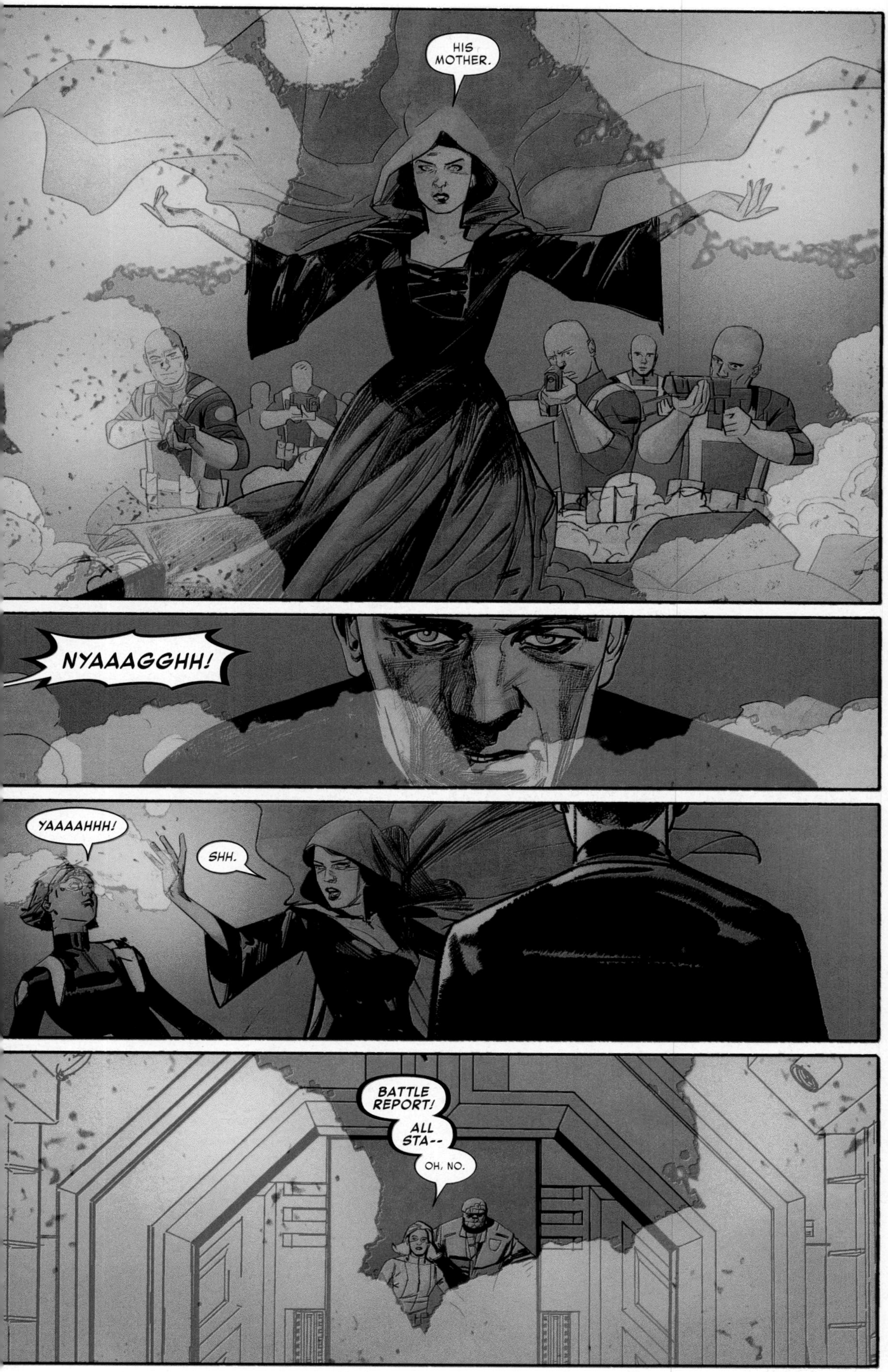
HIS MOTHER.
NYAAAGGHH!
YAAAAHHH!
SHH.
BATTLE REPORT!
ALL STA--
OH, NO.

GRIMM, BACK!

NOT ON THIS FLOATING SHIP!

I'LL GET HER OFF THE--

ALL AGENTS! CODE RED! BATTLE STATIONS!

THIS IS NOT A DRILL!

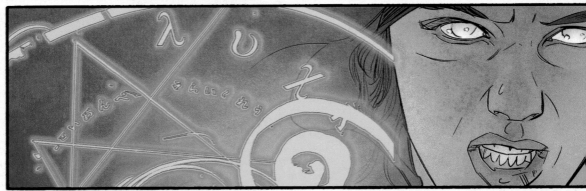

WHA--!

AAGGH!

ALL HANDS!

YOU, IN THE ROCKS.

I *TOLD* YOU TO LEAVE MY SON ALONE.

I WAS *VERY* CLEAR.

GRIMM, NO!

CAN'T DO NUTHIN'.

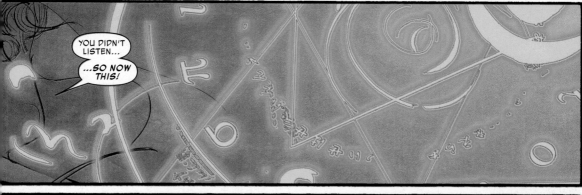

YOU DIDN'T LISTEN...

...SO NOW THIS!

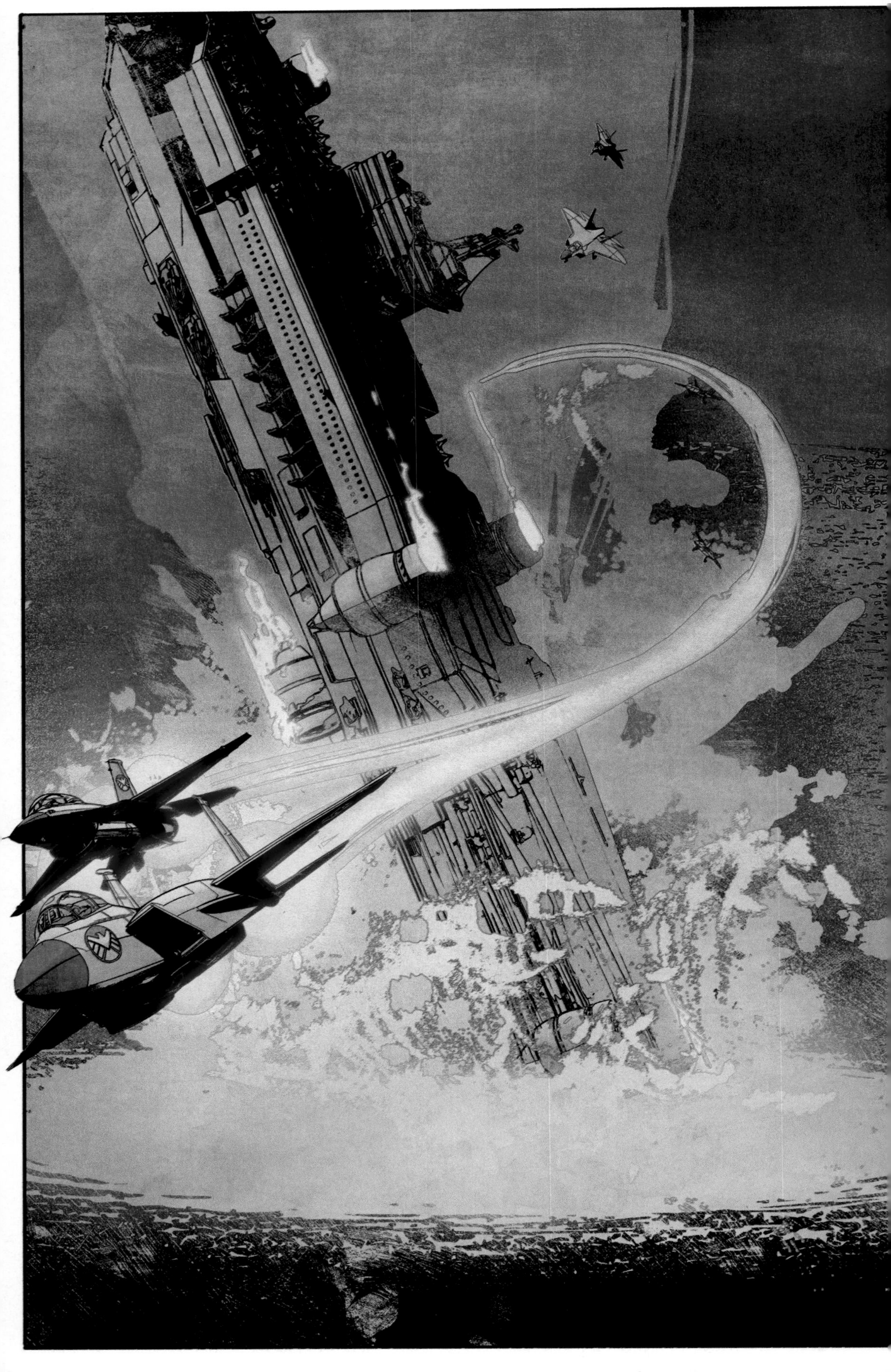

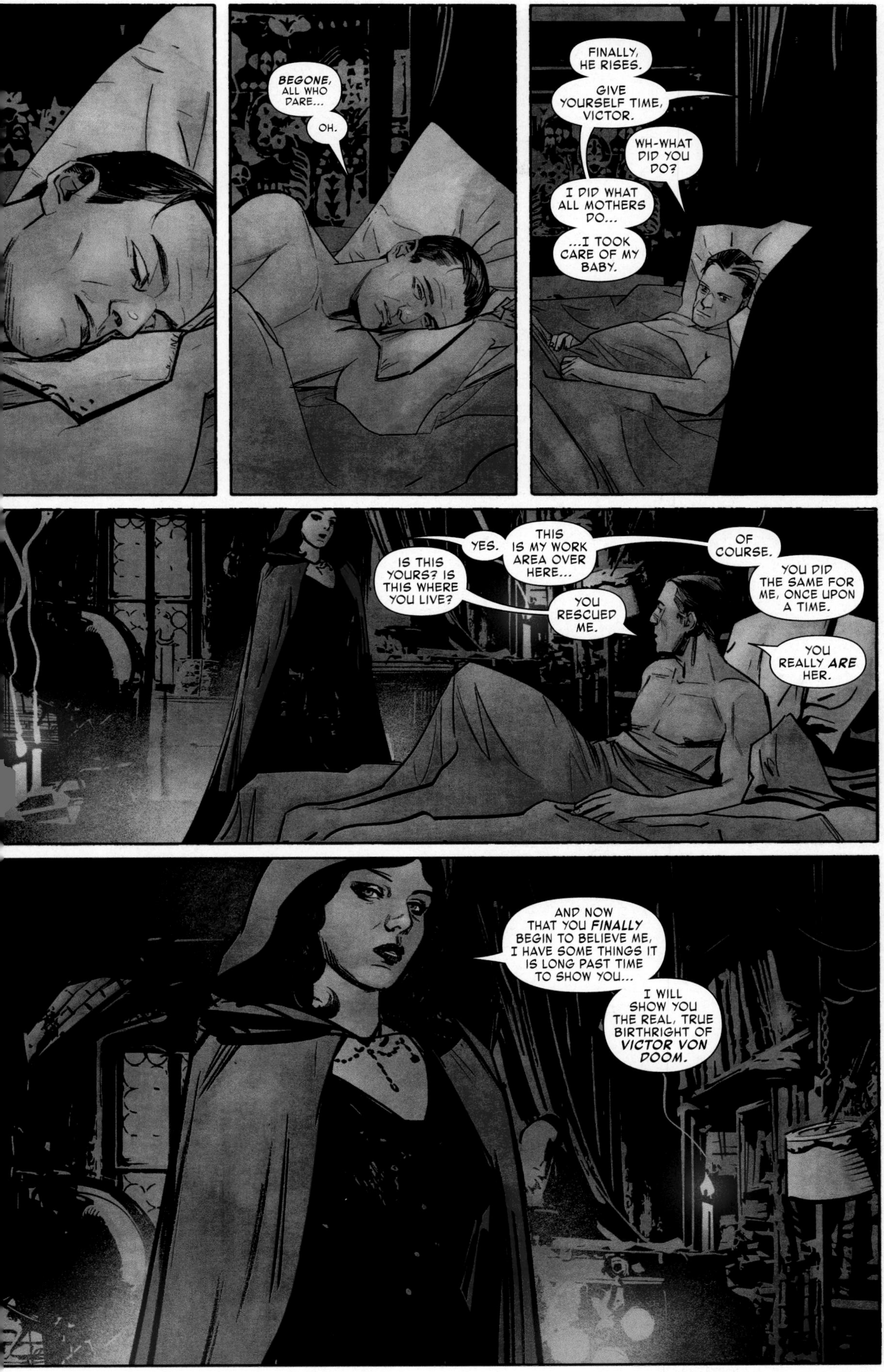
BEGONE, ALL WHO DARE...
OH.
FINALLY, HE RISES.
GIVE YOURSELF TIME, VICTOR.
WH-WHAT DID YOU DO?
I DID WHAT ALL MOTHERS DO...
...I TOOK CARE OF MY BABY.
IS THIS YOURS? IS THIS WHERE YOU LIVE?
YES.
THIS IS MY WORK AREA OVER HERE...
OF COURSE.
YOU RESCUED ME.
YOU DID THE SAME FOR ME, ONCE UPON A TIME.
YOU REALLY ARE HER.
AND NOW THAT YOU FINALLY BEGIN TO BELIEVE ME, I HAVE SOME THINGS IT IS LONG PAST TIME TO SHOW YOU...
I WILL SHOW YOU THE REAL, TRUE BIRTHRIGHT OF VICTOR VON DOOM.

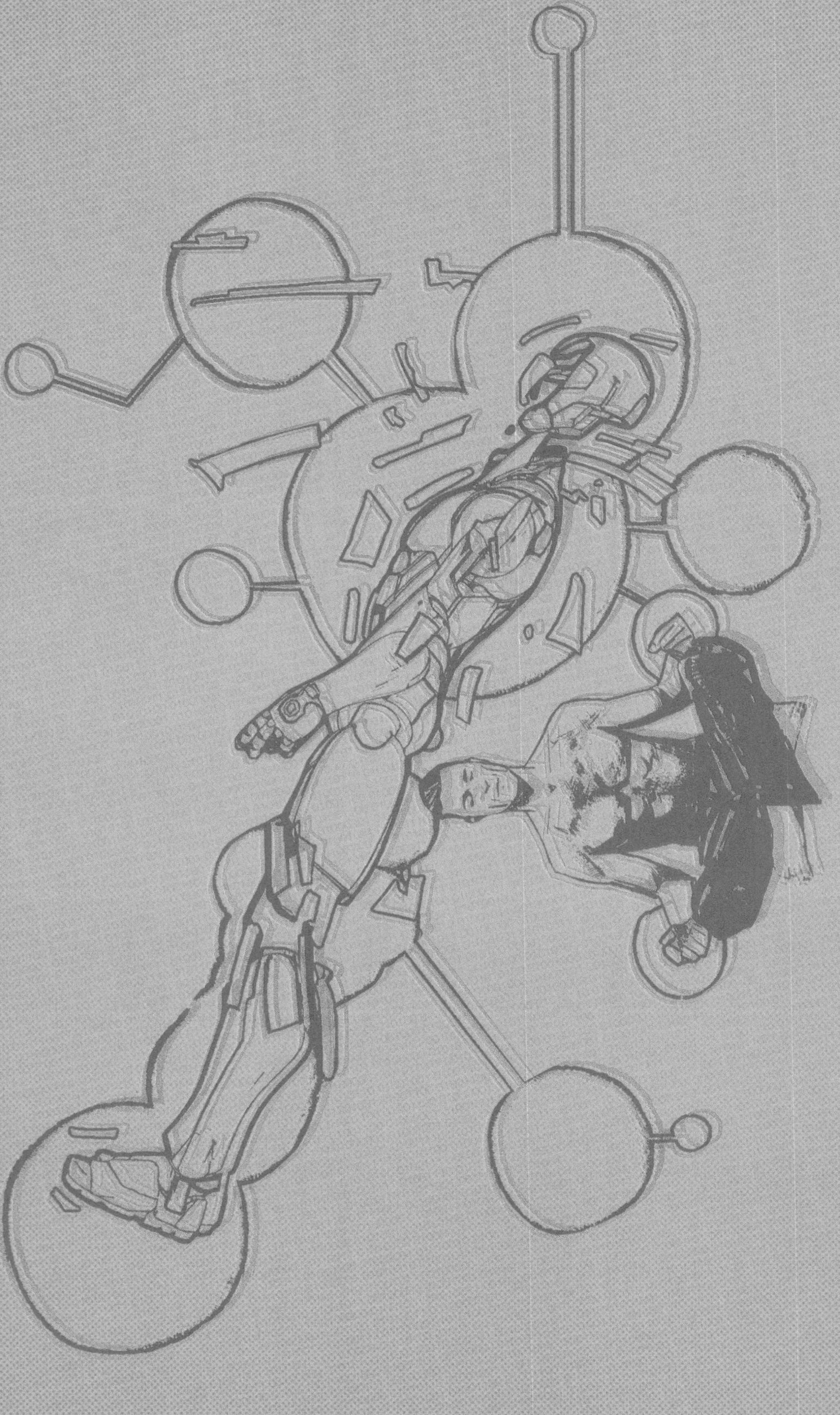

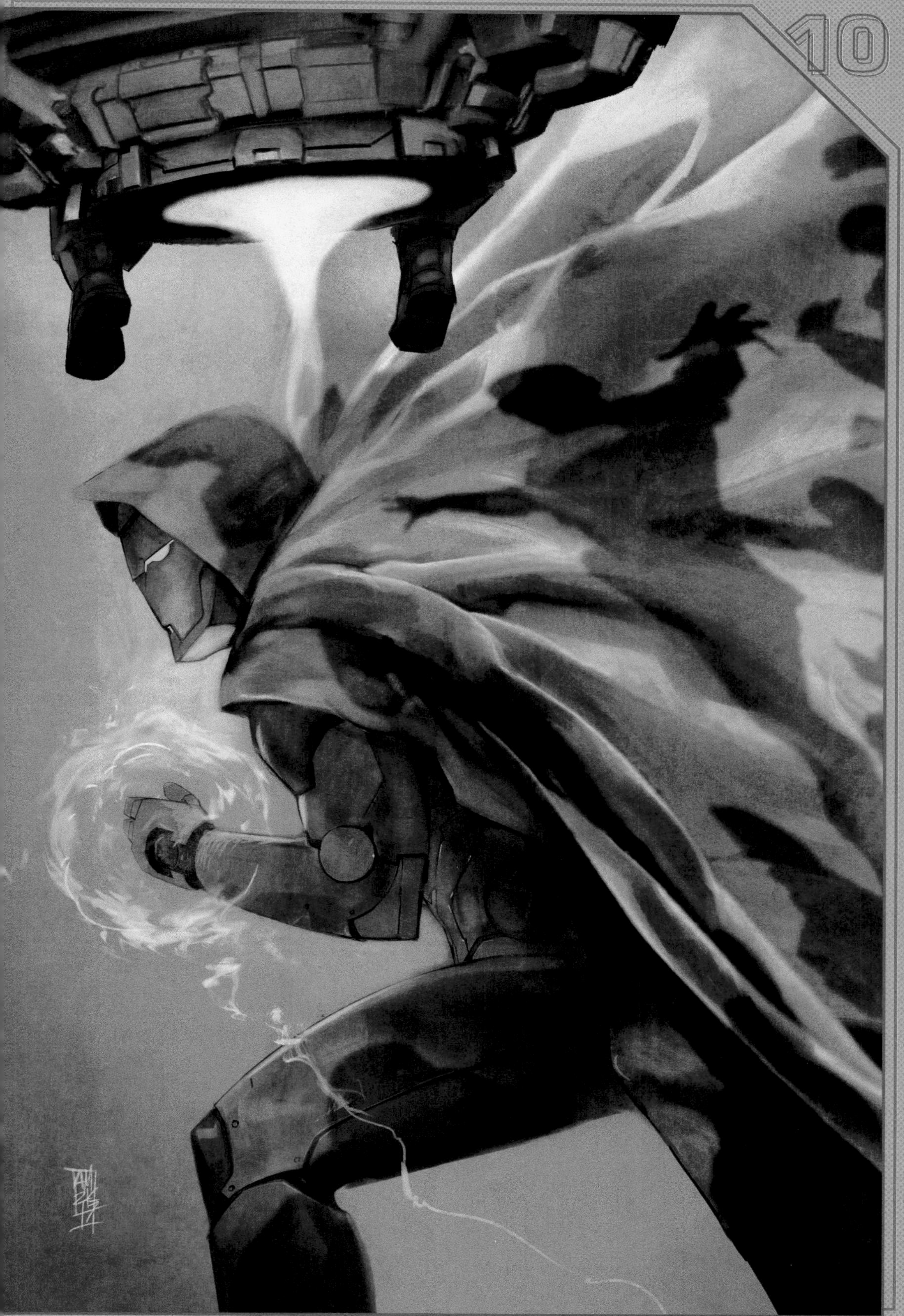
10

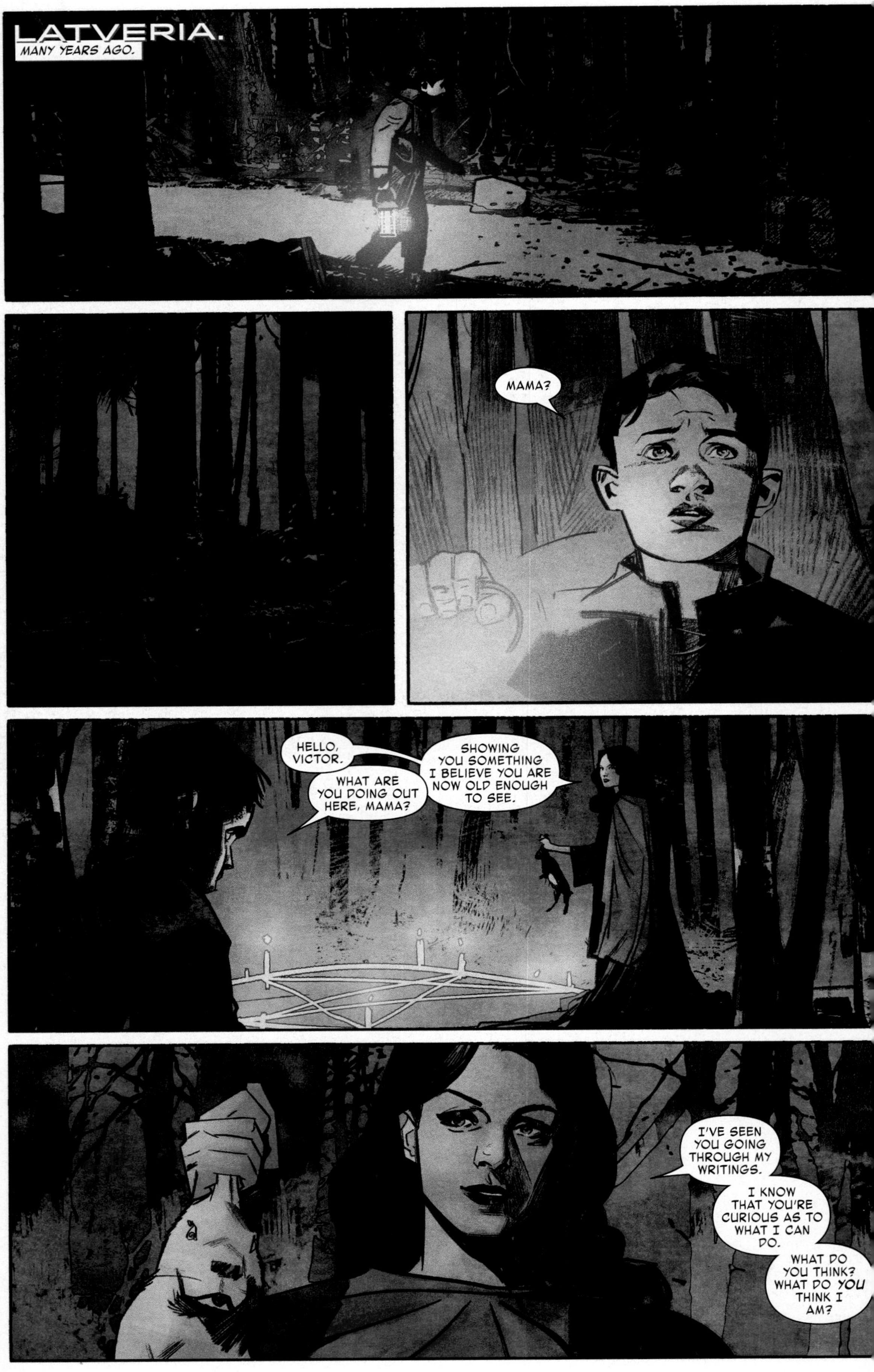
LATVERIA.
MANY YEARS AGO.
MAMA?
HELLO, VICTOR.
WHAT ARE YOU DOING OUT HERE, MAMA?
SHOWING YOU SOMETHING I BELIEVE YOU ARE NOW OLD ENOUGH TO SEE.
I'VE SEEN YOU GOING THROUGH MY WRITINGS.
I KNOW THAT YOU'RE CURIOUS AS TO WHAT I CAN DO.
WHAT DO YOU THINK? WHAT DO *YOU* THINK I AM?

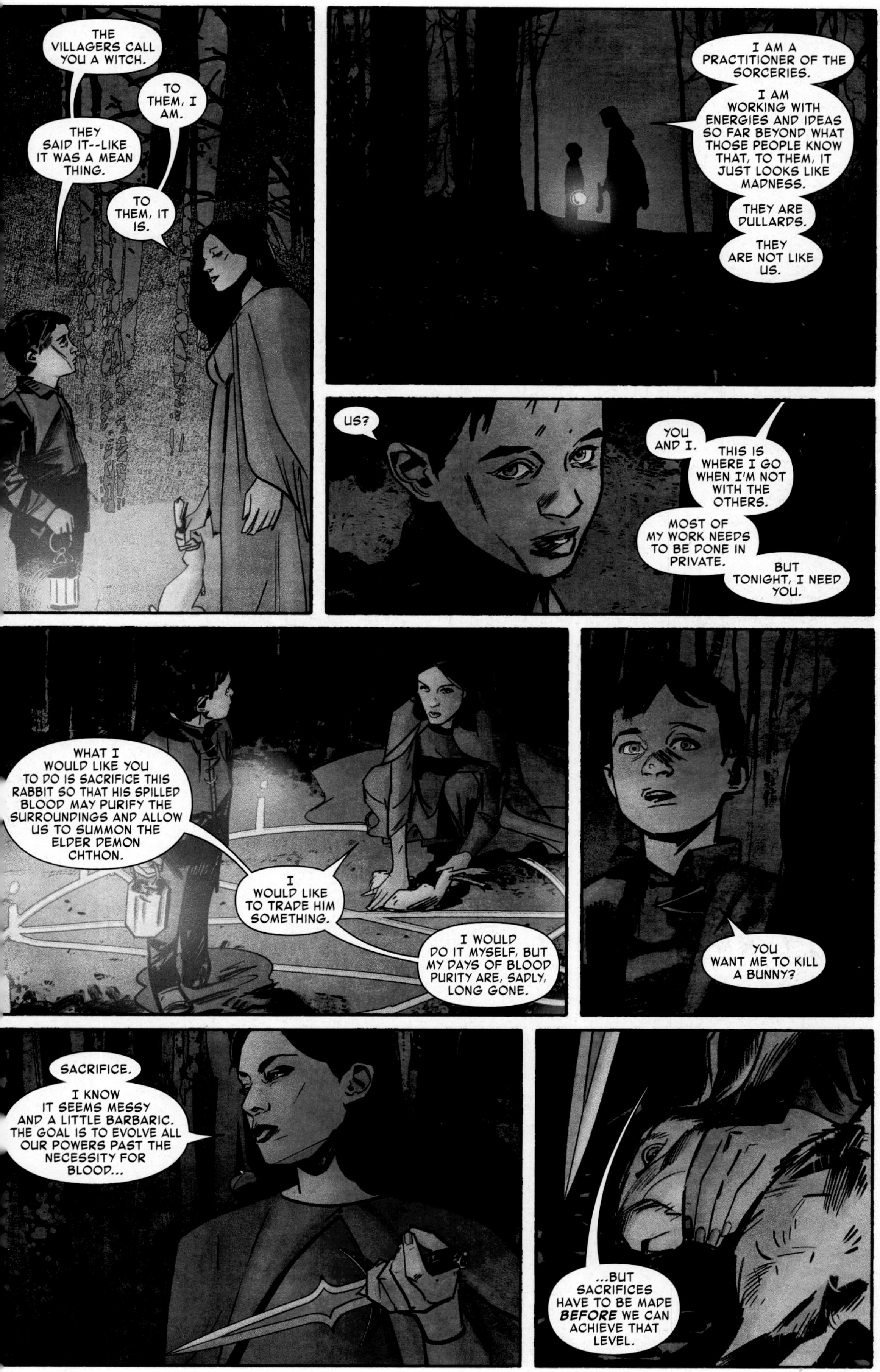
THE VILLAGERS CALL YOU A WITCH.
TO THEM, I AM.
THEY SAID IT--LIKE IT WAS A MEAN THING.
TO THEM, IT IS.
I AM A PRACTITIONER OF THE SORCERIES.
I AM WORKING WITH ENERGIES AND IDEAS SO FAR BEYOND WHAT THOSE PEOPLE KNOW THAT, TO THEM, IT JUST LOOKS LIKE MADNESS.
THEY ARE DULLARDS.
THEY ARE NOT LIKE US.
US?
YOU AND I.
THIS IS WHERE I GO WHEN I'M NOT WITH THE OTHERS.
MOST OF MY WORK NEEDS TO BE DONE IN PRIVATE.
BUT TONIGHT, I NEED YOU.
WHAT I WOULD LIKE YOU TO DO IS SACRIFICE THIS RABBIT SO THAT HIS SPILLED BLOOD MAY PURIFY THE SURROUNDINGS AND ALLOW US TO SUMMON THE ELDER DEMON CHTHON.
I WOULD LIKE TO TRADE HIM SOMETHING.
I WOULD DO IT MYSELF, BUT MY DAYS OF BLOOD PURITY ARE, SADLY, LONG GONE.
YOU WANT ME TO KILL A BUNNY?
SACRIFICE.
I KNOW IT SEEMS MESSY AND A LITTLE BARBARIC. THE GOAL IS TO EVOLVE ALL OUR POWERS PAST THE NECESSITY FOR BLOOD...
...BUT SACRIFICES HAVE TO BE MADE *BEFORE* WE CAN ACHIEVE THAT LEVEL.

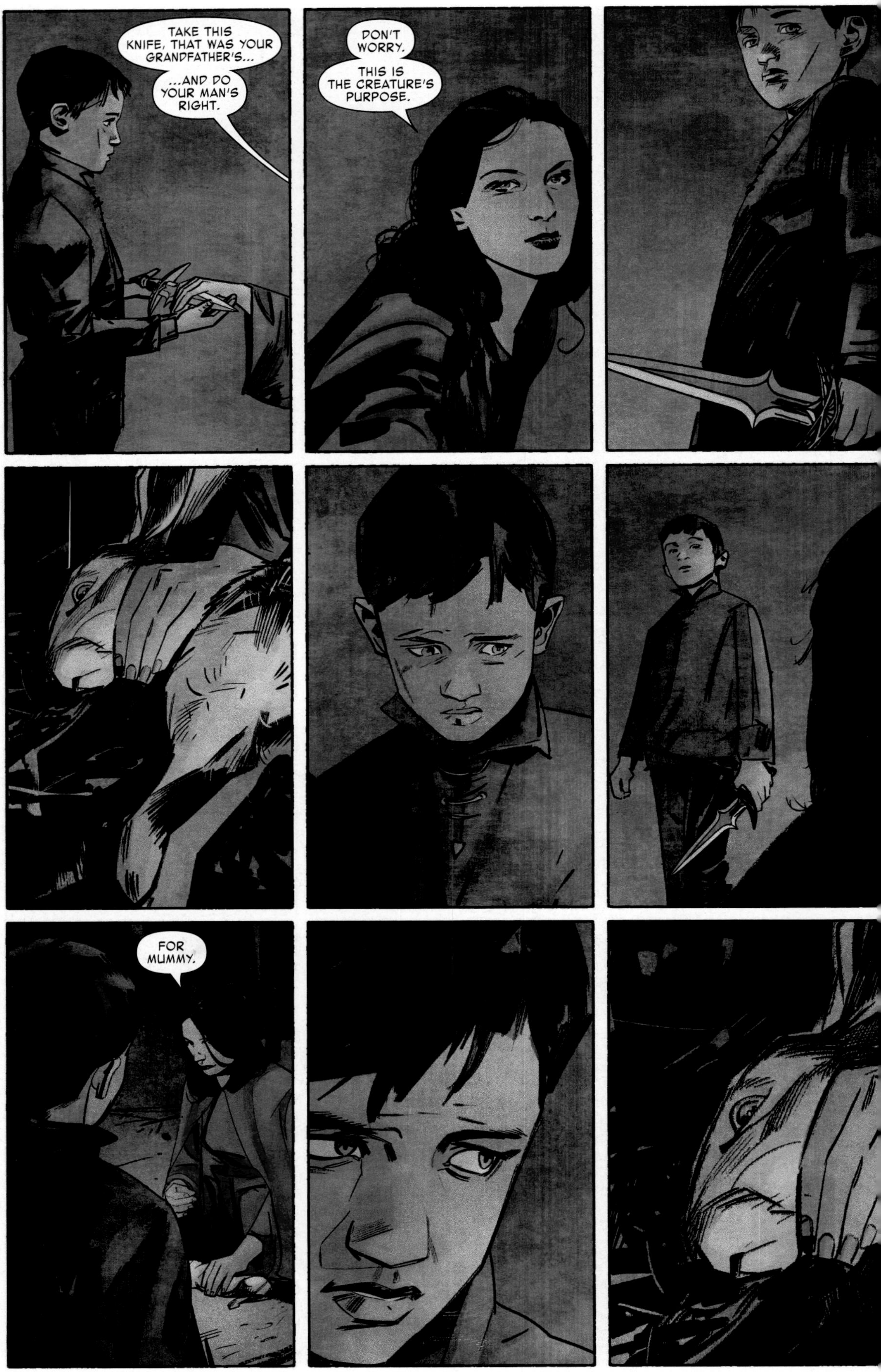
TAKE THIS KNIFE, THAT WAS YOUR GRANDFATHER'S...
...AND DO YOUR MAN'S RIGHT.
DON'T WORRY.
THIS IS THE CREATURE'S PURPOSE.
FOR MUMMY.

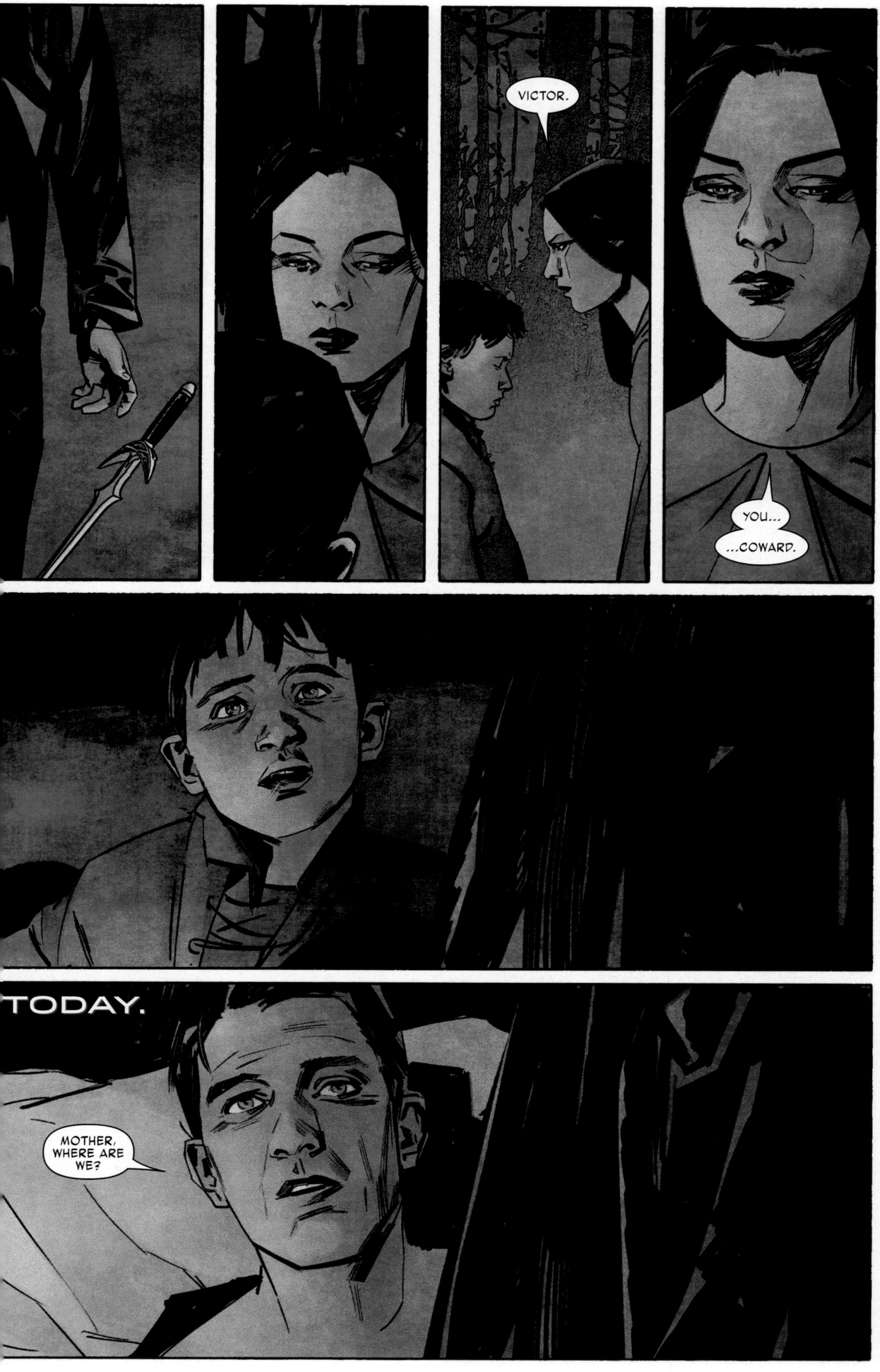
VICTOR.
YOU...
...COWARD.
TODAY.
MOTHER, WHERE ARE WE?

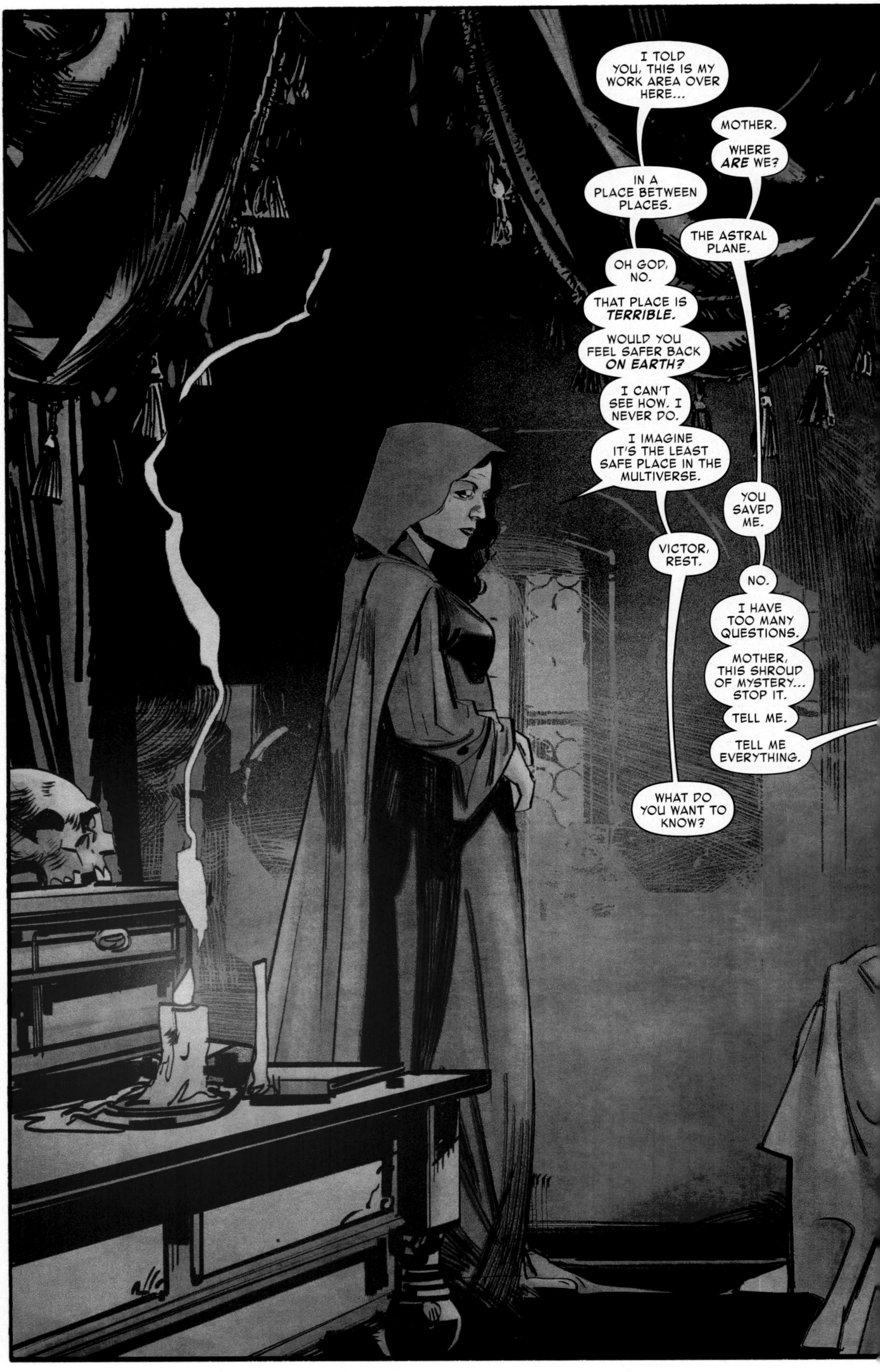

I TOLD YOU, THIS IS MY WORK AREA OVER HERE...
MOTHER.
WHERE ARE WE?
IN A PLACE BETWEEN PLACES.
THE ASTRAL PLANE.
OH GOD, NO.
THAT PLACE IS TERRIBLE.
WOULD YOU FEEL SAFER BACK ON EARTH?
I CAN'T SEE HOW. I NEVER DO.
I IMAGINE IT'S THE LEAST SAFE PLACE IN THE MULTIVERSE.
YOU SAVED ME.
VICTOR, REST.
NO.
I HAVE TOO MANY QUESTIONS.
MOTHER, THIS SHROUD OF MYSTERY... STOP IT.
TELL ME.
TELL ME EVERYTHING.
WHAT DO YOU WANT TO KNOW?

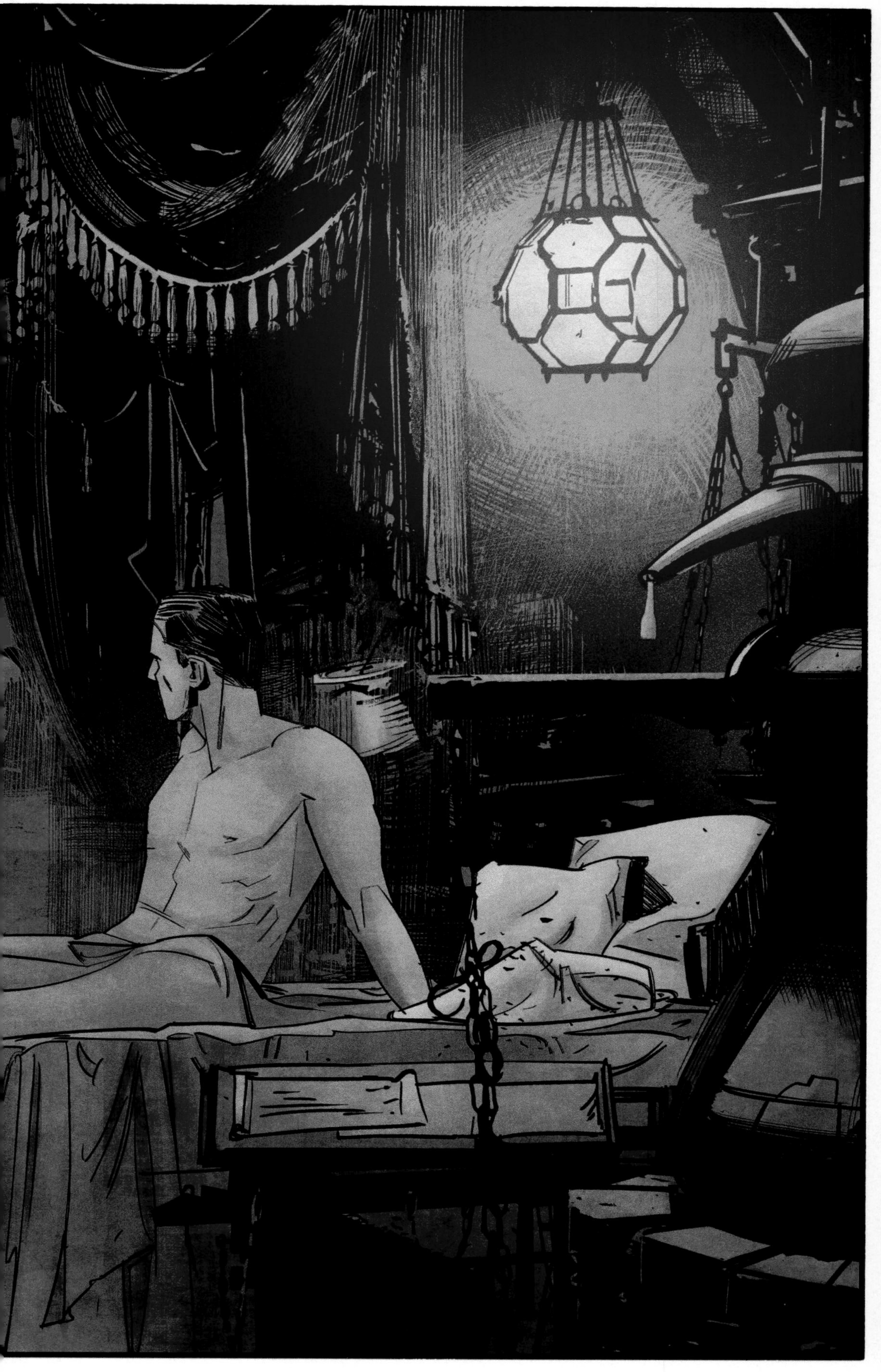

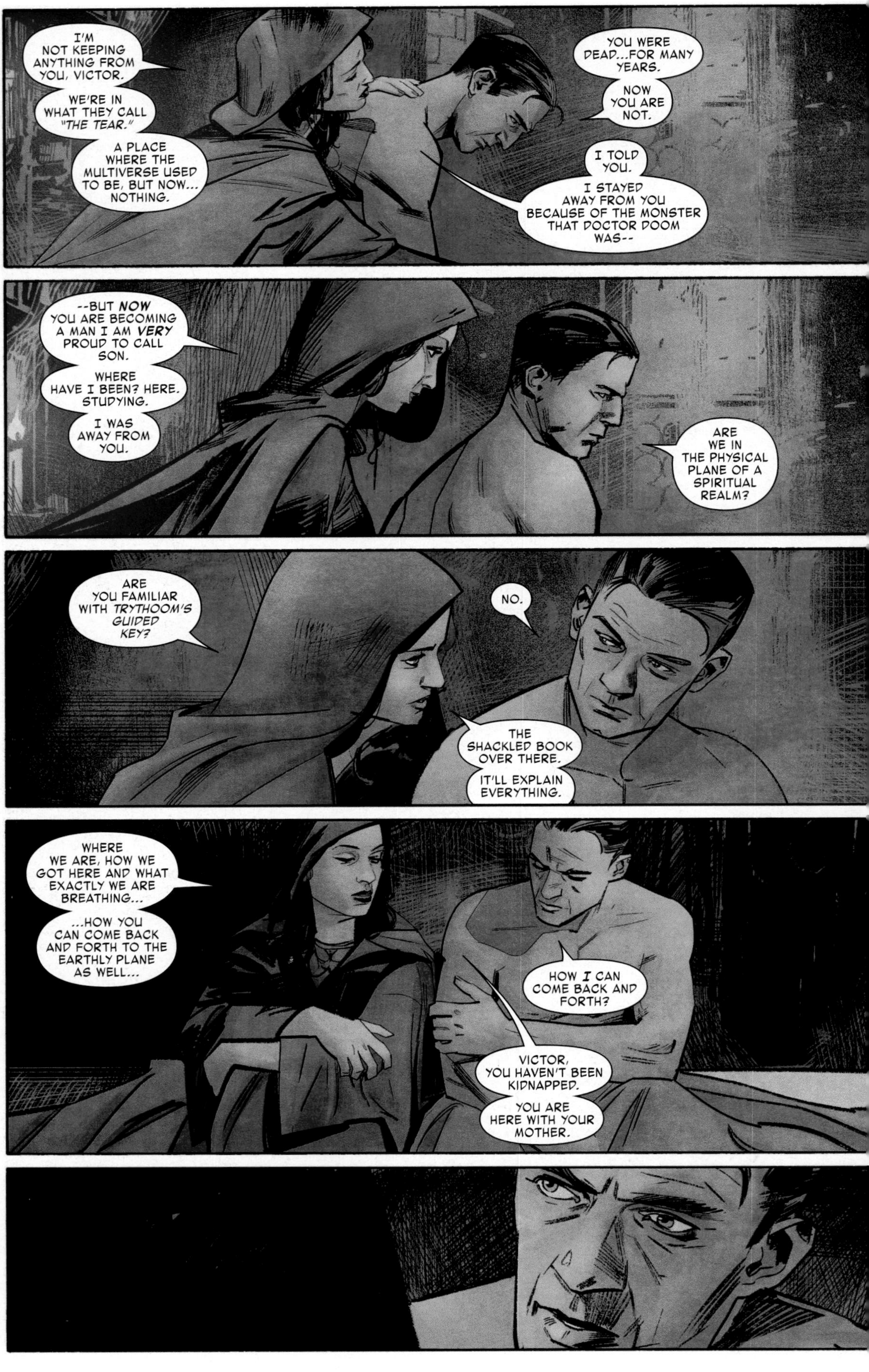
I'M NOT KEEPING ANYTHING FROM YOU, VICTOR.
WE'RE IN WHAT THEY CALL "THE TEAR."
A PLACE WHERE THE MULTIVERSE USED TO BE, BUT NOW... NOTHING.
YOU WERE DEAD...FOR MANY YEARS.
NOW YOU ARE NOT.
I TOLD YOU.
I STAYED AWAY FROM YOU BECAUSE OF THE MONSTER THAT DOCTOR DOOM WAS--
--BUT NOW YOU ARE BECOMING A MAN I AM VERY PROUD TO CALL SON.
WHERE HAVE I BEEN? HERE. STUDYING.
I WAS AWAY FROM YOU.
ARE WE IN THE PHYSICAL PLANE OF A SPIRITUAL REALM?
ARE YOU FAMILIAR WITH TRYTHOOM'S GUIDED KEY?
NO.
THE SHACKLED BOOK OVER THERE.
IT'LL EXPLAIN EVERYTHING.
WHERE WE ARE, HOW WE GOT HERE AND WHAT EXACTLY WE ARE BREATHING...
...HOW YOU CAN COME BACK AND FORTH TO THE EARTHLY PLANE AS WELL...
HOW I CAN COME BACK AND FORTH?
VICTOR, YOU HAVEN'T BEEN KIDNAPPED.
YOU ARE HERE WITH YOUR MOTHER.

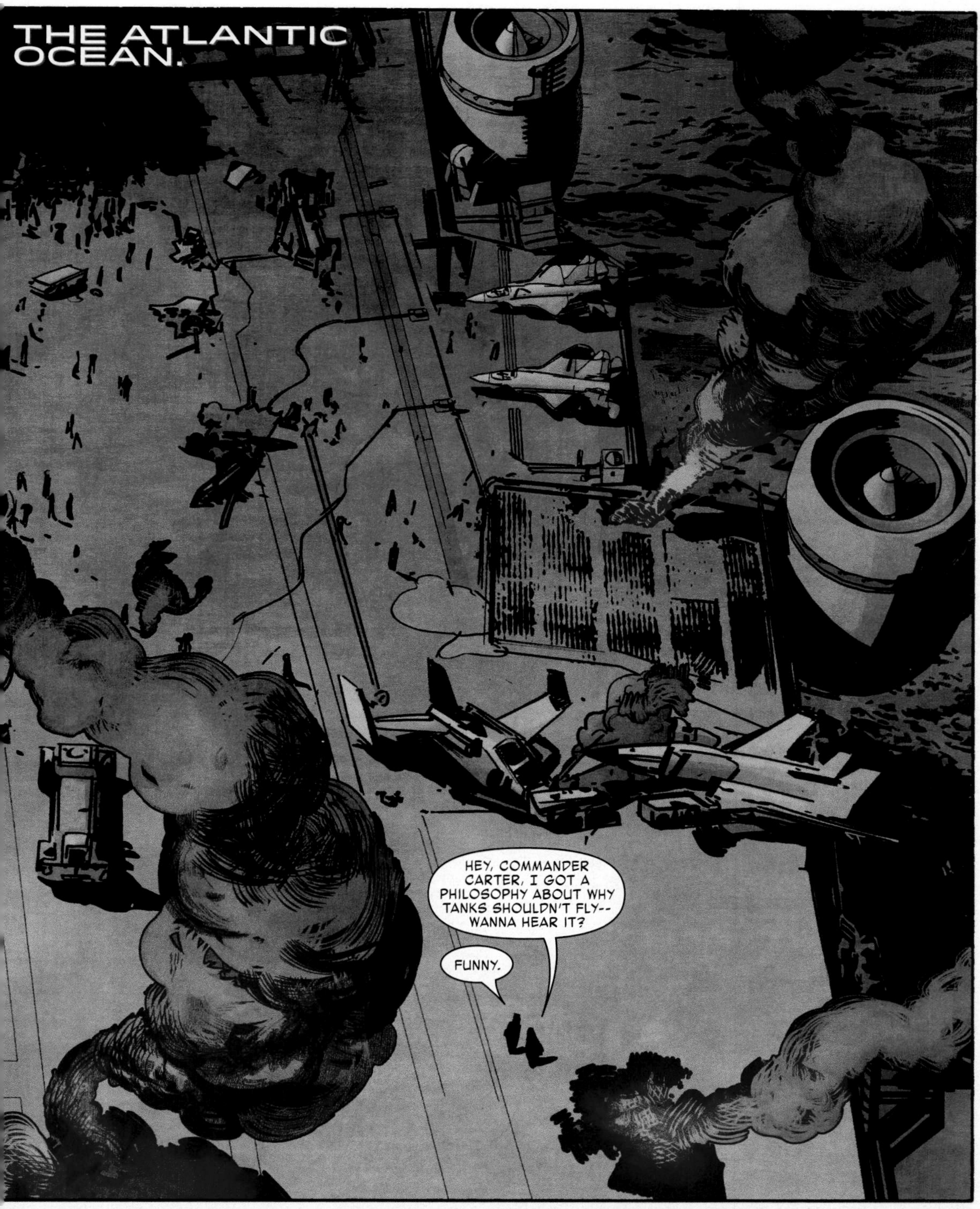
THE ATLANTIC OCEAN.
HEY, COMMANDER CARTER, I GOT A PHILOSOPHY ABOUT WHY TANKS SHOULDN'T FLY-- WANNA HEAR IT?
FUNNY.

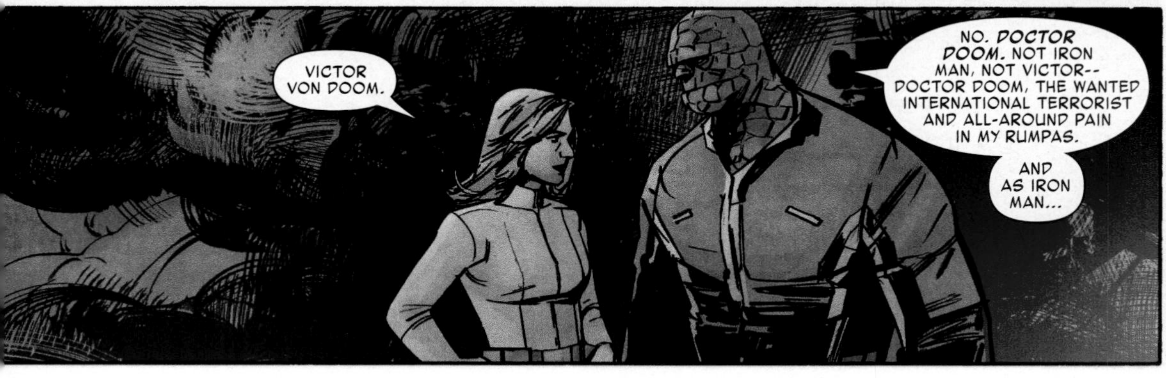
VICTOR VON DOOM.
NO. *DOCTOR DOOM.* NOT IRON MAN, NOT VICTOR-- DOCTOR DOOM, THE WANTED INTERNATIONAL TERRORIST AND ALL-AROUND PAIN IN MY RUMPAS.
AND AS IRON MAN...

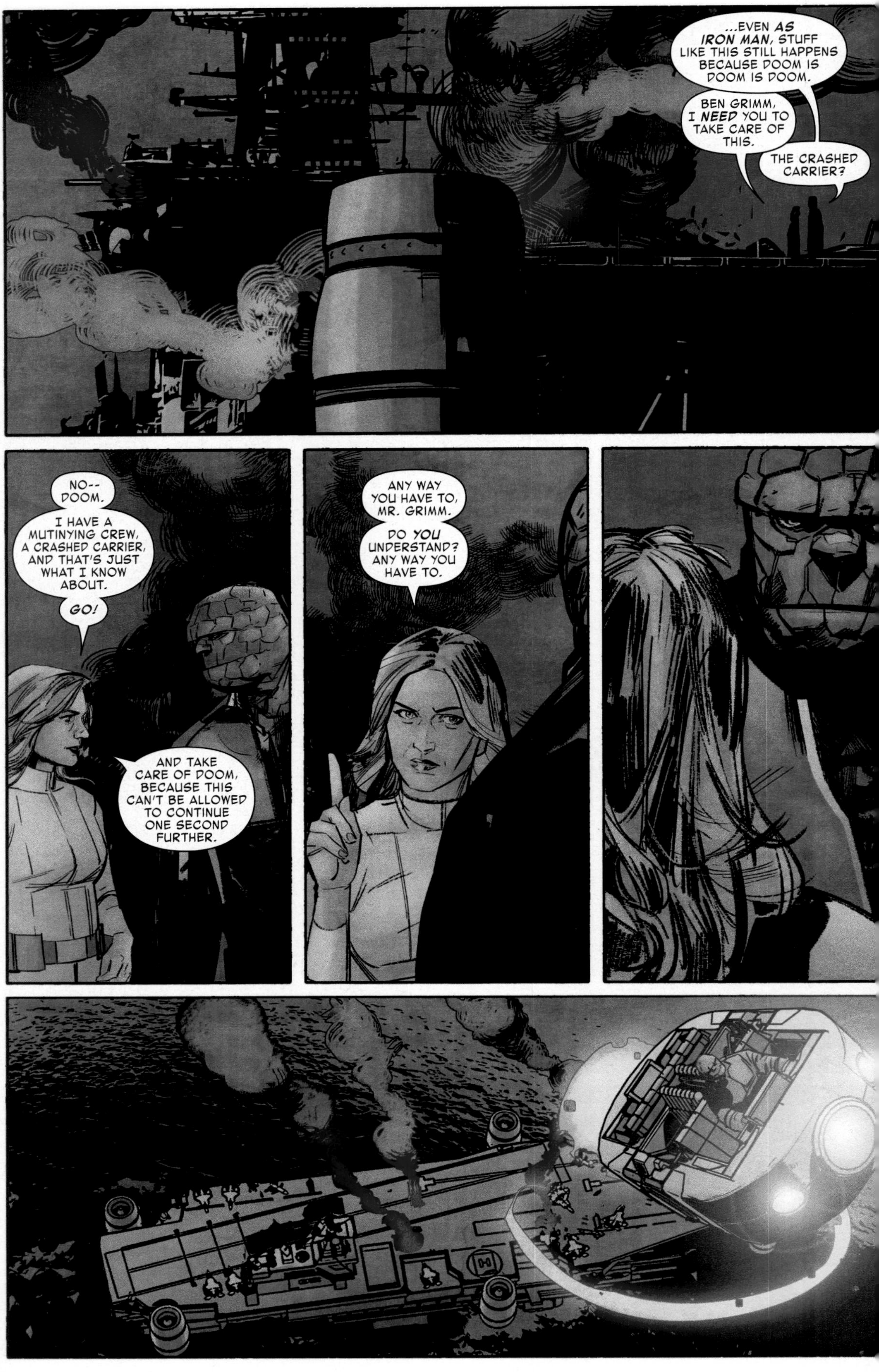
...EVEN AS IRON MAN, STUFF LIKE THIS STILL HAPPENS BECAUSE DOOM IS DOOM IS DOOM.
BEN GRIMM, I NEED YOU TO TAKE CARE OF THIS.
THE CRASHED CARRIER?
NO-- DOOM.
I HAVE A MUTINYING CREW, A CRASHED CARRIER, AND THAT'S JUST WHAT I KNOW ABOUT.
GO!
AND TAKE CARE OF DOOM, BECAUSE THIS CAN'T BE ALLOWED TO CONTINUE ONE SECOND FURTHER.
ANY WAY YOU HAVE TO, MR. GRIMM.
DO YOU UNDERSTAND? ANY WAY YOU HAVE TO.

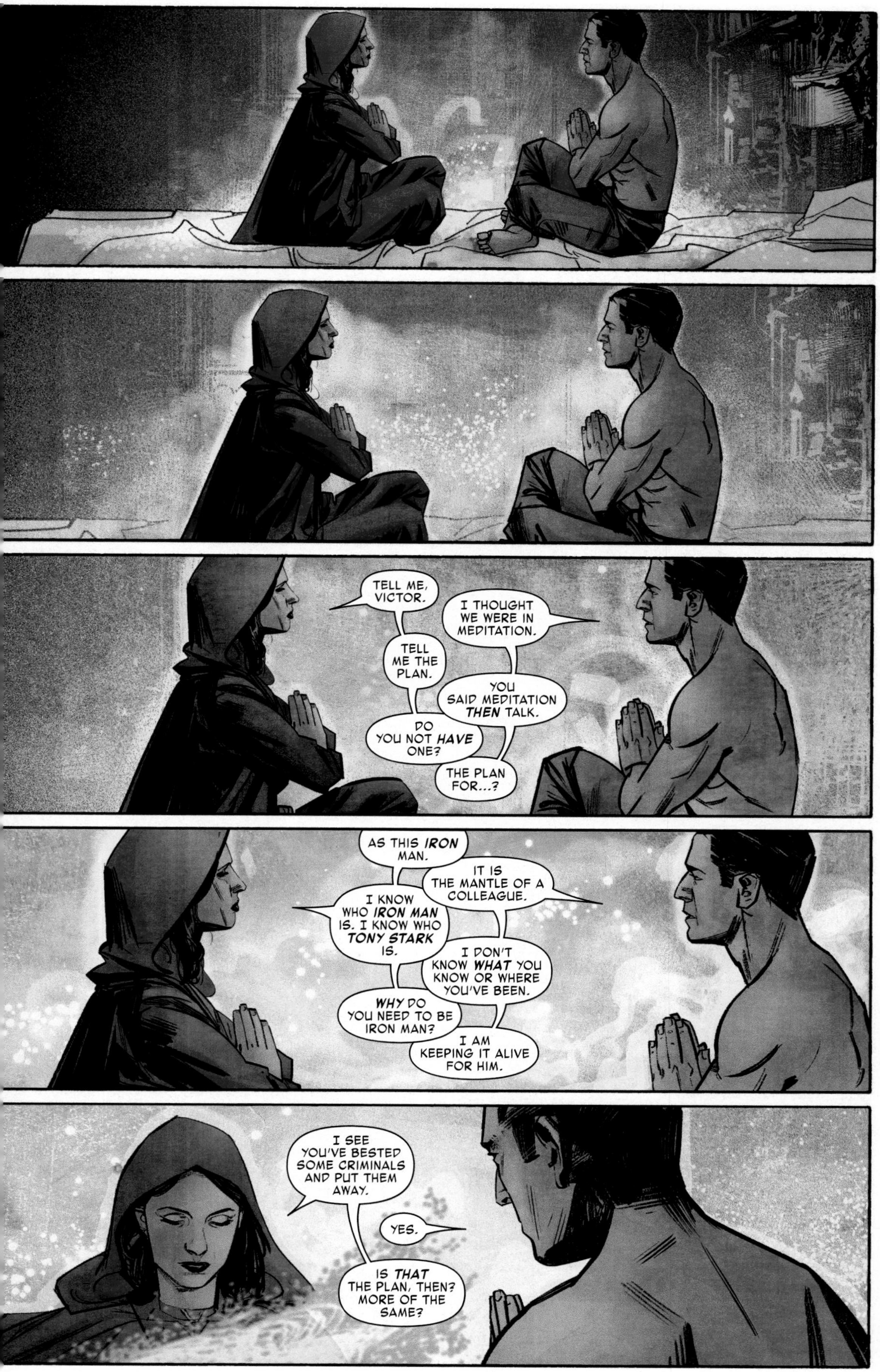
TELL ME, VICTOR.
TELL ME THE PLAN.
I THOUGHT WE WERE IN MEDITATION.
YOU SAID MEDITATION *THEN* TALK.
DO YOU NOT *HAVE* ONE?
THE PLAN FOR...?
AS THIS *IRON* MAN.
IT IS THE MANTLE OF A COLLEAGUE.
I KNOW WHO *IRON MAN* IS. I KNOW WHO *TONY STARK* IS.
I DON'T KNOW *WHAT* YOU KNOW OR WHERE YOU'VE BEEN.
WHY DO YOU NEED TO BE IRON MAN?
I AM KEEPING IT ALIVE FOR HIM.
I SEE YOU'VE BESTED SOME CRIMINALS AND PUT THEM AWAY.
YES.
IS *THAT* THE PLAN, THEN? MORE OF THE SAME?

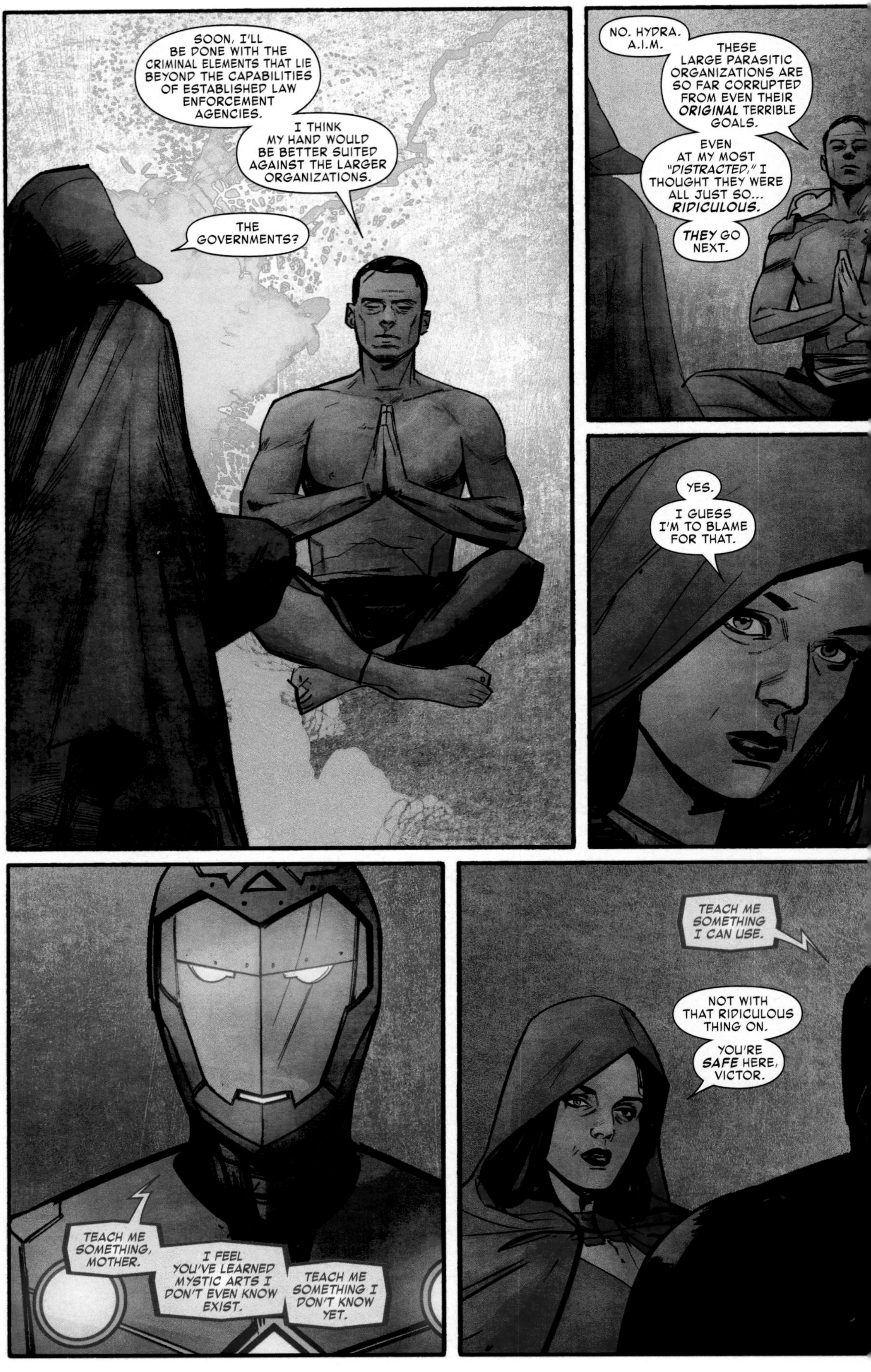
SOON, I'LL BE DONE WITH THE CRIMINAL ELEMENTS THAT LIE BEYOND THE CAPABILITIES OF ESTABLISHED LAW ENFORCEMENT AGENCIES.
I THINK MY HAND WOULD BE BETTER SUITED AGAINST THE LARGER ORGANIZATIONS.
THE GOVERNMENTS?
NO. HYDRA. A.I.M.
THESE LARGE PARASITIC ORGANIZATIONS ARE SO FAR CORRUPTED FROM EVEN THEIR *ORIGINAL* TERRIBLE GOALS.
EVEN AT MY MOST "*DISTRACTED*," I THOUGHT THEY WERE ALL JUST SO... ***RIDICULOUS.***
THEY GO NEXT.
YES.
I GUESS I'M TO BLAME FOR THAT.
TEACH ME SOMETHING, MOTHER.
I FEEL YOU'VE LEARNED MYSTIC ARTS I DON'T EVEN KNOW EXIST.
TEACH ME SOMETHING I DON'T KNOW YET.
TEACH ME SOMETHING I CAN USE.
NOT WITH THAT RIDICULOUS THING ON.
YOU'RE ***SAFE*** HERE, VICTOR.

DO YOU REALLY THINK YOU CAN *DO* THAT?

RID MANKIND OF ALL THOSE THAT WOULD PREY ON THE WEAKER?

I THINK I CAN MAKE THE FIGHT FAIR.

MY SHAME IS THAT I COULD HAVE DONE THIS SO MANY YEARS AGO, HAD I SEEN THINGS WITH A CLEAR MIND.

THAT IS *NOT* WHAT I MEANT.

I AM AN ADULT MAN.

I MADE MY OWN CHOICES.

THAT IS KIND OF YOU TO SAY, BUT WE BOTH KNOW IF I ONLY SHOWED YOU THE WORLD ONE WAY...

...HOW ARE YOU TO GROW UP AND SEE IT AS ANYTHING ELSE?

YOU'RE SAFE.

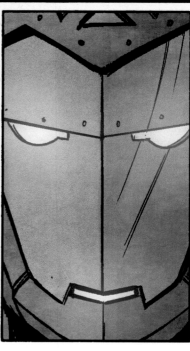

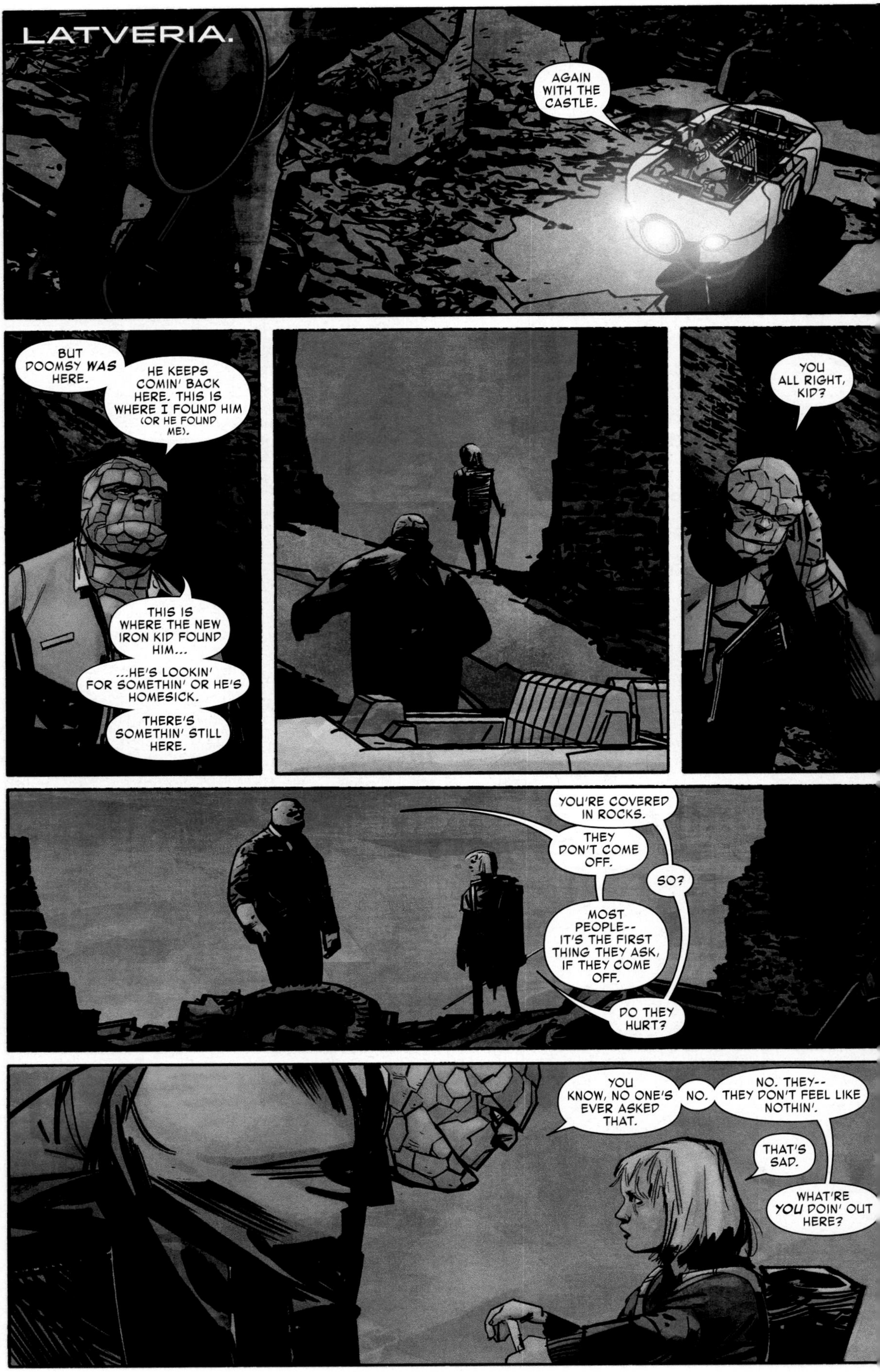
LATVERIA.
AGAIN WITH THE CASTLE.
BUT DOOMSY *WAS* HERE.
HE KEEPS COMIN' BACK HERE. THIS IS WHERE I FOUND HIM (OR HE FOUND ME).
THIS IS WHERE THE NEW IRON KID FOUND HIM...
...HE'S LOOKIN' FOR SOMETHIN' OR HE'S HOMESICK.
THERE'S SOMETHIN' STILL HERE.
YOU ALL RIGHT, KID?
YOU'RE COVERED IN ROCKS.
THEY DON'T COME OFF.
SO?
MOST PEOPLE-- IT'S THE FIRST THING THEY ASK, IF THEY COME OFF.
DO THEY HURT?
YOU KNOW, NO ONE'S EVER ASKED THAT.
NO.
NO. THEY-- THEY DON'T FEEL LIKE NOTHIN'.
THAT'S SAD.
WHAT'RE *YOU* DOIN' OUT HERE?

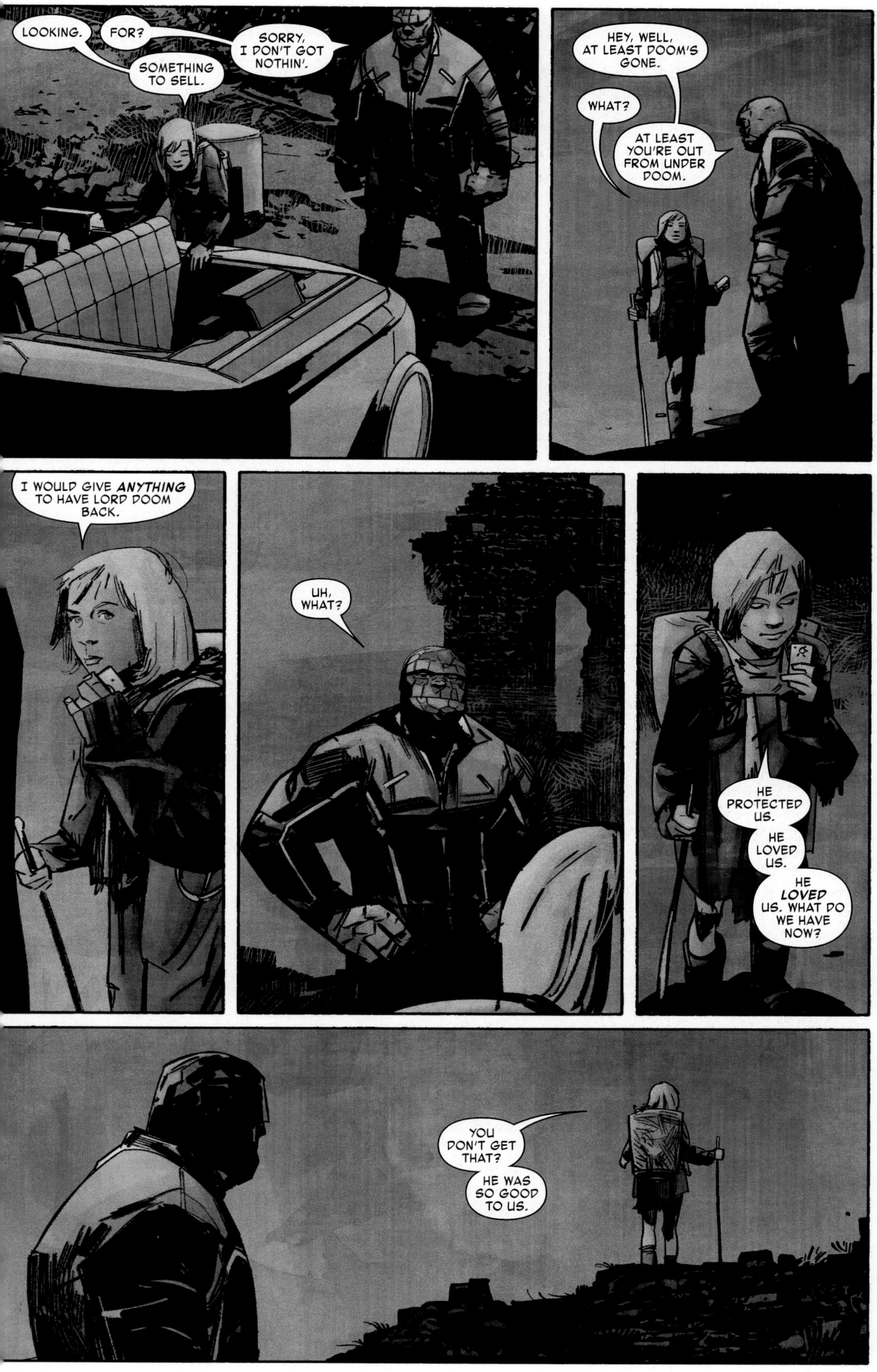
LOOKING.
FOR?
SOMETHING TO SELL.
SORRY, I DON'T GOT NOTHIN'.
HEY, WELL, AT LEAST DOOM'S GONE.
WHAT?
AT LEAST YOU'RE OUT FROM UNDER DOOM.
I WOULD GIVE ANYTHING TO HAVE LORD DOOM BACK.
UH, WHAT?
HE PROTECTED US.
HE LOVED US.
HE LOVED US. WHAT DO WE HAVE NOW?
YOU DON'T GET THAT?
HE WAS SO GOOD TO US.

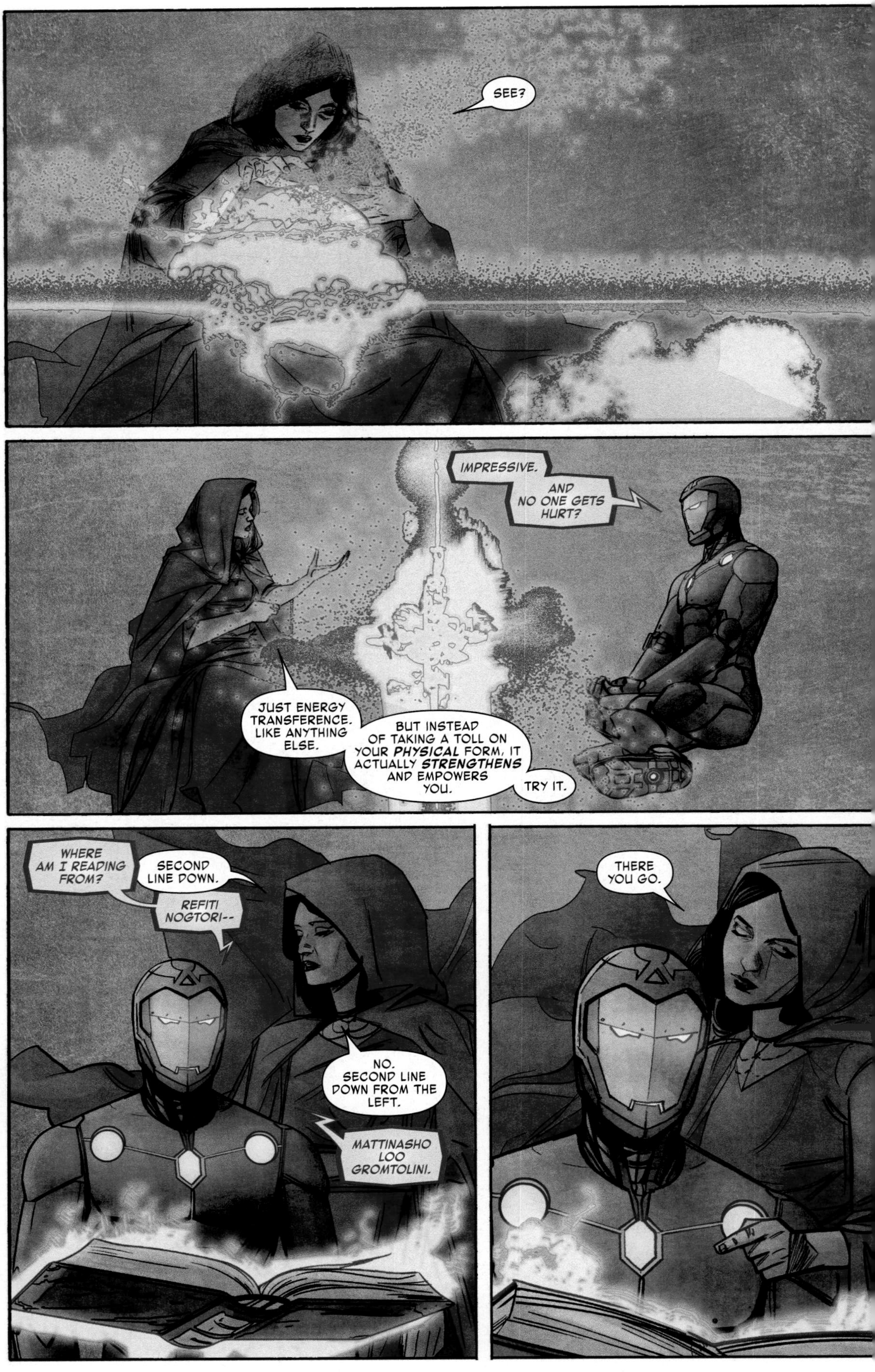
SEE?
IMPRESSIVE.
AND NO ONE GETS HURT?
JUST ENERGY TRANSFERENCE. LIKE ANYTHING ELSE.
BUT INSTEAD OF TAKING A TOLL ON YOUR PHYSICAL FORM, IT ACTUALLY STRENGTHENS AND EMPOWERS YOU.
TRY IT.
WHERE AM I READING FROM?
SECOND LINE DOWN.
REFITI NOGTORI--
NO. SECOND LINE DOWN FROM THE LEFT.
MATTINASHO LOO GROMTOLINI.
THERE YOU GO.

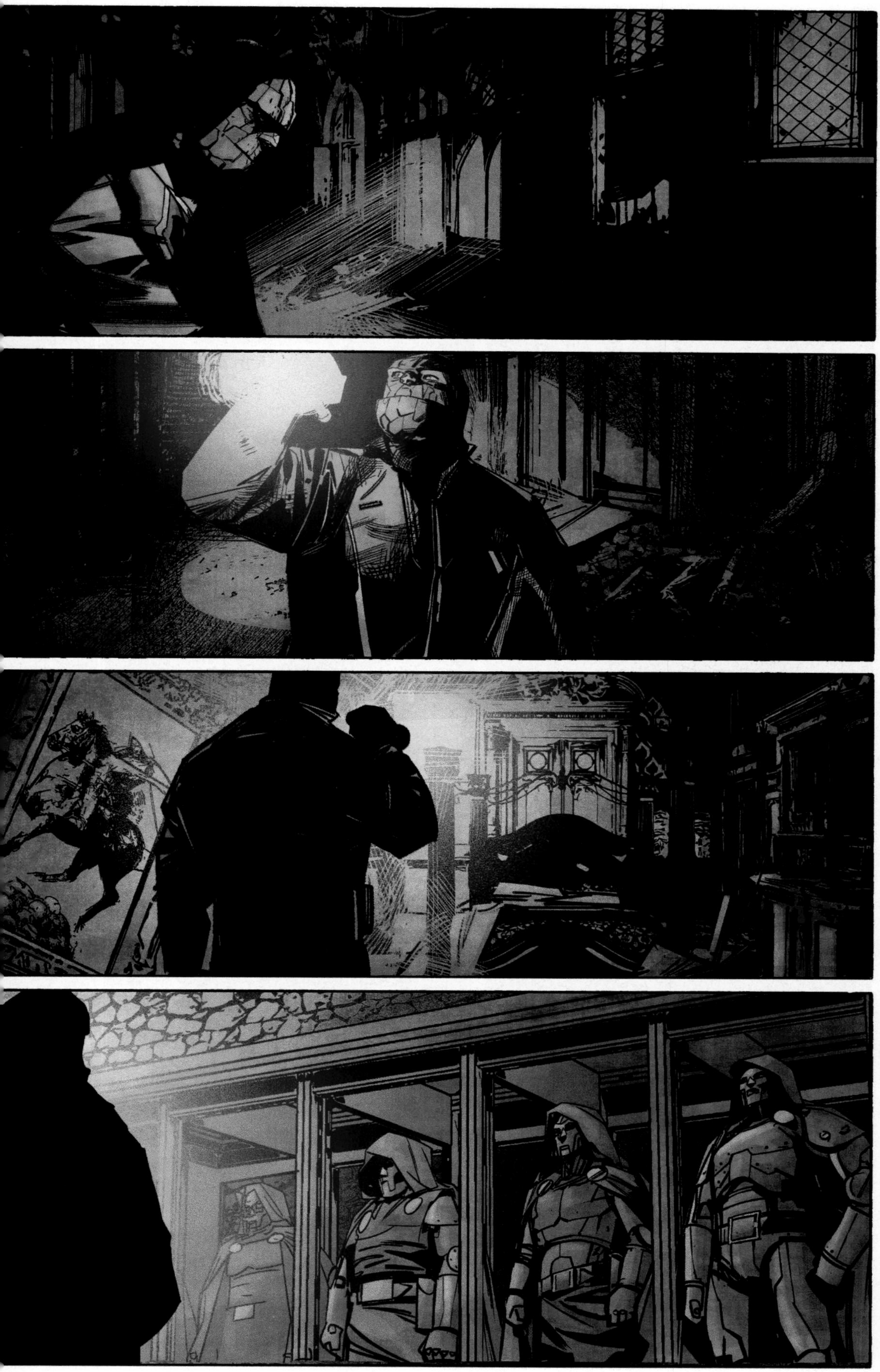

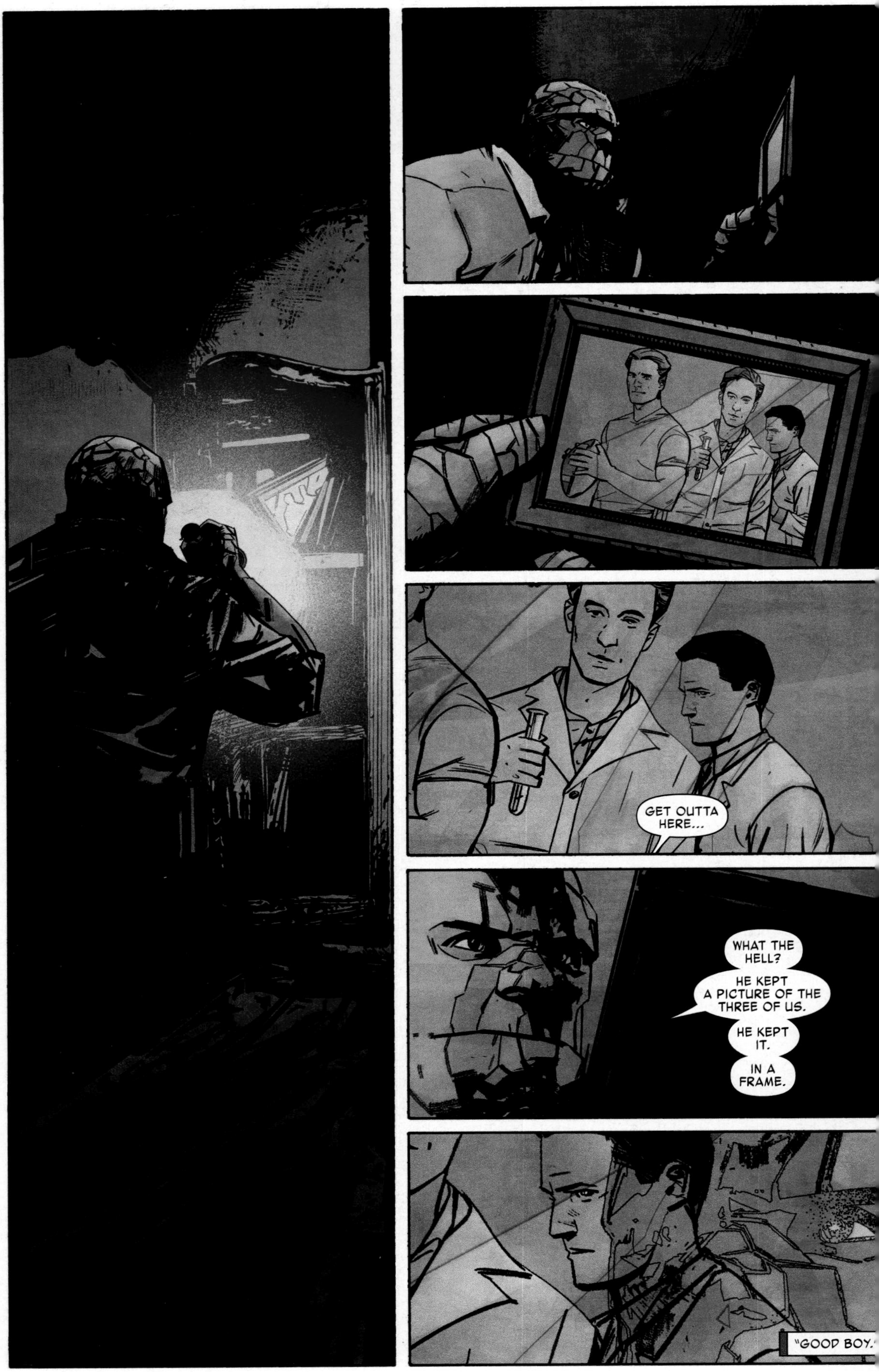
GET OUTTA HERE...
WHAT THE HELL?
HE KEPT A PICTURE OF THE THREE OF US.
HE KEPT IT.
IN A FRAME.
"GOOD BOY."

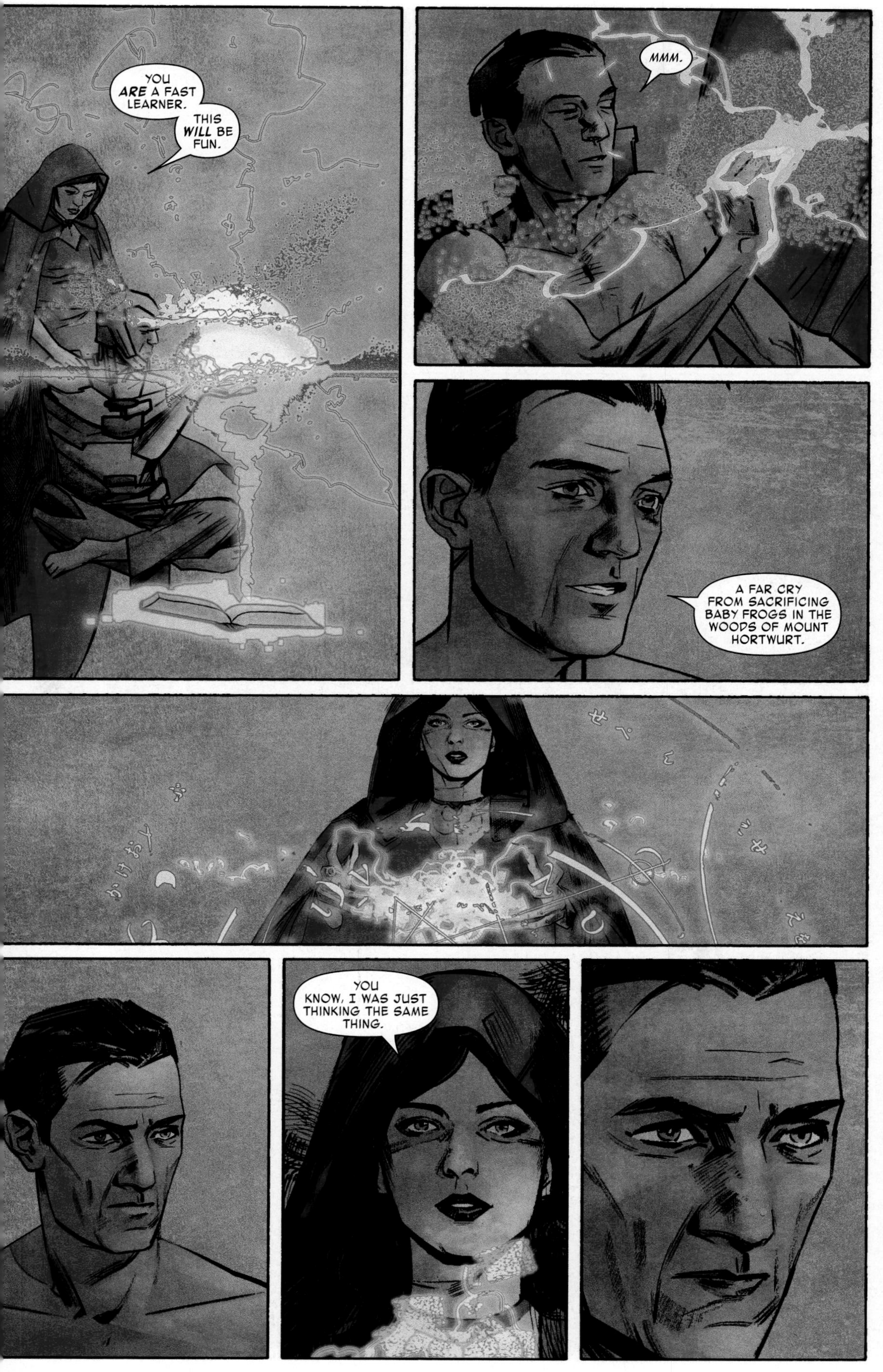
YOU ARE A FAST LEARNER.
THIS WILL BE FUN.
MMM.
A FAR CRY FROM SACRIFICING BABY FROGS IN THE WOODS OF MOUNT HORTWURT.
YOU KNOW, I WAS JUST THINKING THE SAME THING.

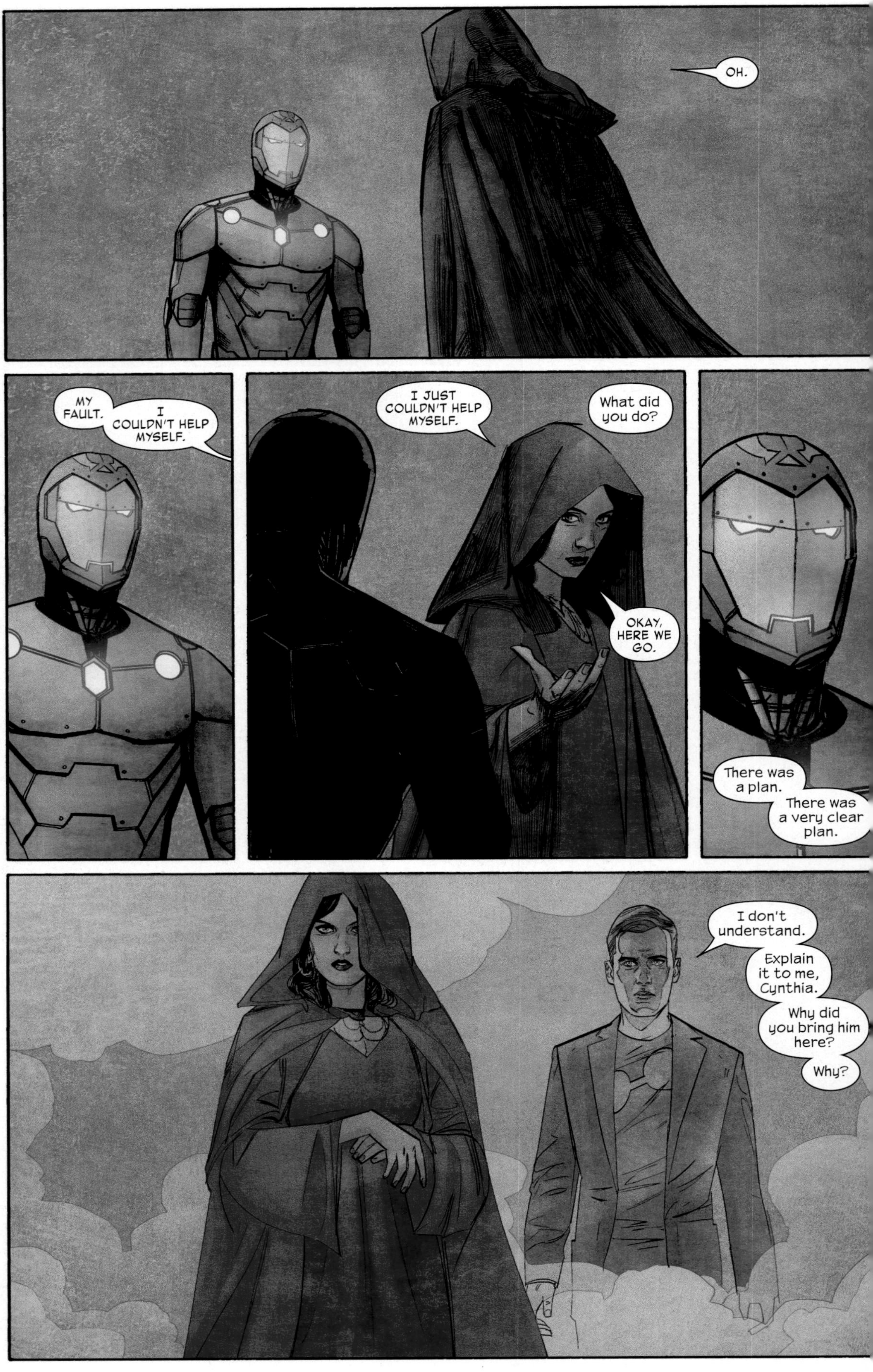
OH.
MY FAULT.
I COULDN'T HELP MYSELF.
I JUST COULDN'T HELP MYSELF.
What did you do?
OKAY, HERE WE GO.
There was a plan.
There was a very clear plan.
I don't understand.
Explain it to me, Cynthia.
Why did you bring him here?
Why?

AAGH!

GEEZ LOUISE!

THE HELL, VIC?

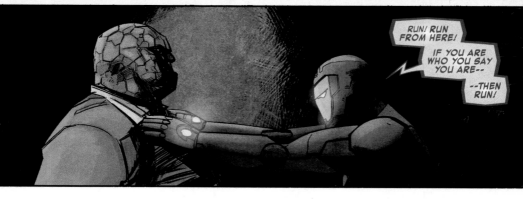

RUN! RUN FROM HERE!

IF YOU ARE WHO YOU SAY YOU ARE--

--THEN RUN!

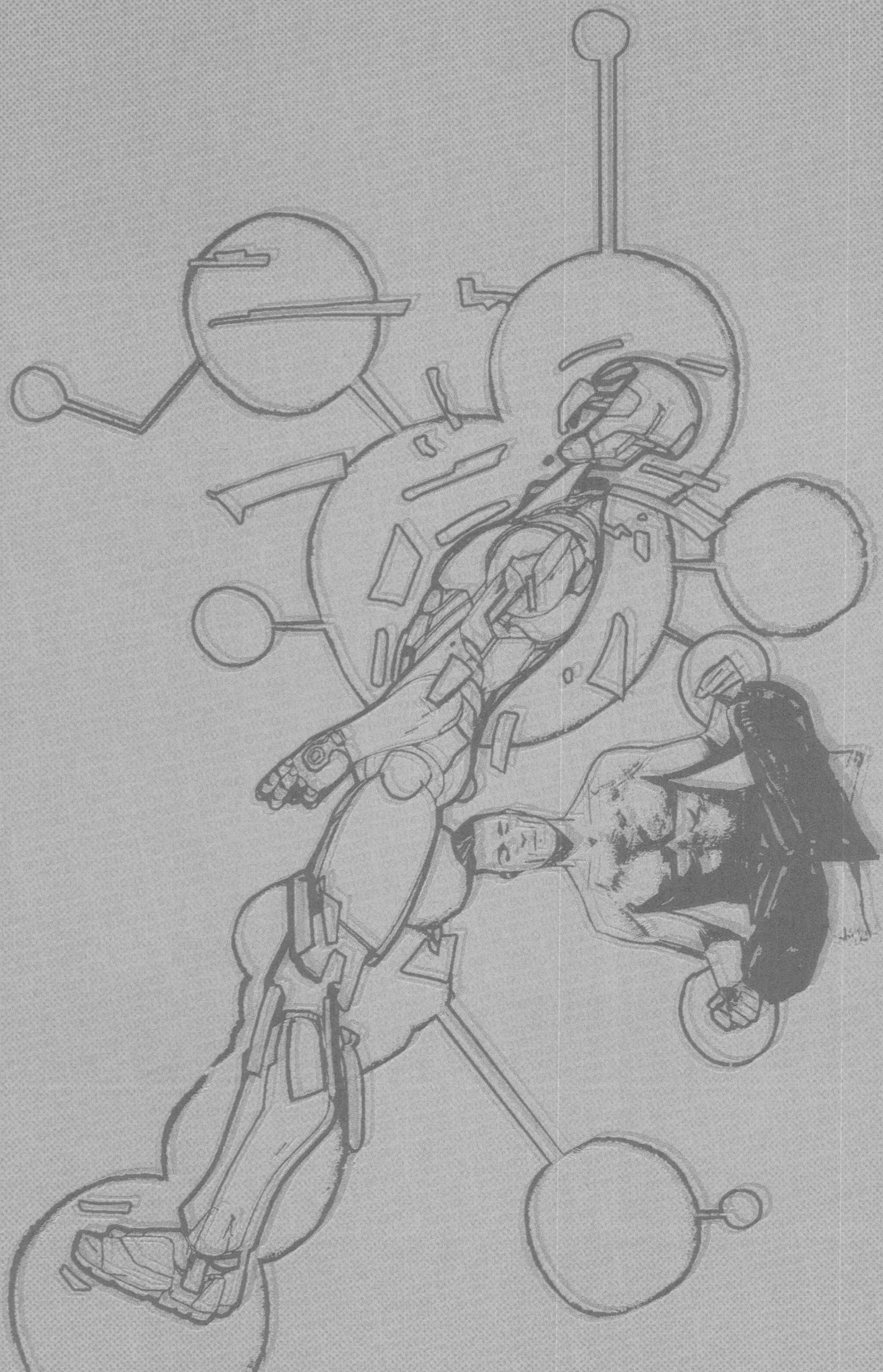

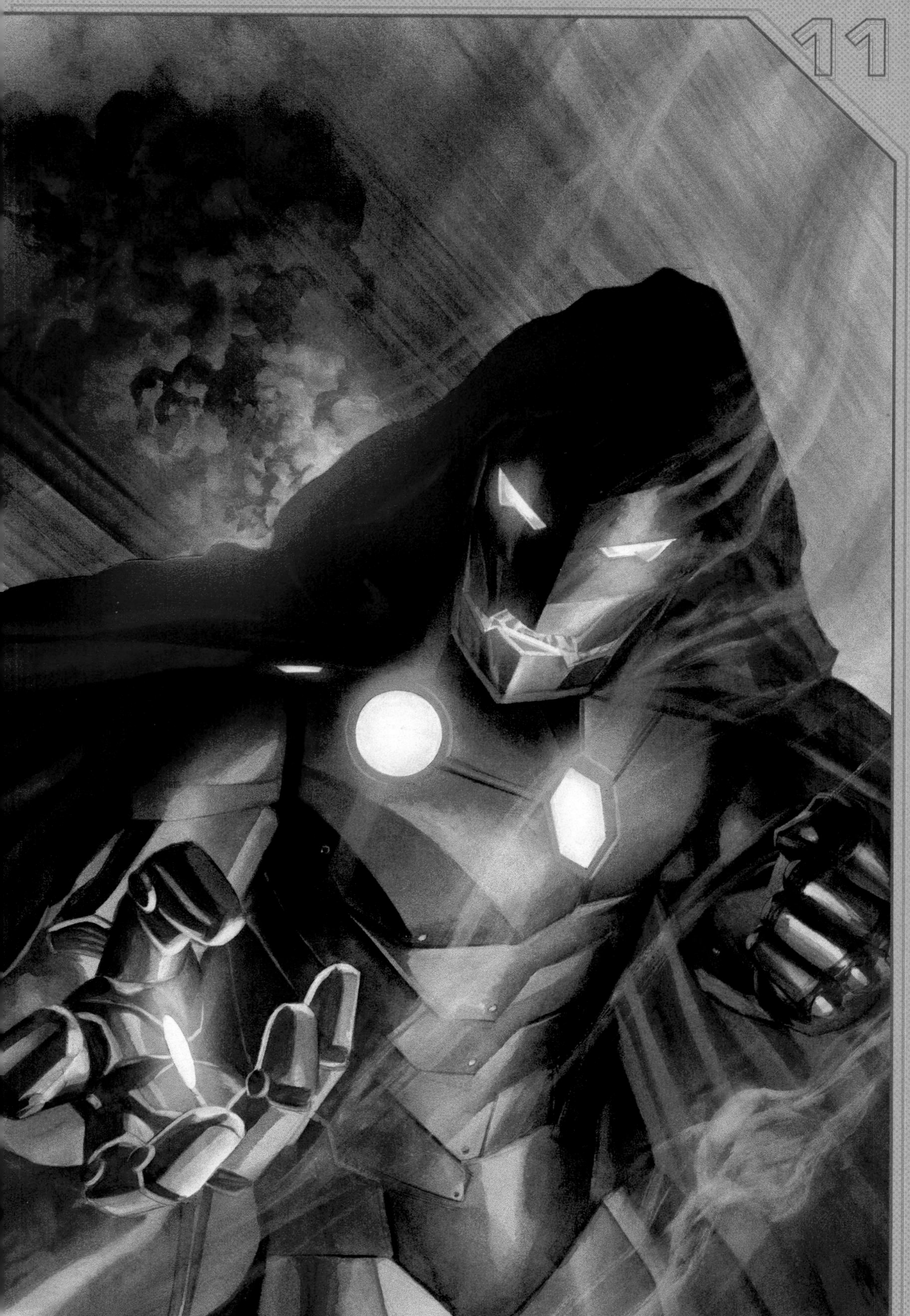

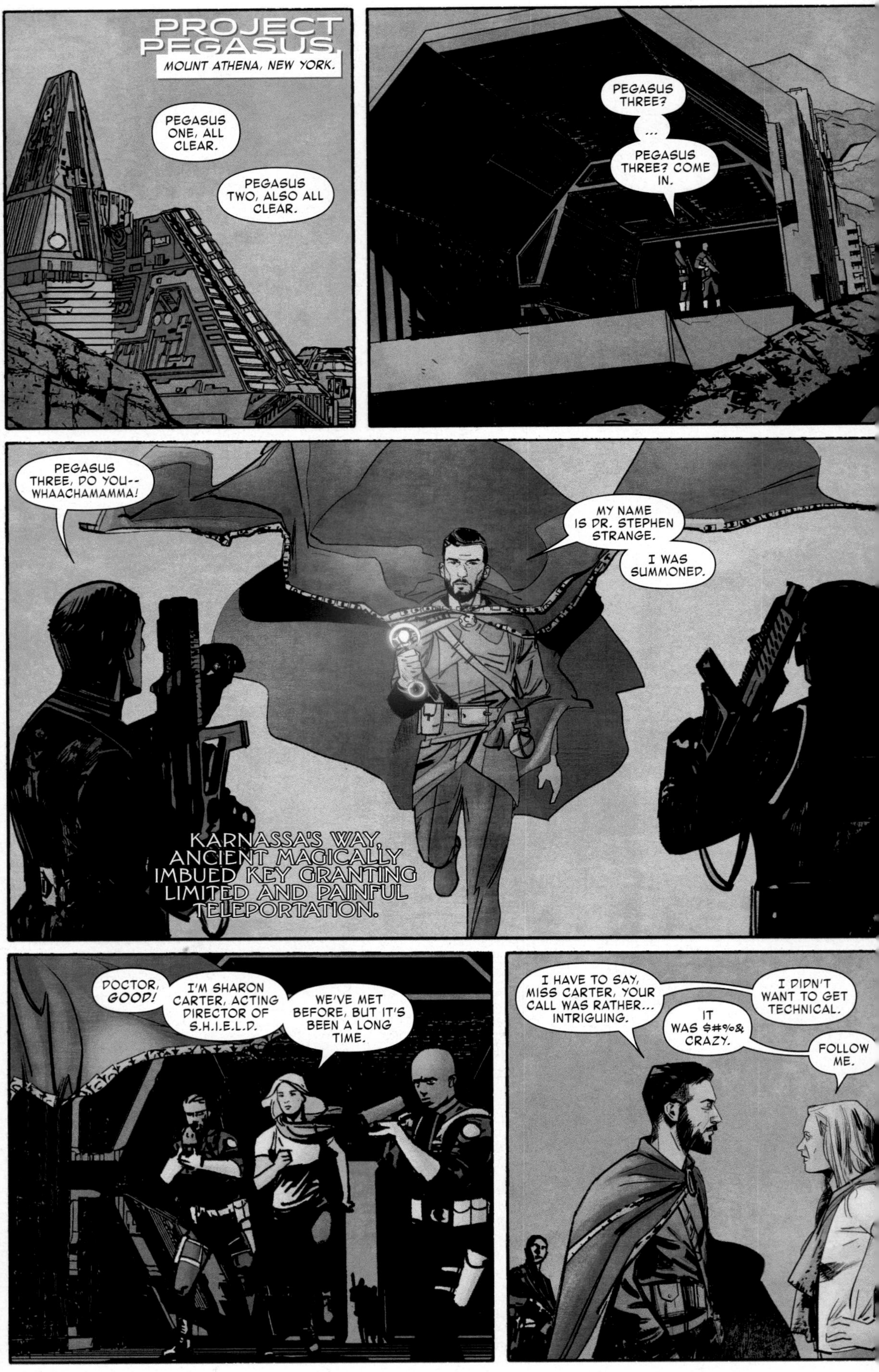
PROJECT PEGASUS
MOUNT ATHENA, NEW YORK.
PEGASUS ONE, ALL CLEAR.
PEGASUS TWO, ALSO ALL CLEAR.
PEGASUS THREE?
...
PEGASUS THREE? COME IN.
PEGASUS THREE, DO YOU-- WHAACHAMAMMA!
MY NAME IS DR. STEPHEN STRANGE.
I WAS SUMMONED.
KARNASSA'S WAY, ANCIENT MAGICALLY IMBUED KEY GRANTING LIMITED AND PAINFUL TELEPORTATION.
DOCTOR, GOOD!
I'M SHARON CARTER, ACTING DIRECTOR OF S.H.I.E.L.D.
WE'VE MET BEFORE, BUT IT'S BEEN A LONG TIME.
I HAVE TO SAY, MISS CARTER, YOUR CALL WAS RATHER... INTRIGUING.
I DIDN'T WANT TO GET TECHNICAL.
IT WAS $#%& CRAZY.
FOLLOW ME.

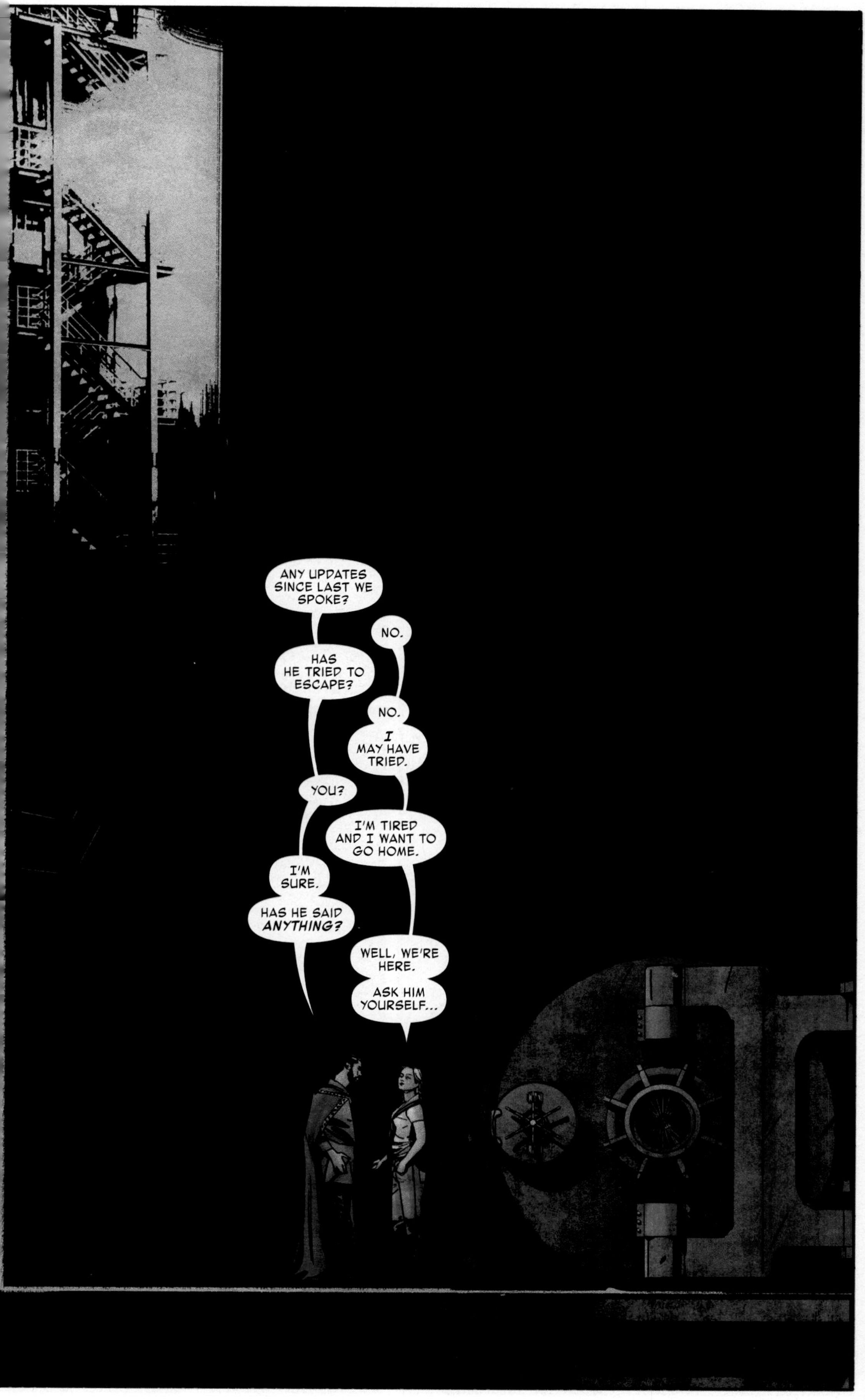
ANY UPDATES SINCE LAST WE SPOKE?
NO.
HAS HE TRIED TO ESCAPE?
NO.
I MAY HAVE TRIED.
YOU?
I'M TIRED AND I WANT TO GO HOME.
I'M SURE.
HAS HE SAID ANYTHING?
WELL, WE'RE HERE.
ASK HIM YOURSELF...

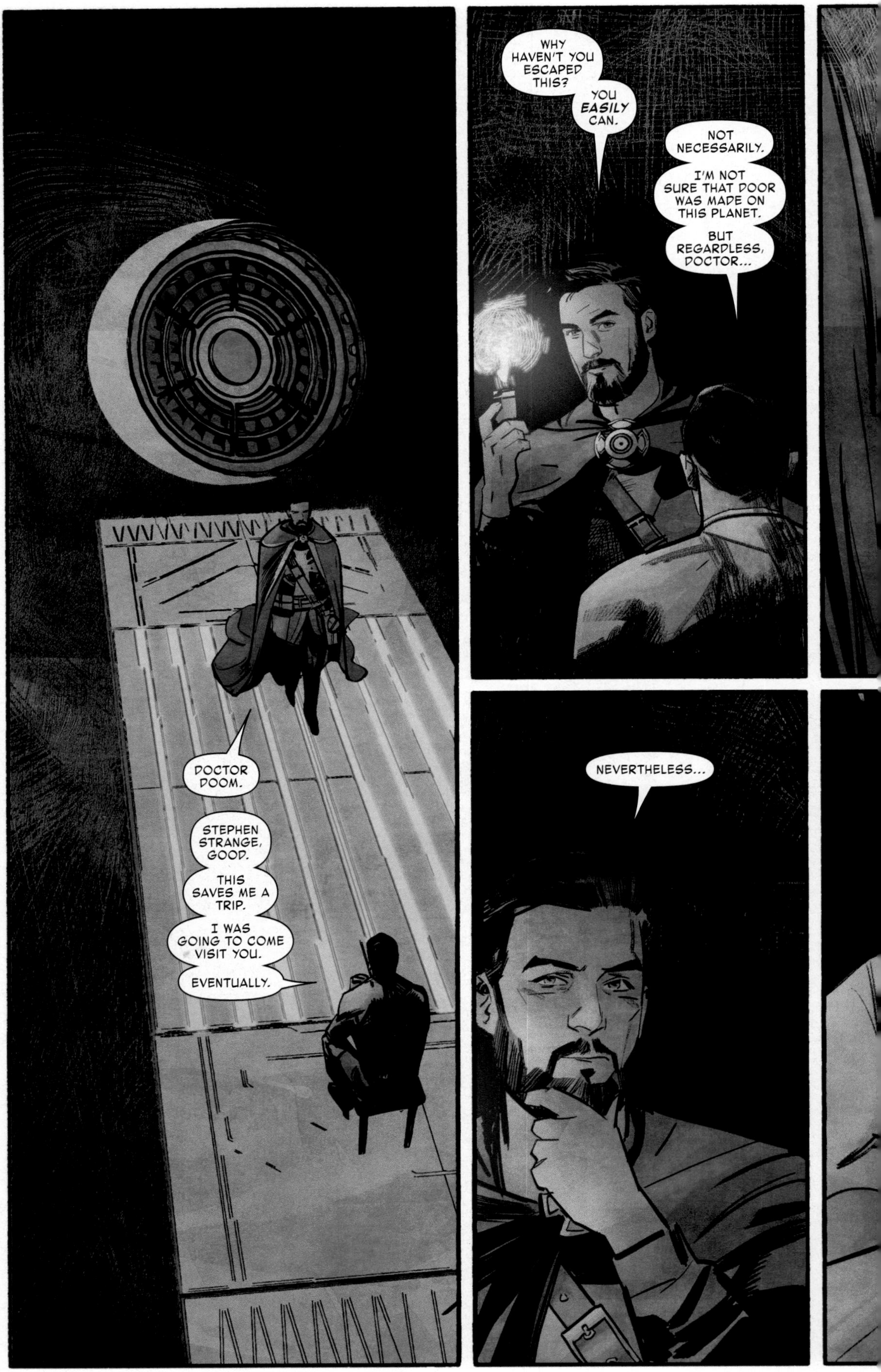
DOCTOR DOOM.
STEPHEN STRANGE, GOOD.
THIS SAVES ME A TRIP.
I WAS GOING TO COME VISIT YOU.
EVENTUALLY.
WHY HAVEN'T YOU ESCAPED THIS?
YOU EASILY CAN.
NOT NECESSARILY.
I'M NOT SURE THAT DOOR WAS MADE ON THIS PLANET.
BUT REGARDLESS, DOCTOR...
NEVERTHELESS...

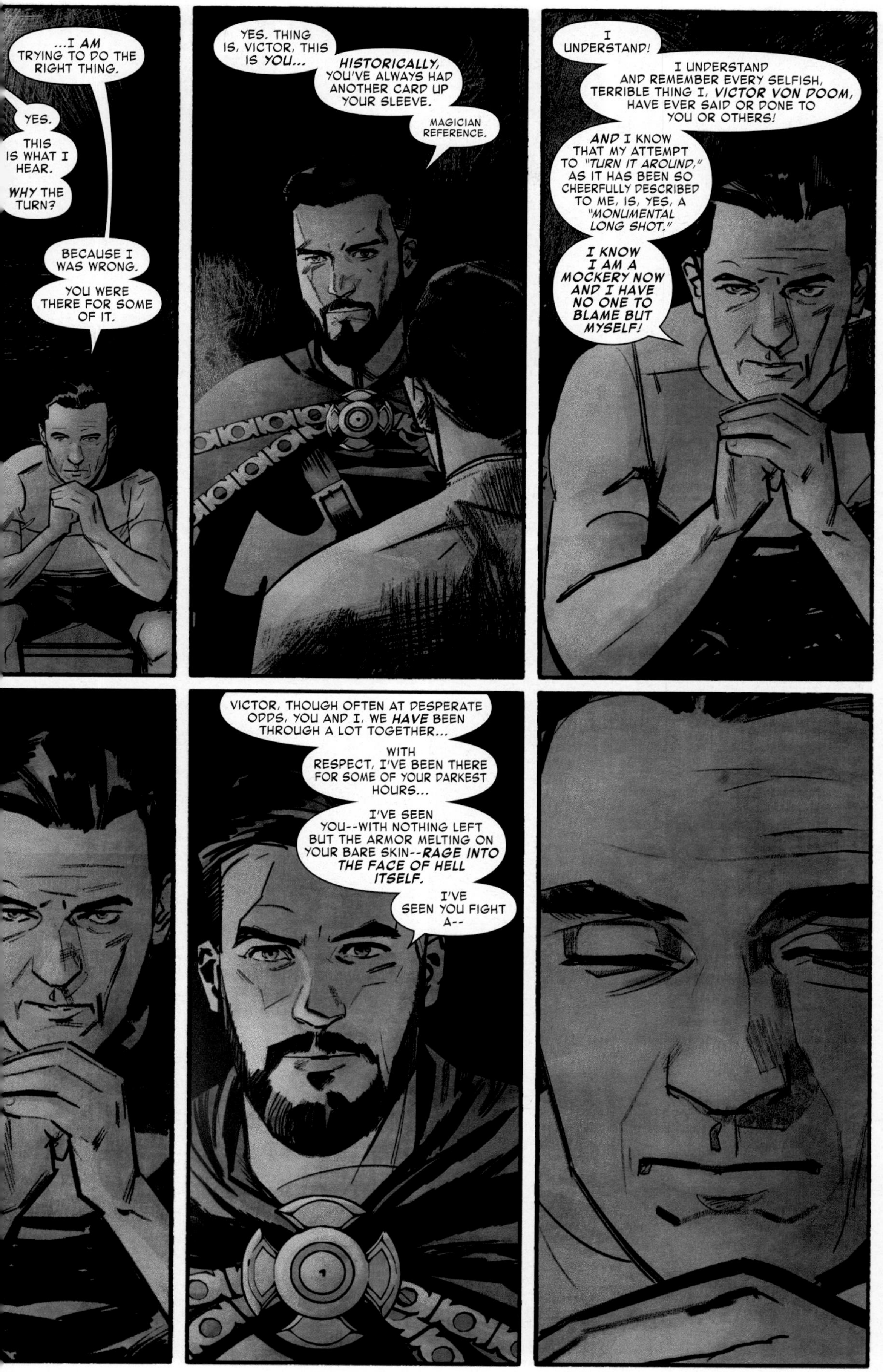
...I AM TRYING TO DO THE RIGHT THING.
YES.
THIS IS WHAT I HEAR.
WHY THE TURN?
BECAUSE I WAS WRONG.
YOU WERE THERE FOR SOME OF IT.
YES. THING IS, VICTOR, THIS IS YOU...
HISTORICALLY, YOU'VE ALWAYS HAD ANOTHER CARD UP YOUR SLEEVE.
MAGICIAN REFERENCE.
I UNDERSTAND!
I UNDERSTAND AND REMEMBER EVERY SELFISH, TERRIBLE THING I, VICTOR VON DOOM, HAVE EVER SAID OR DONE TO YOU OR OTHERS!
AND I KNOW THAT MY ATTEMPT TO "TURN IT AROUND," AS IT HAS BEEN SO CHEERFULLY DESCRIBED TO ME, IS, YES, A "MONUMENTAL LONG SHOT."
I KNOW I AM A MOCKERY NOW AND I HAVE NO ONE TO BLAME BUT MYSELF!
VICTOR, THOUGH OFTEN AT DESPERATE ODDS, YOU AND I, WE HAVE BEEN THROUGH A LOT TOGETHER...
WITH RESPECT, I'VE BEEN THERE FOR SOME OF YOUR DARKEST HOURS...
I'VE SEEN YOU--WITH NOTHING LEFT BUT THE ARMOR MELTING ON YOUR BARE SKIN--RAGE INTO THE FACE OF HELL ITSELF.
I'VE SEEN YOU FIGHT A--

BY THE HOARY HOSTS...

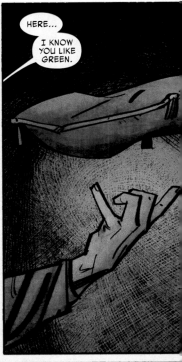

HERE... I KNOW YOU LIKE GREEN.

IF I FELT LIKE LEAVING THIS PLANE, I *WOULD* HAVE.

SHHH! I'M ALREADY IN THE ZONE.

AUTOZONE.

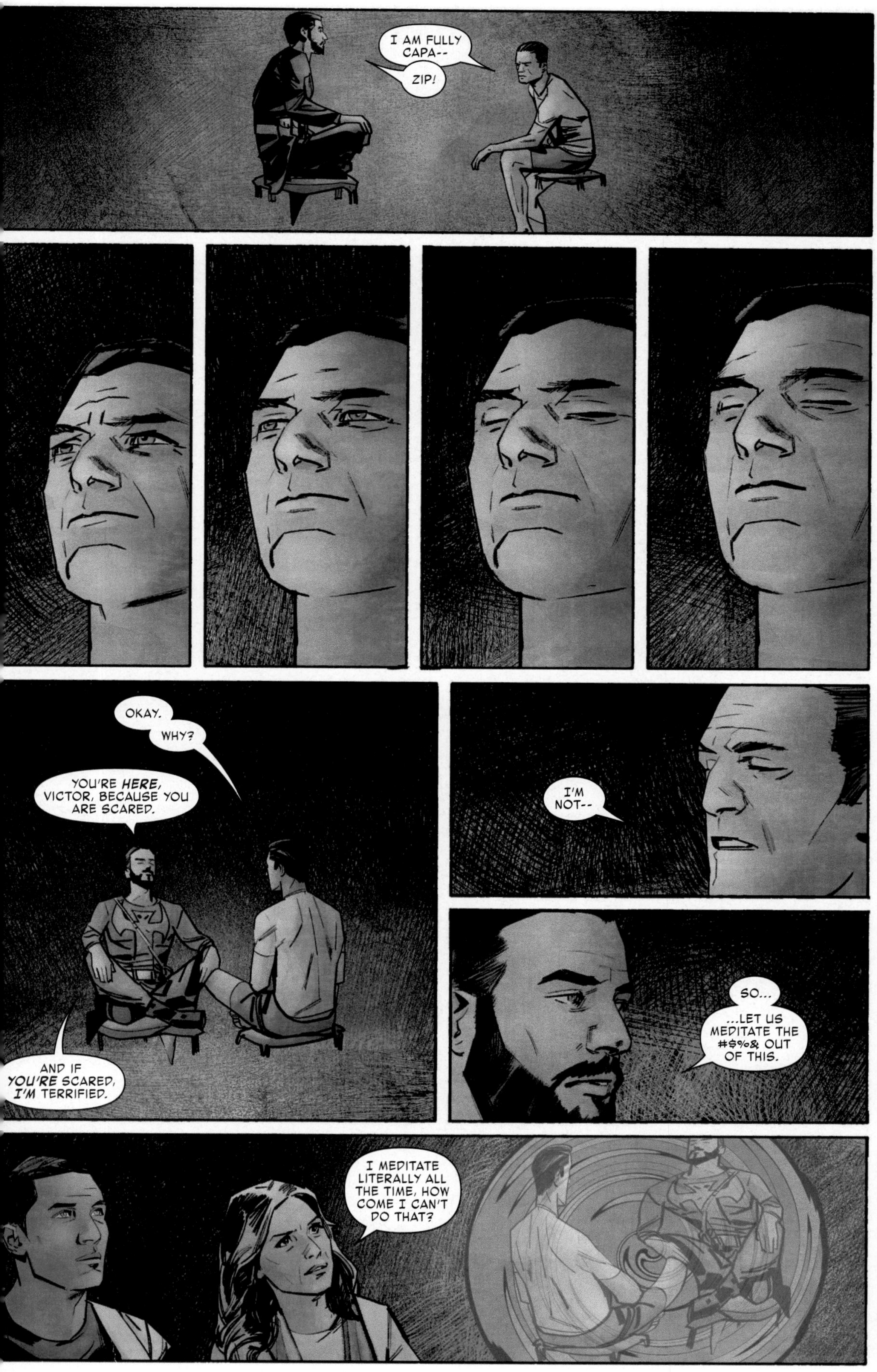
I AM FULLY CAPA--
ZIP!
OKAY.
WHY?
YOU'RE HERE, VICTOR, BECAUSE YOU ARE SCARED.
AND IF YOU'RE SCARED, I'M TERRIFIED.
I'M NOT--
SO...
...LET US MEDITATE THE #$%& OUT OF THIS.
I MEDITATE LITERALLY ALL THE TIME, HOW COME I CAN'T DO THAT?

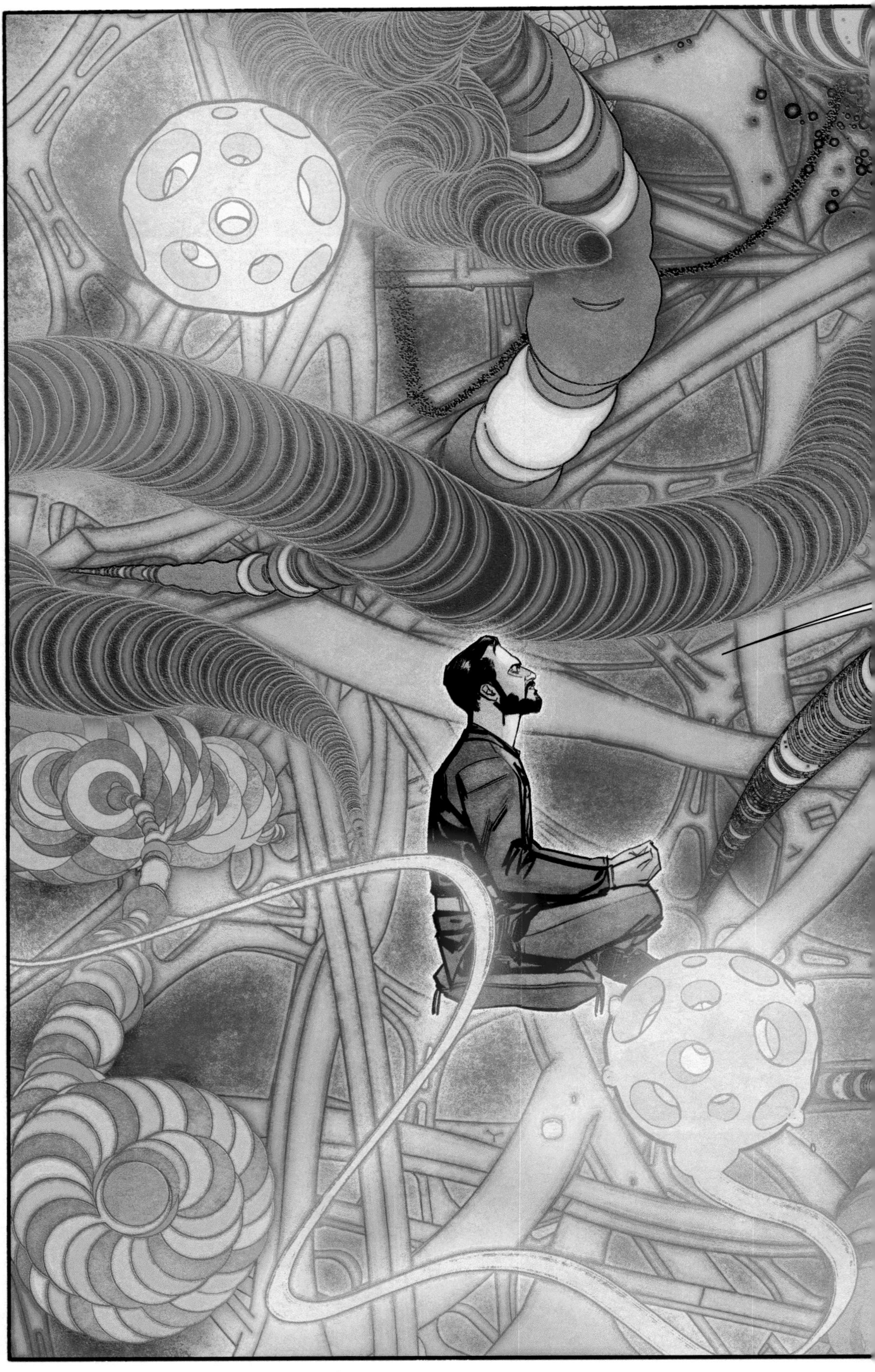

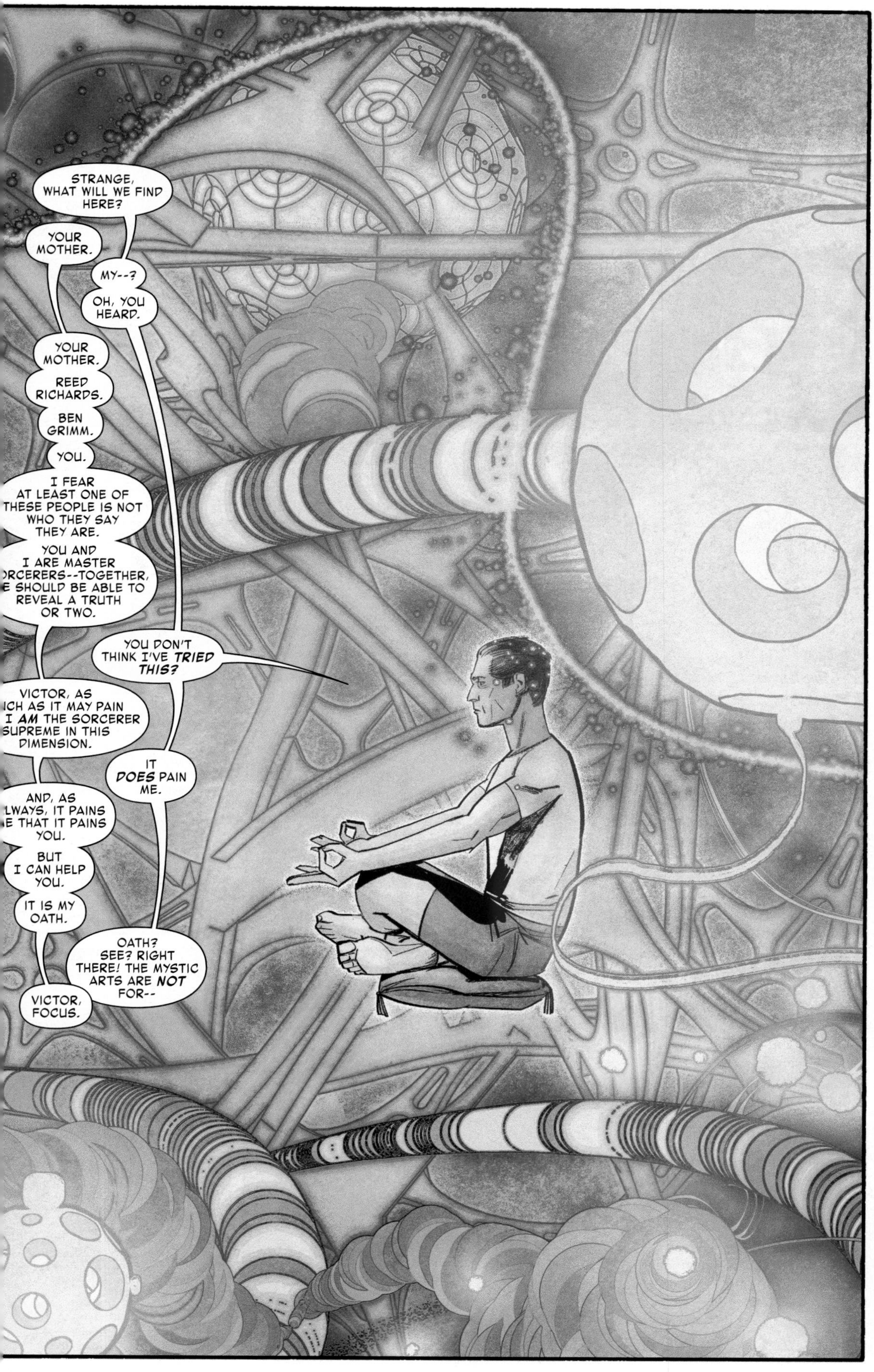
STRANGE, WHAT WILL WE FIND HERE?
YOUR MOTHER.
MY--?
OH, YOU HEARD.
YOUR MOTHER.
REED RICHARDS.
BEN GRIMM.
YOU.
I FEAR AT LEAST ONE OF THESE PEOPLE IS NOT WHO THEY SAY THEY ARE.
YOU AND I ARE MASTER ORCERERS--TOGETHER, E SHOULD BE ABLE TO REVEAL A TRUTH OR TWO.
YOU DON'T THINK I'VE TRIED THIS?
VICTOR, AS ICH AS IT MAY PAIN I AM THE SORCERER SUPREME IN THIS DIMENSION.
IT DOES PAIN ME.
AND, AS LWAYS, IT PAINS E THAT IT PAINS YOU.
BUT I CAN HELP YOU.
IT IS MY OATH.
OATH? SEE? RIGHT THERE! THE MYSTIC ARTS ARE NOT FOR--
VICTOR, FOCUS.

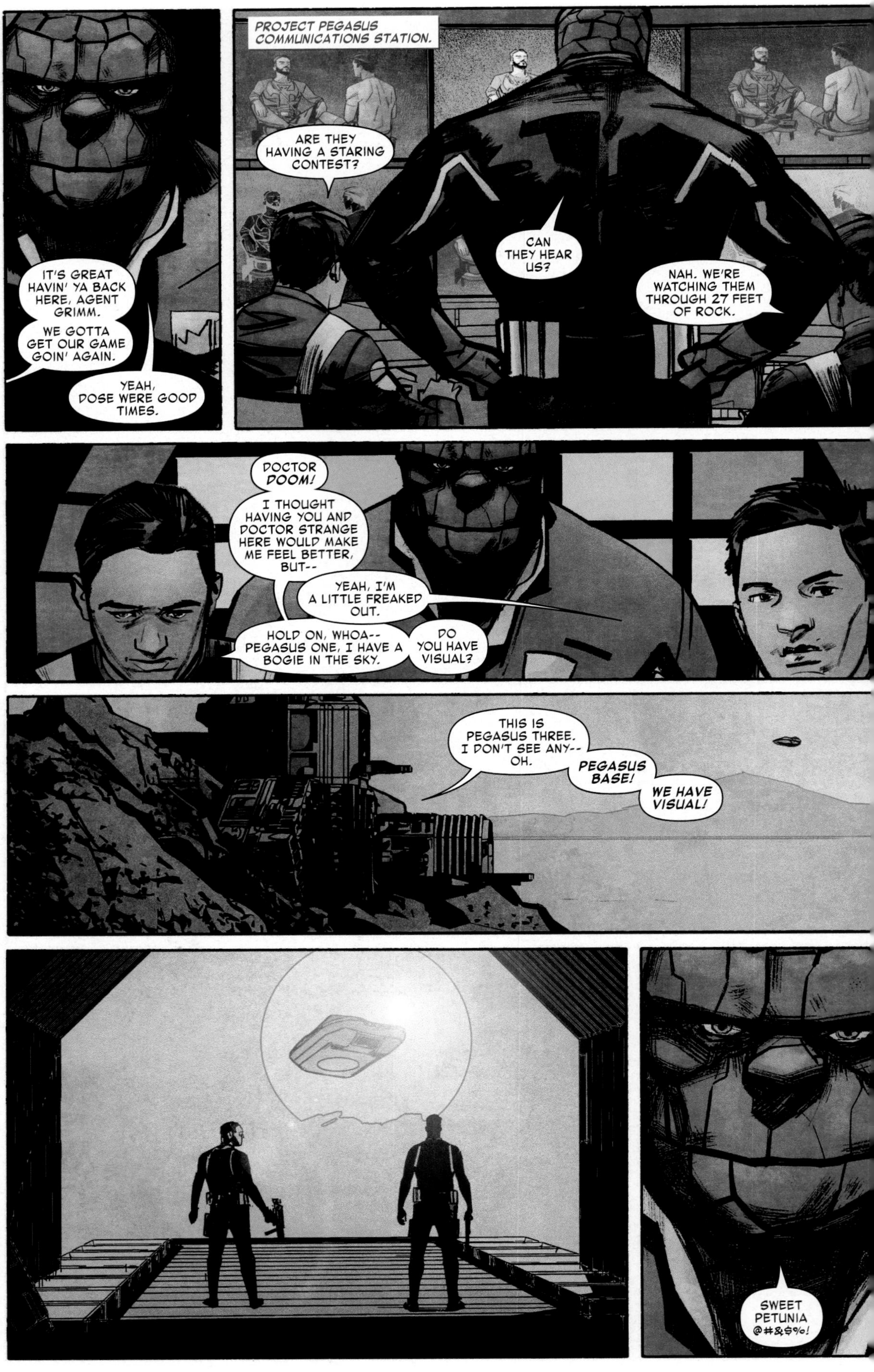
PROJECT PEGASUS COMMUNICATIONS STATION.
IT'S GREAT HAVIN' YA BACK HERE, AGENT GRIMM.
WE GOTTA GET OUR GAME GOIN' AGAIN.
YEAH, DOSE WERE GOOD TIMES.
ARE THEY HAVING A STARING CONTEST?
CAN THEY HEAR US?
NAH. WE'RE WATCHING THEM THROUGH 27 FEET OF ROCK.
DOCTOR DOOM!
I THOUGHT HAVING YOU AND DOCTOR STRANGE HERE WOULD MAKE ME FEEL BETTER, BUT--
YEAH, I'M A LITTLE FREAKED OUT.
HOLD ON, WHOA-- PEGASUS ONE, I HAVE A BOGIE IN THE SKY.
DO YOU HAVE VISUAL?
THIS IS PEGASUS THREE. I DON'T SEE ANY-- OH.
PEGASUS BASE!
WE HAVE VISUAL!
SWEET PETUNIA @#&$%!

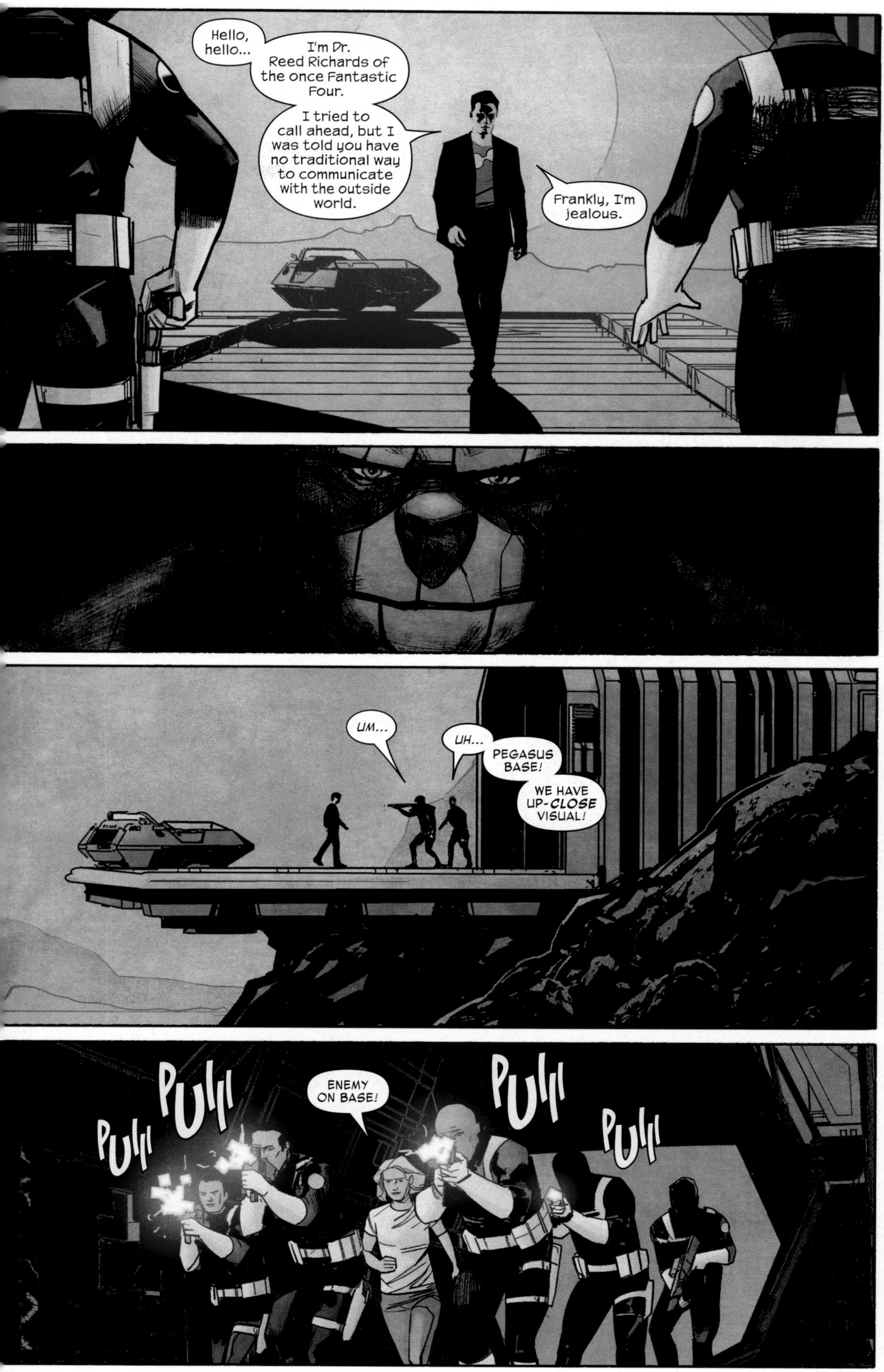
Hello, hello...
I'm Dr. Reed Richards of the once Fantastic Four.
I tried to call ahead, but I was told you have no traditional way to communicate with the outside world.
Frankly, I'm jealous.
UM...
UH...
PEGASUS BASE!
WE HAVE UP-CLOSE VISUAL!
PUH
PUH
ENEMY ON BASE!
PUH
PUH

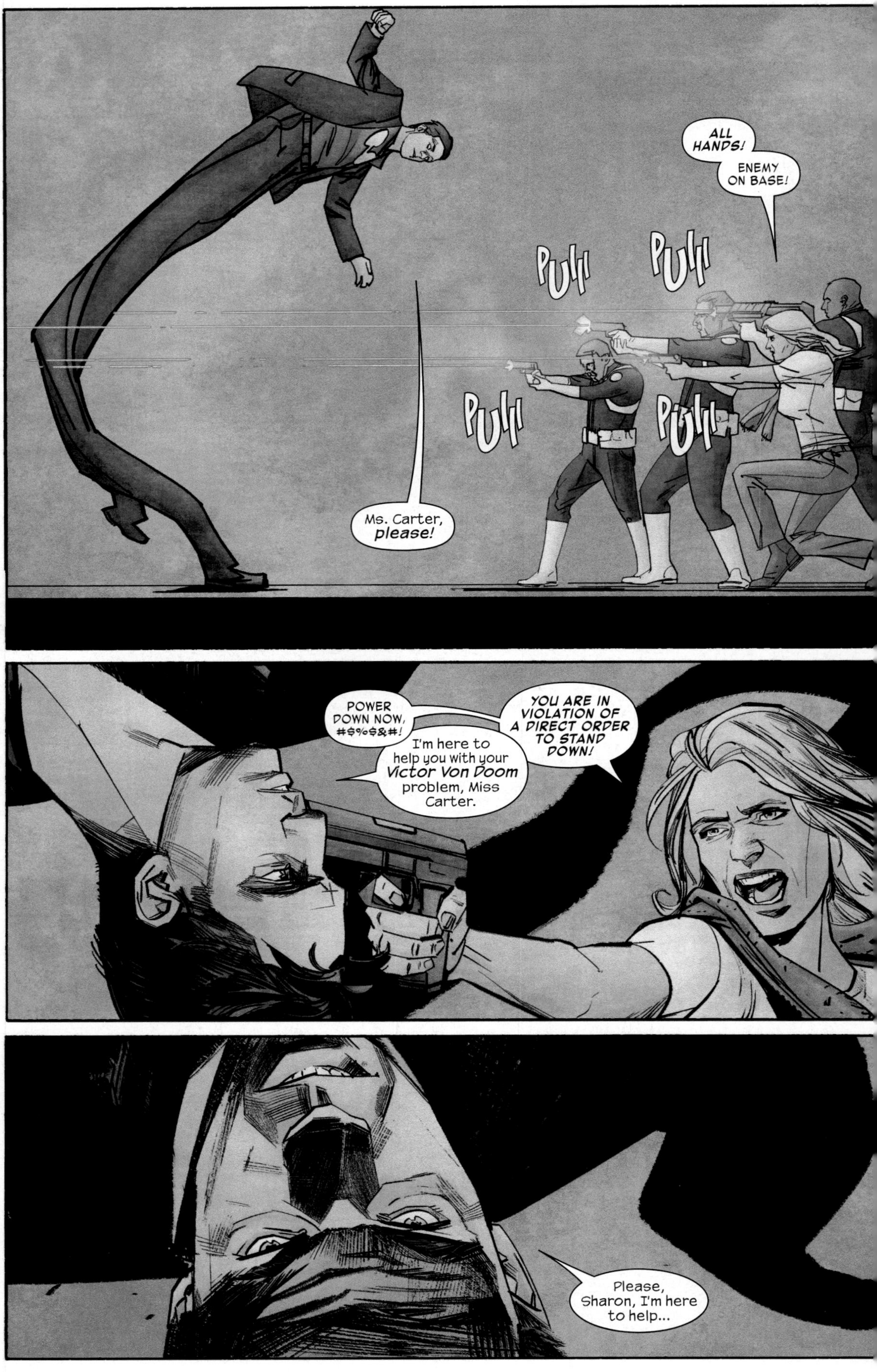
ALL HANDS!
ENEMY ON BASE!
PUH
PUH
PUH
PUH
Ms. Carter, please!
POWER DOWN NOW, #$%$&#!
YOU ARE IN VIOLATION OF A DIRECT ORDER TO STAND DOWN!
I'm here to help you with your Victor Von Doom problem, Miss Carter.
Please, Sharon, I'm here to help...

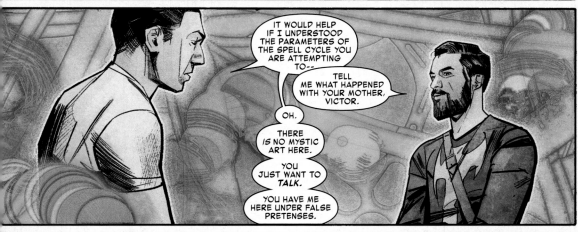

IT WOULD HELP IF I UNDERSTOOD THE PARAMETERS OF THE SPELL CYCLE YOU ARE ATTEMPTING TO--

TELL ME WHAT HAPPENED WITH YOUR MOTHER, VICTOR.

OH.

THERE *IS* NO MYSTIC ART HERE.

YOU JUST WANT TO *TALK.*

YOU HAVE ME HERE UNDER FALSE PRETENSES.

I HAVE YOU HERE BECAUSE I THINK THAT, AWAY FROM MAN, YOU MIGHT SPEAK FREELY.

HERE, YOU MIGHT TELL ME WHAT SENT *YOU,* OF ALL PEOPLE, RUNNING INTO THE ARMS OF YOUR JAILERS.

TELL ME ABOUT YOUR MOTHER.

DAMN YOU.

BENJAMIN SAID HE SAW HER WITH HIS--

THIS IS INTOLERABLE.

WHAT *HAPPENED* TO YOU, VICTOR?

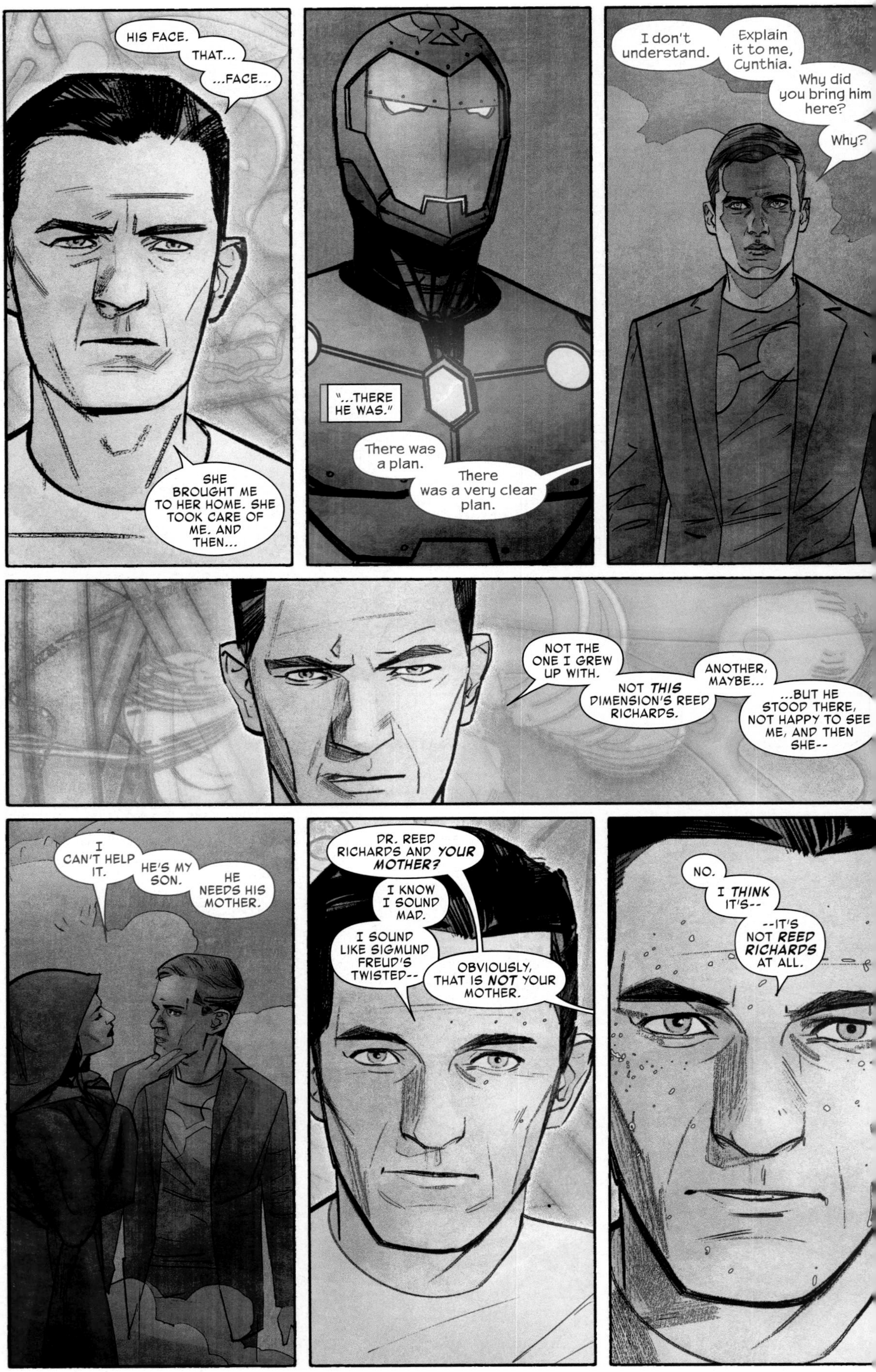

HIS FACE.
THAT...
...FACE...
SHE BROUGHT ME TO HER HOME. SHE TOOK CARE OF ME. AND THEN...
"...THERE HE WAS."
There was a plan.
There was a very clear plan.
I don't understand.
Explain it to me, Cynthia.
Why did you bring him here?
Why?
NOT THE ONE I GREW UP WITH.
NOT THIS DIMENSION'S REED RICHARDS.
ANOTHER, MAYBE...
...BUT HE STOOD THERE, NOT HAPPY TO SEE ME, AND THEN SHE--
I CAN'T HELP IT.
HE'S MY SON.
HE NEEDS HIS MOTHER.
DR. REED RICHARDS AND YOUR MOTHER?
I KNOW I SOUND MAD.
I SOUND LIKE SIGMUND FREUD'S TWISTED--
OBVIOUSLY, THAT IS NOT YOUR MOTHER.
NO.
I THINK IT'S--
--IT'S NOT REED RICHARDS AT ALL.

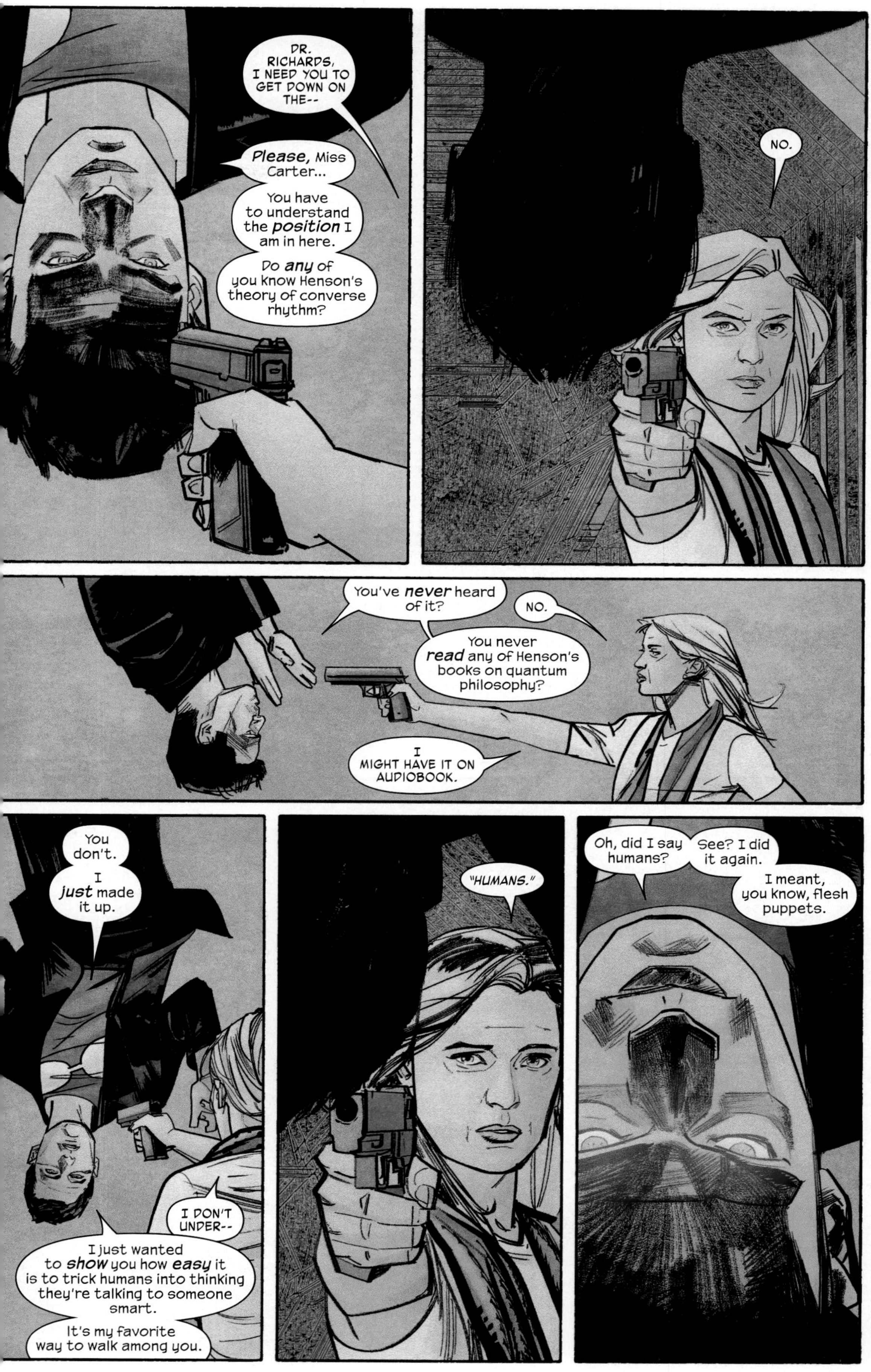
DR. RICHARDS, I NEED YOU TO GET DOWN ON THE--
Please, Miss Carter...
You have to understand the position I am in here.
Do any of you know Henson's theory of converse rhythm?
NO.
You've never heard of it?
NO.
You never read any of Henson's books on quantum philosophy?
I MIGHT HAVE IT ON AUDIOBOOK.
You don't.
I just made it up.
I DON'T UNDER--
I just wanted to show you how easy it is to trick humans into thinking they're talking to someone smart.
It's my favorite way to walk among you.
"HUMANS."
Oh, did I say humans?
See? I did it again.
I meant, you know, flesh puppets.

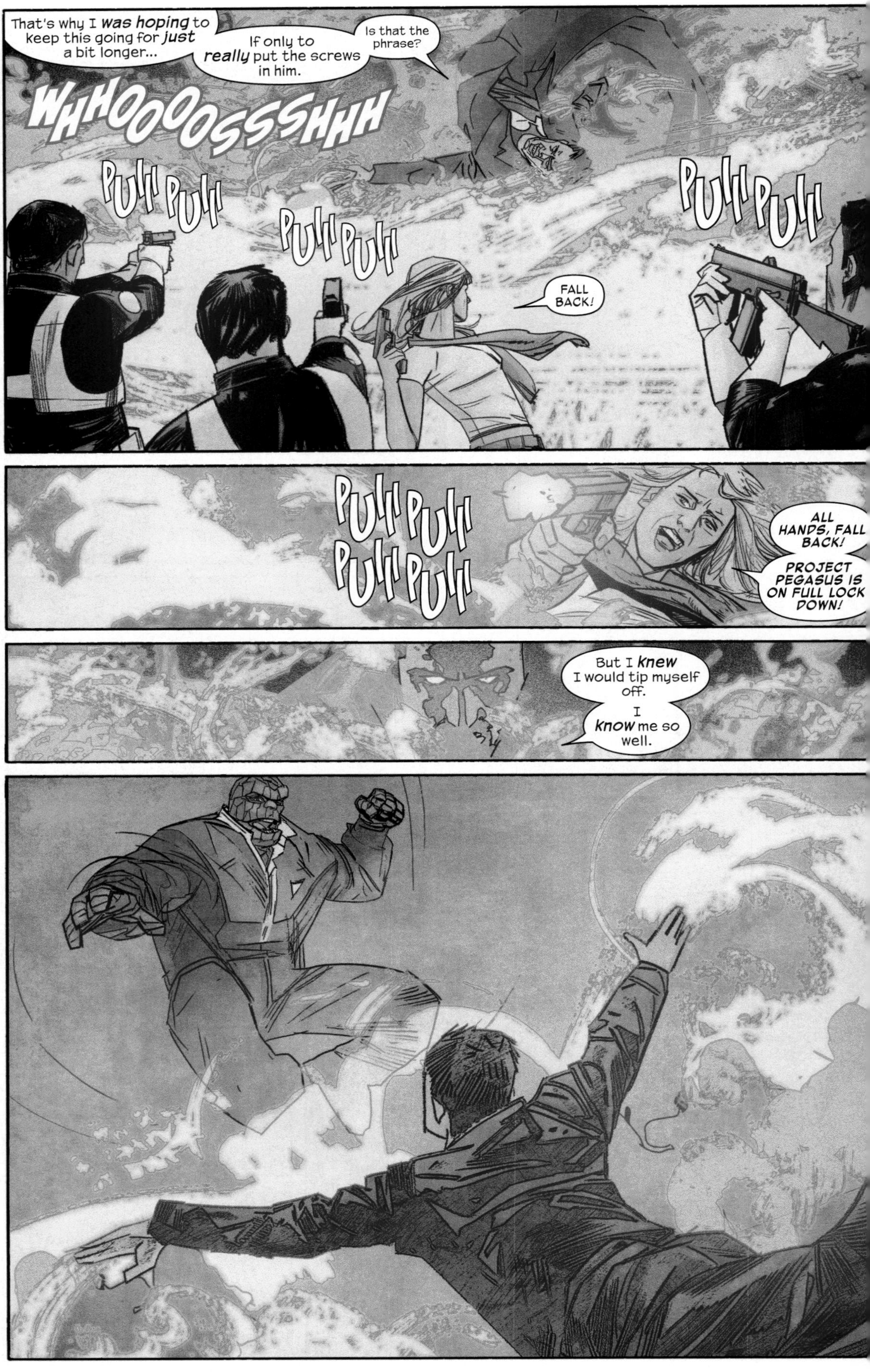
That's why I was hoping to keep this going for just a bit longer...
If only to really put the screws in him.
Is that the phrase?
WHHOOOOOSSSSHHH
PUH PUH
PUH PUH
FALL BACK!
PUH PUH
PUH PUH
PUH PUH
ALL HANDS, FALL BACK!
PROJECT PEGASUS IS ON FULL LOCK DOWN!
But I knew I would tip myself off.
I know me so well.

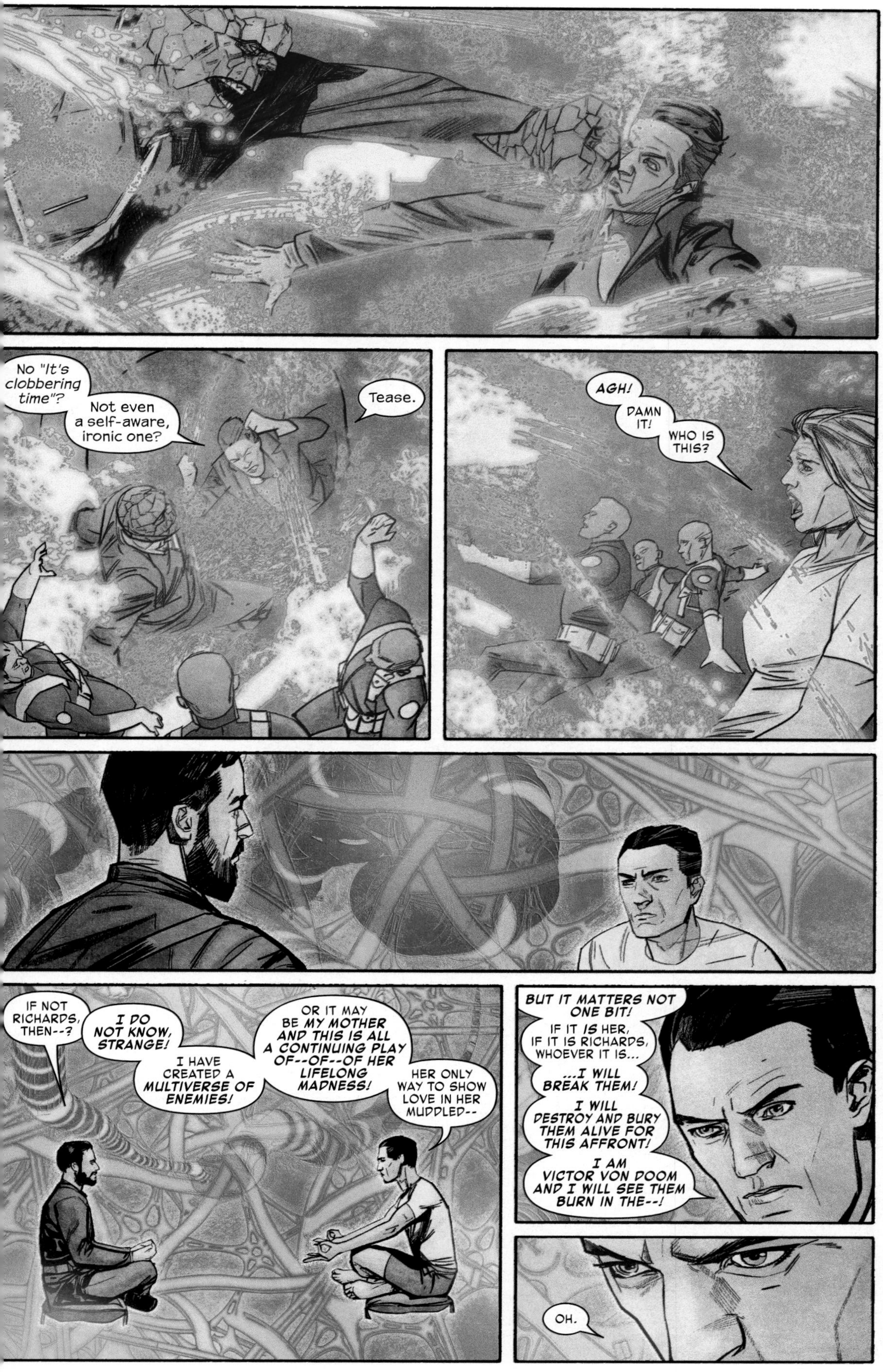

No "It's clobbering time"?
Not even a self-aware, ironic one?
Tease.
AGH!
DAMN IT!
WHO IS THIS?
IF NOT RICHARDS, THEN--?
I DO NOT KNOW, STRANGE!
I HAVE CREATED A MULTIVERSE OF ENEMIES!
OR IT MAY BE MY MOTHER AND THIS IS ALL A CONTINUING PLAY OF--OF--OF HER LIFELONG MADNESS!
HER ONLY WAY TO SHOW LOVE IN HER MUDDLED--
BUT IT MATTERS NOT ONE BIT!
IF IT IS HER, IF IT IS RICHARDS, WHOEVER IT IS...
...I WILL BREAK THEM!
I WILL DESTROY AND BURY THEM ALIVE FOR THIS AFFRONT!
I AM VICTOR VON DOOM AND I WILL SEE THEM BURN IN THE--!
OH.

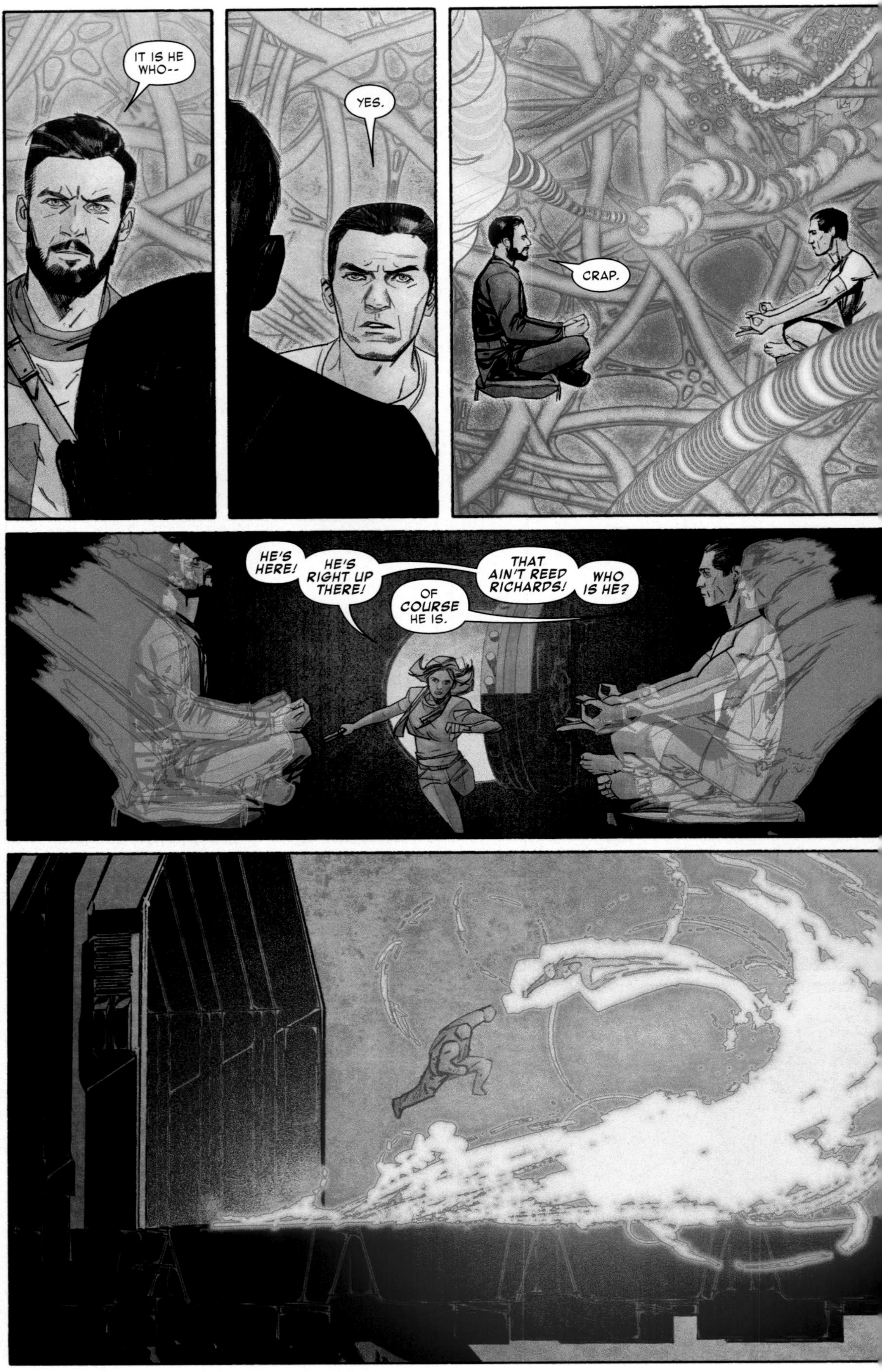
IT IS HE WHO--
YES.
CRAP.
HE'S HERE!
HE'S RIGHT UP THERE!
THAT AIN'T REED RICHARDS!
WHO IS HE?
OF COURSE HE IS.

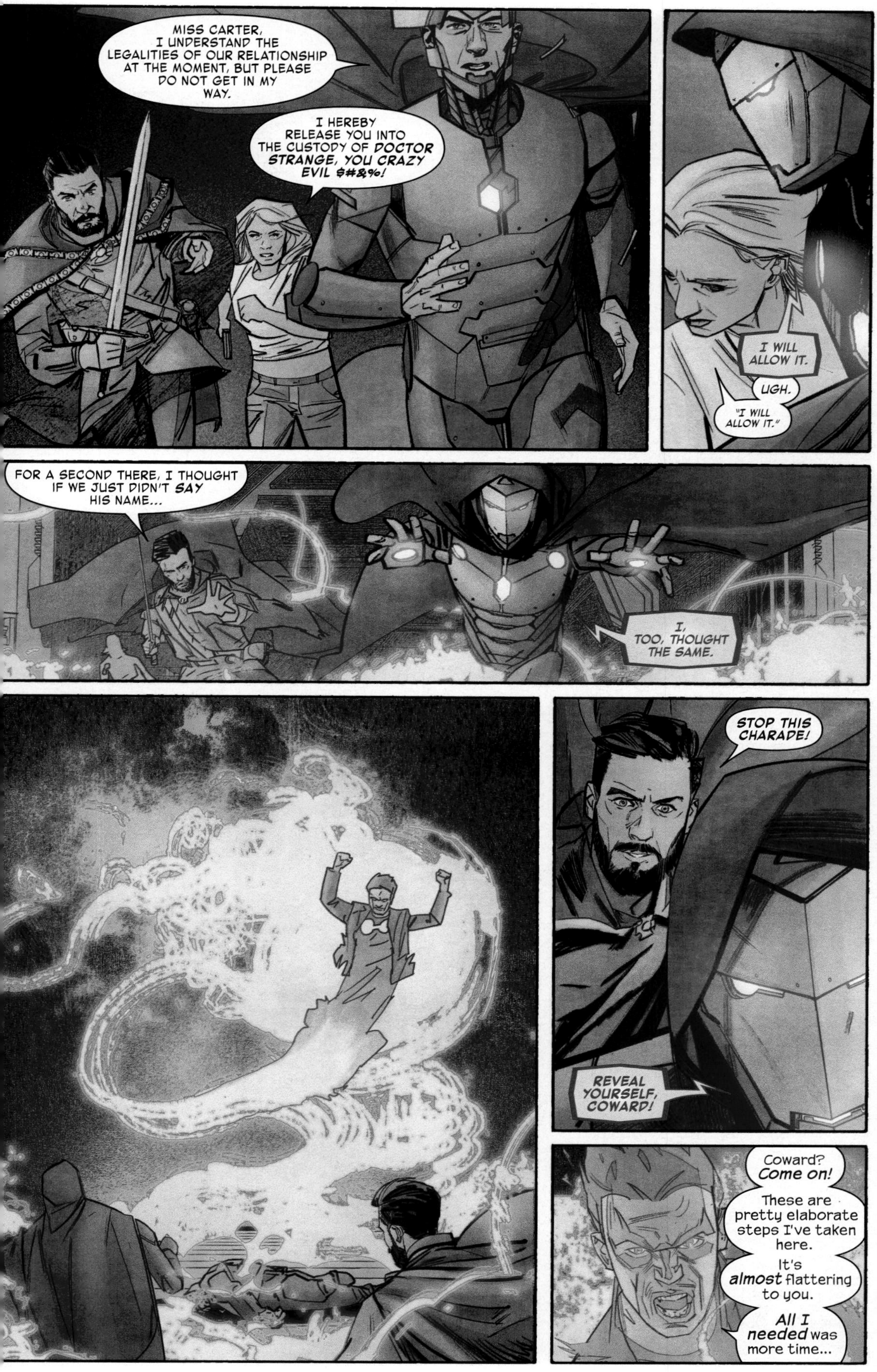

MISS CARTER, I UNDERSTAND THE LEGALITIES OF OUR RELATIONSHIP AT THE MOMENT, BUT PLEASE DO NOT GET IN MY WAY.
I HEREBY RELEASE YOU INTO THE CUSTODY OF DOCTOR STRANGE, YOU CRAZY EVIL $#&%!
I WILL ALLOW IT.
UGH.
"I WILL ALLOW IT."
FOR A SECOND THERE, I THOUGHT IF WE JUST DIDN'T SAY HIS NAME...
I, TOO, THOUGHT THE SAME.
STOP THIS CHARADE!
REVEAL YOURSELF, COWARD!
Coward? Come on!
These are pretty elaborate steps I've taken here.
It's almost flattering to you.
All I needed was more time...

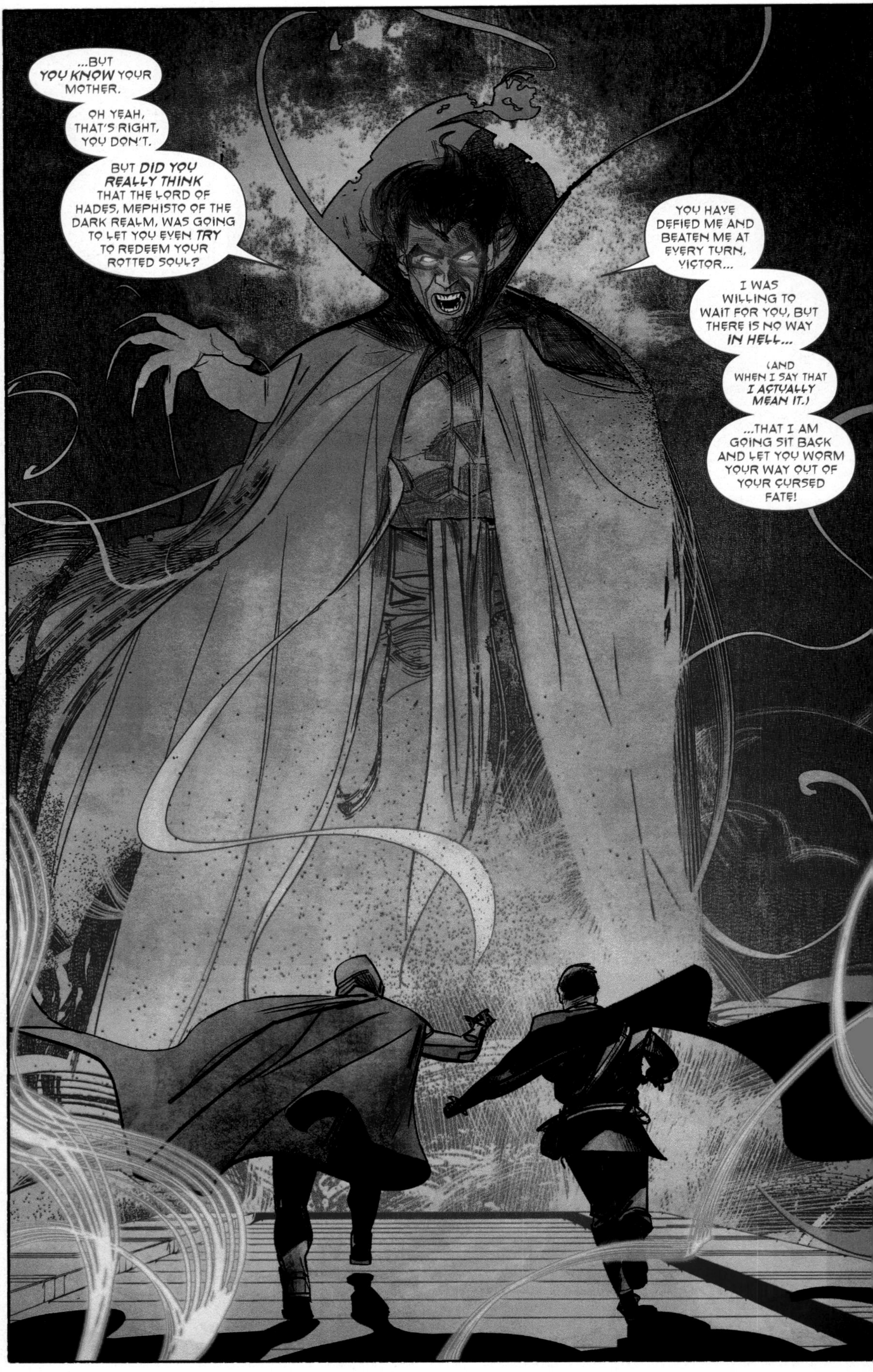
...BUT YOU KNOW YOUR MOTHER.
OH YEAH, THAT'S RIGHT, YOU DON'T.
BUT DID YOU REALLY THINK THAT THE LORD OF HADES, MEPHISTO OF THE DARK REALM, WAS GOING TO LET YOU EVEN TRY TO REDEEM YOUR ROTTED SOUL?
YOU HAVE DEFIED ME AND BEATEN ME AT EVERY TURN, VICTOR...
I WAS WILLING TO WAIT FOR YOU, BUT THERE IS NO WAY IN HELL...
(AND WHEN I SAY THAT I ACTUALLY MEAN IT.)
...THAT I AM GOING SIT BACK AND LET YOU WORM YOUR WAY OUT OF YOUR CURSED FATE!

12

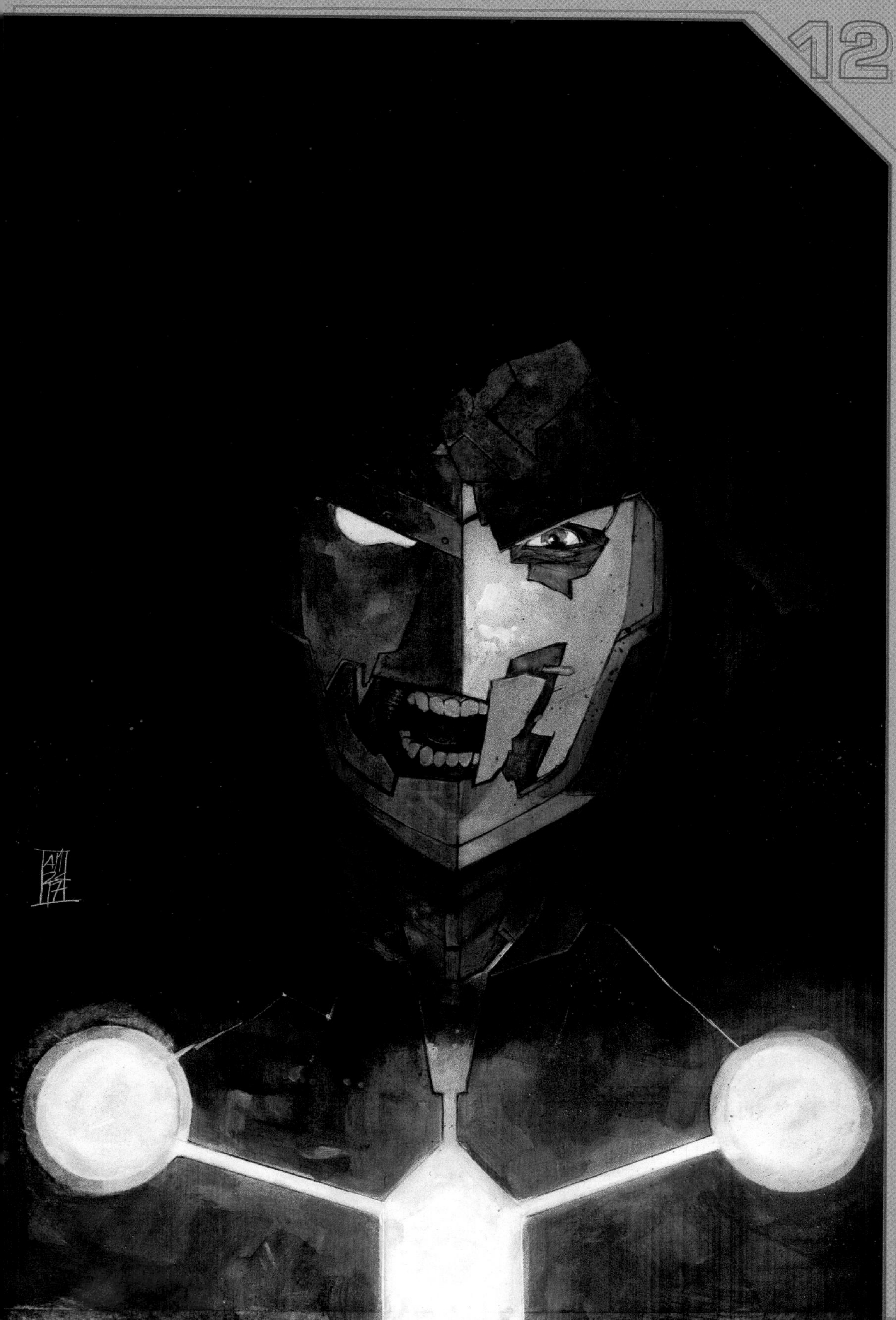

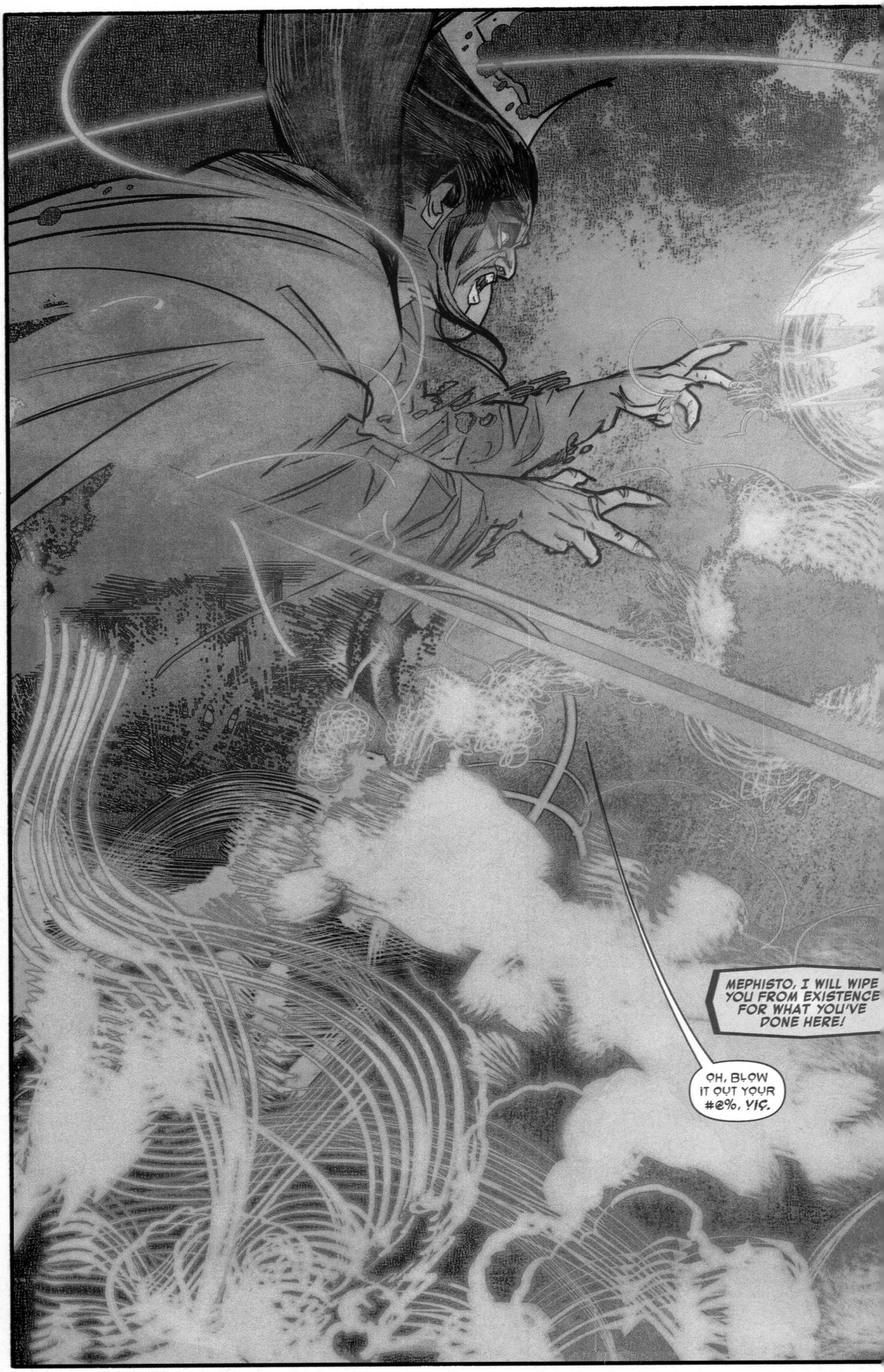
MEPHISTO, I WILL WIPE YOU FROM EXISTENCE FOR WHAT YOU'VE DONE HERE!
OH, BLOW IT OUT YOUR #@%, VIC.

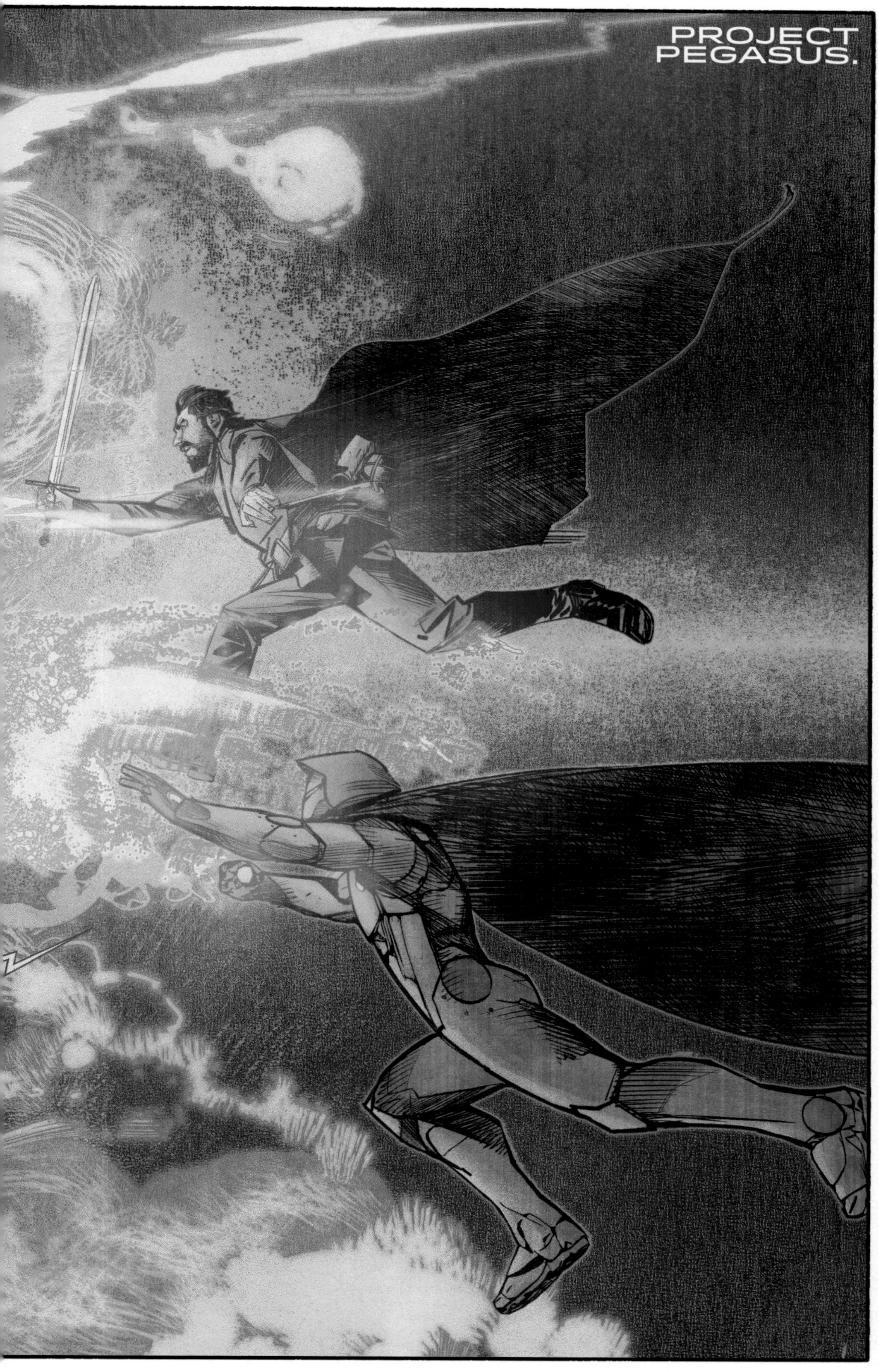
PROJECT PEGASUS.

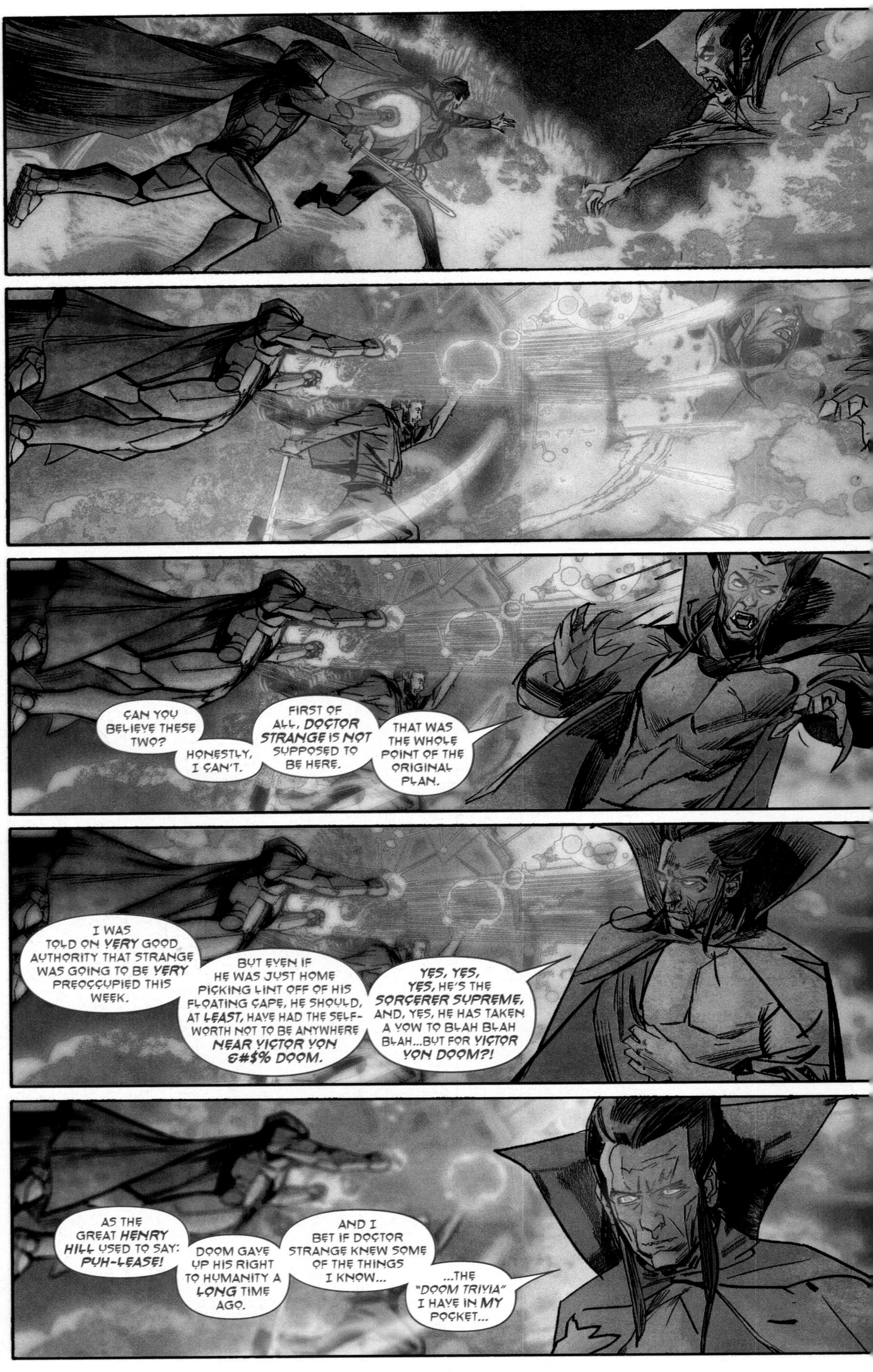
CAN YOU BELIEVE THESE TWO?
HONESTLY, I CAN'T.
FIRST OF ALL, DOCTOR STRANGE IS NOT SUPPOSED TO BE HERE.
THAT WAS THE WHOLE POINT OF THE ORIGINAL PLAN.
I WAS TOLD ON VERY GOOD AUTHORITY THAT STRANGE WAS GOING TO BE VERY PREOCCUPIED THIS WEEK.
BUT EVEN IF HE WAS JUST HOME PICKING LINT OFF OF HIS FLOATING CAPE, HE SHOULD, AT LEAST, HAVE HAD THE SELF-WORTH NOT TO BE ANYWHERE NEAR VICTOR VON &#$% DOOM.
YES, YES, YES, HE'S THE SORCERER SUPREME, AND, YES, HE HAS TAKEN A VOW TO BLAH BLAH BLAH...BUT FOR VICTOR VON DOOM?!
AS THE GREAT HENRY HILL USED TO SAY: PUH-LEASE!
DOOM GAVE UP HIS RIGHT TO HUMANITY A LONG TIME AGO.
AND I BET IF DOCTOR STRANGE KNEW SOME OF THE THINGS I KNOW...
...THE "DOOM TRIVIA" I HAVE IN MY POCKET...

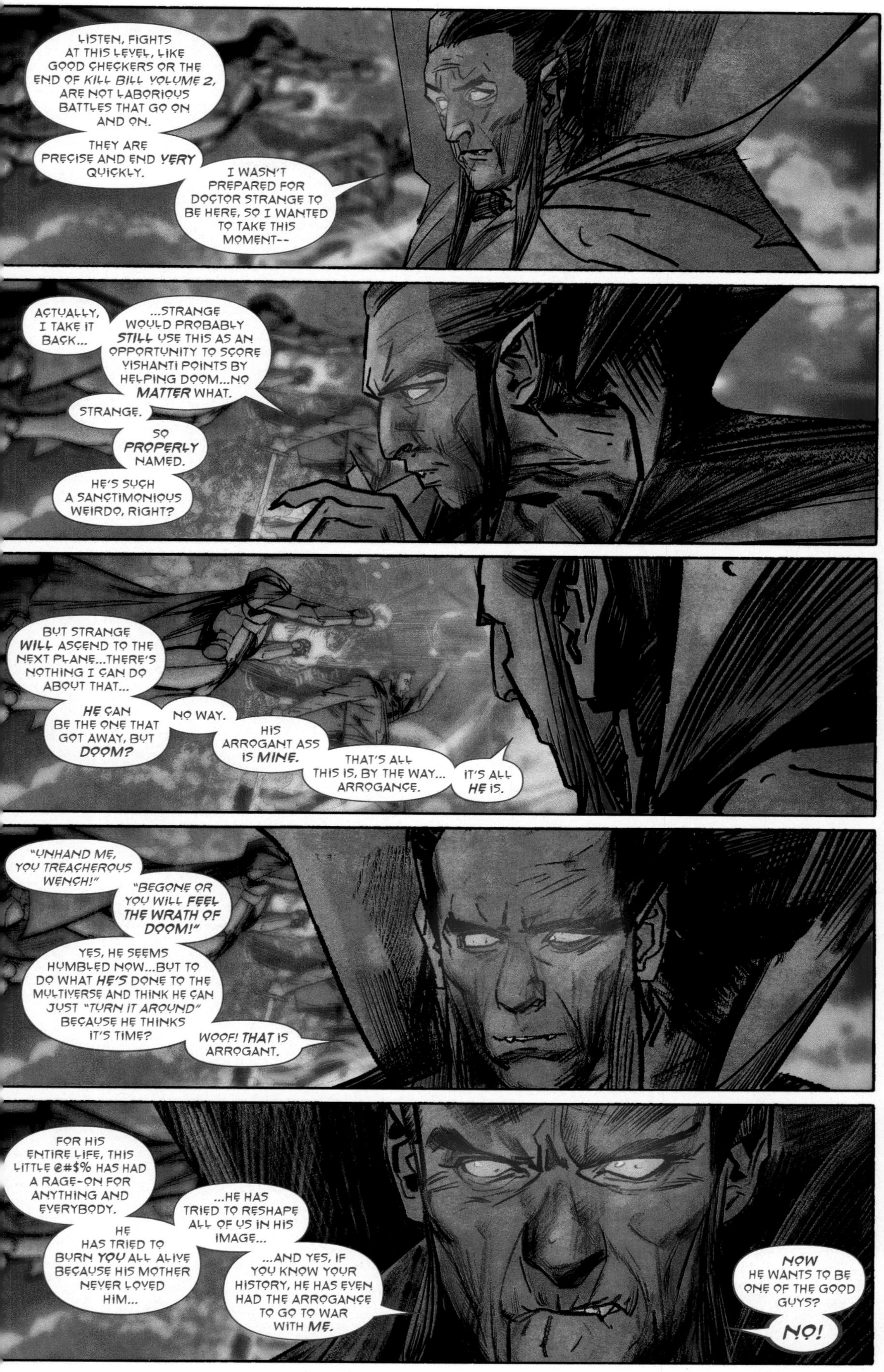

LISTEN, FIGHTS AT THIS LEVEL, LIKE GOOD CHECKERS OR THE END OF *KILL BILL VOLUME 2*, ARE NOT LABORIOUS BATTLES THAT GO ON AND ON.
THEY ARE PRECISE AND END *VERY* QUICKLY.
I WASN'T PREPARED FOR DOCTOR STRANGE TO BE HERE, SO I WANTED TO TAKE THIS MOMENT--
ACTUALLY, I TAKE IT BACK...
...STRANGE WOULD PROBABLY *STILL* USE THIS AS AN OPPORTUNITY TO SCORE VISHANTI POINTS BY HELPING DOOM...NO *MATTER* WHAT.
STRANGE.
SO *PROPERLY* NAMED.
HE'S SUCH A SANCTIMONIOUS WEIRDO, RIGHT?
BUT STRANGE *WILL* ASCEND TO THE NEXT PLANE...THERE'S NOTHING I CAN DO ABOUT THAT...
HE CAN BE THE ONE THAT GOT AWAY, BUT *DOOM?*
NO WAY.
HIS ARROGANT ASS IS *MINE.*
THAT'S ALL THIS IS, BY THE WAY... ARROGANCE.
IT'S ALL *HE* IS.
"UNHAND ME, YOU TREACHEROUS WENCH!"
"BEGONE OR YOU WILL FEEL THE WRATH OF DOOM!"
YES, HE SEEMS HUMBLED NOW...BUT TO DO WHAT *HE'S* DONE TO THE MULTIVERSE AND THINK HE CAN JUST *"TURN IT AROUND"* BECAUSE HE THINKS IT'S TIME?
WOOF! THAT IS ARROGANT.
FOR HIS ENTIRE LIFE, THIS LITTLE @#$% HAS HAD A RAGE-ON FOR ANYTHING AND EVERYBODY.
...HE HAS TRIED TO RESHAPE ALL OF US IN HIS IMAGE...
HE HAS TRIED TO BURN *YOU* ALL ALIVE BECAUSE HIS MOTHER NEVER LOVED HIM...
...AND YES, IF YOU KNOW YOUR HISTORY, HE HAS EVEN HAD THE ARROGANCE TO GO TO WAR WITH *ME.*
NOW HE WANTS TO BE ONE OF THE GOOD GUYS?
NO!

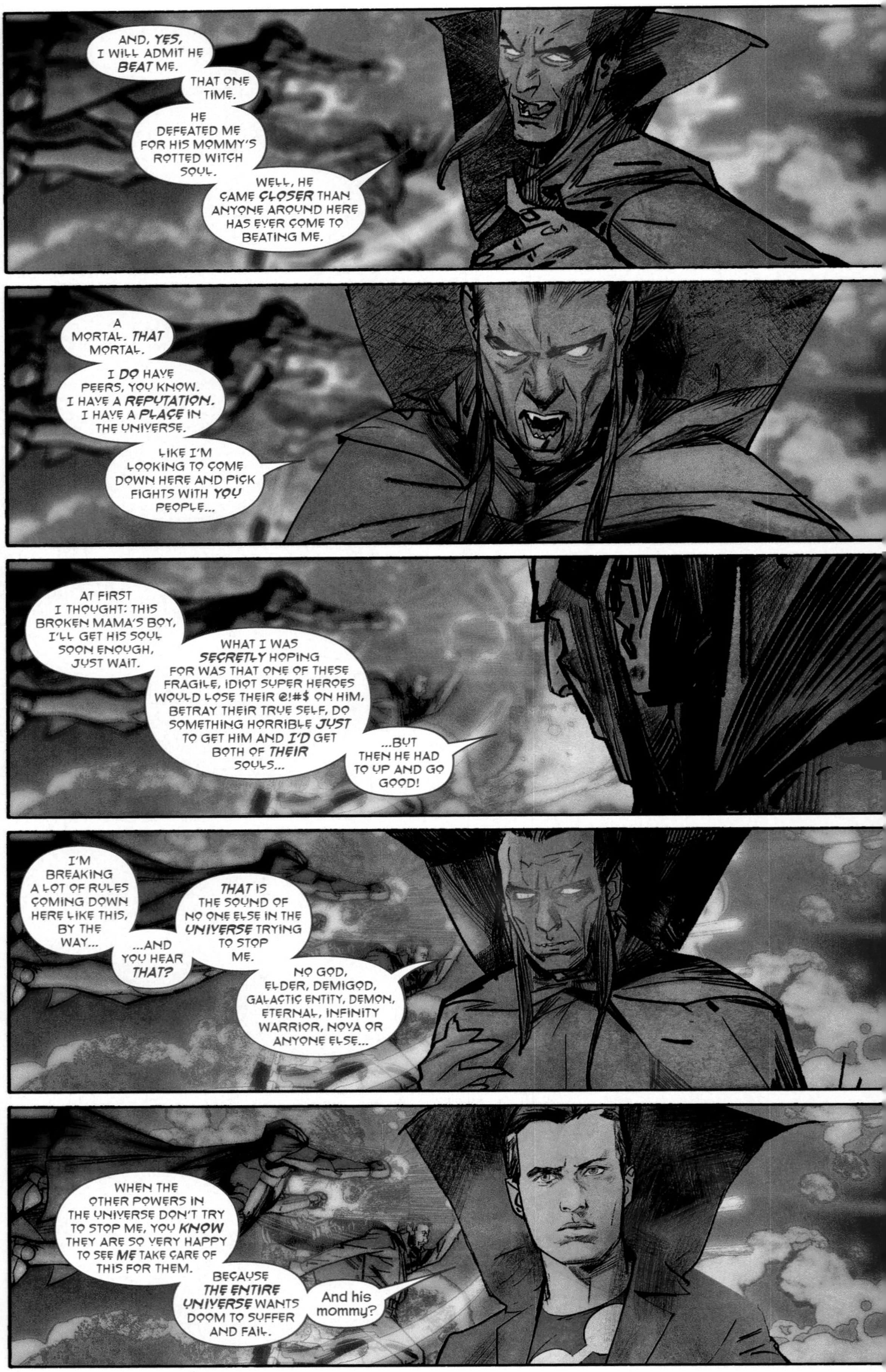
AND, YES, I WILL ADMIT HE BEAT ME.
THAT ONE TIME.
HE DEFEATED ME FOR HIS MOMMY'S ROTTED WITCH SOUL.
WELL, HE CAME CLOSER THAN ANYONE AROUND HERE HAS EVER COME TO BEATING ME.
A MORTAL. THAT MORTAL.
I DO HAVE PEERS, YOU KNOW. I HAVE A REPUTATION. I HAVE A PLACE IN THE UNIVERSE.
LIKE I'M LOOKING TO COME DOWN HERE AND PICK FIGHTS WITH YOU PEOPLE...
AT FIRST I THOUGHT: THIS BROKEN MAMA'S BOY, I'LL GET HIS SOUL SOON ENOUGH, JUST WAIT.
WHAT I WAS SECRETLY HOPING FOR WAS THAT ONE OF THESE FRAGILE, IDIOT SUPER HEROES WOULD LOSE THEIR @!#$ ON HIM, BETRAY THEIR TRUE SELF, DO SOMETHING HORRIBLE JUST TO GET HIM AND I'D GET BOTH OF THEIR SOULS...
...BUT THEN HE HAD TO UP AND GO GOOD!
I'M BREAKING A LOT OF RULES COMING DOWN HERE LIKE THIS, BY THE WAY...
...AND YOU HEAR THAT?
THAT IS THE SOUND OF NO ONE ELSE IN THE UNIVERSE TRYING TO STOP ME.
NO GOD, ELDER, DEMIGOD, GALACTIC ENTITY, DEMON, ETERNAL, INFINITY WARRIOR, NOVA OR ANYONE ELSE...
WHEN THE OTHER POWERS IN THE UNIVERSE DON'T TRY TO STOP ME, YOU KNOW THEY ARE SO VERY HAPPY TO SEE ME TAKE CARE OF THIS FOR THEM.
BECAUSE THE ENTIRE UNIVERSE WANTS DOOM TO SUFFER AND FAIL.
And his mommy?

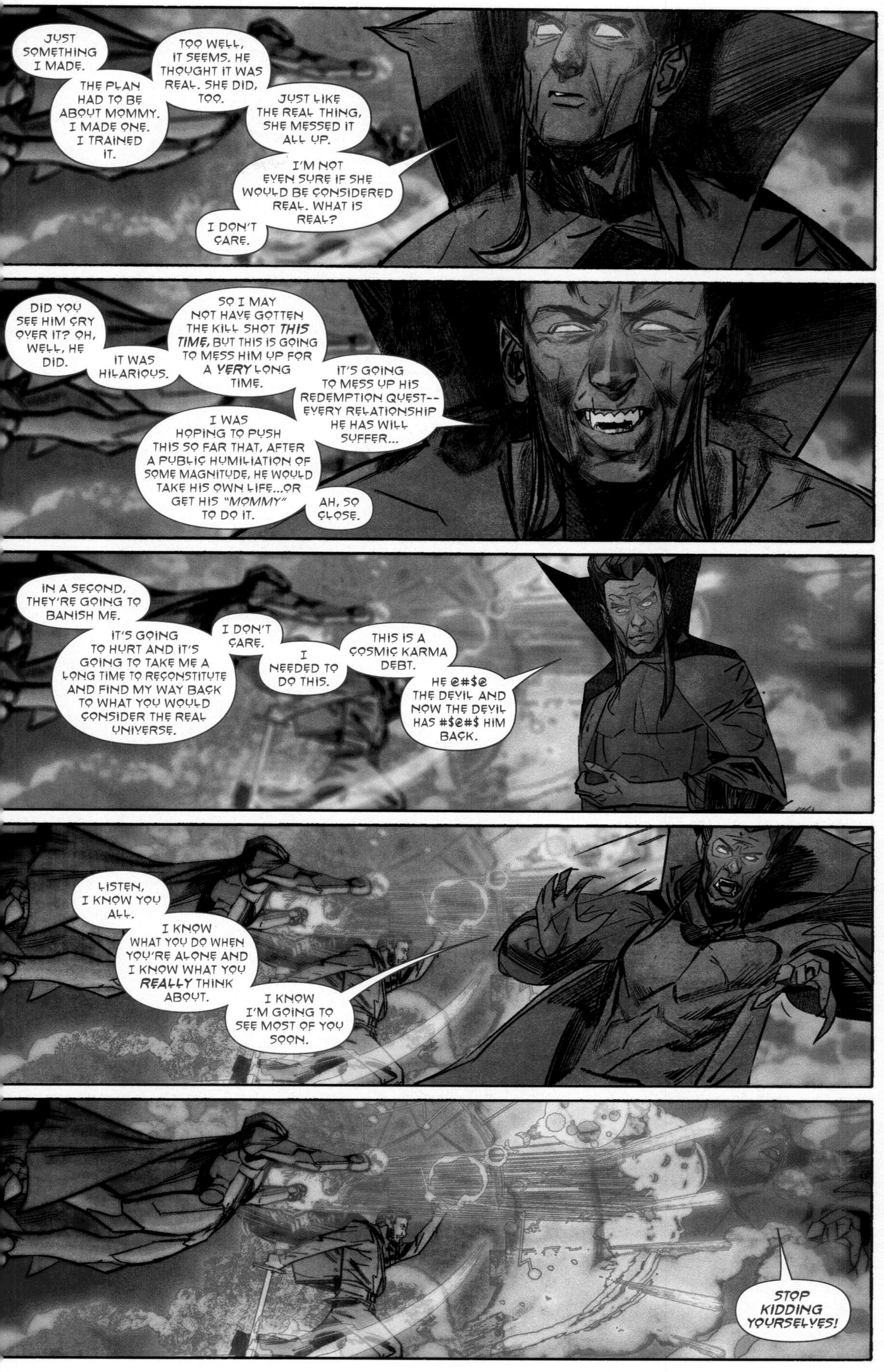
JUST SOMETHING I MADE.
THE PLAN HAD TO BE ABOUT MOMMY. I MADE ONE. I TRAINED IT.
TOO WELL, IT SEEMS. HE THOUGHT IT WAS REAL. SHE DID, TOO.
JUST LIKE THE REAL THING, SHE MESSED IT ALL UP.
I'M NOT EVEN SURE IF SHE WOULD BE CONSIDERED REAL. WHAT IS REAL?
I DON'T CARE.
DID YOU SEE HIM CRY OVER IT? OH, WELL, HE DID.
IT WAS HILARIOUS.
SO I MAY NOT HAVE GOTTEN THE KILL SHOT THIS TIME, BUT THIS IS GOING TO MESS HIM UP FOR A VERY LONG TIME.
IT'S GOING TO MESS UP HIS REDEMPTION QUEST--EVERY RELATIONSHIP HE HAS WILL SUFFER...
I WAS HOPING TO PUSH THIS SO FAR THAT, AFTER A PUBLIC HUMILIATION OF SOME MAGNITUDE, HE WOULD TAKE HIS OWN LIFE...OR GET HIS "MOMMY" TO DO IT.
AH, SO CLOSE.
IN A SECOND, THEY'RE GOING TO BANISH ME.
IT'S GOING TO HURT AND IT'S GOING TO TAKE ME A LONG TIME TO RECONSTITUTE AND FIND MY WAY BACK TO WHAT YOU WOULD CONSIDER THE REAL UNIVERSE.
I DON'T CARE.
I NEEDED TO DO THIS.
THIS IS A COSMIC KARMA DEBT.
HE @#$@ THE DEVIL AND NOW THE DEVIL HAS #$@#$ HIM BACK.
LISTEN, I KNOW YOU ALL.
I KNOW WHAT YOU DO WHEN YOU'RE ALONE AND I KNOW WHAT YOU REALLY THINK ABOUT.
I KNOW I'M GOING TO SEE MOST OF YOU SOON.
STOP KIDDING YOURSELVES!

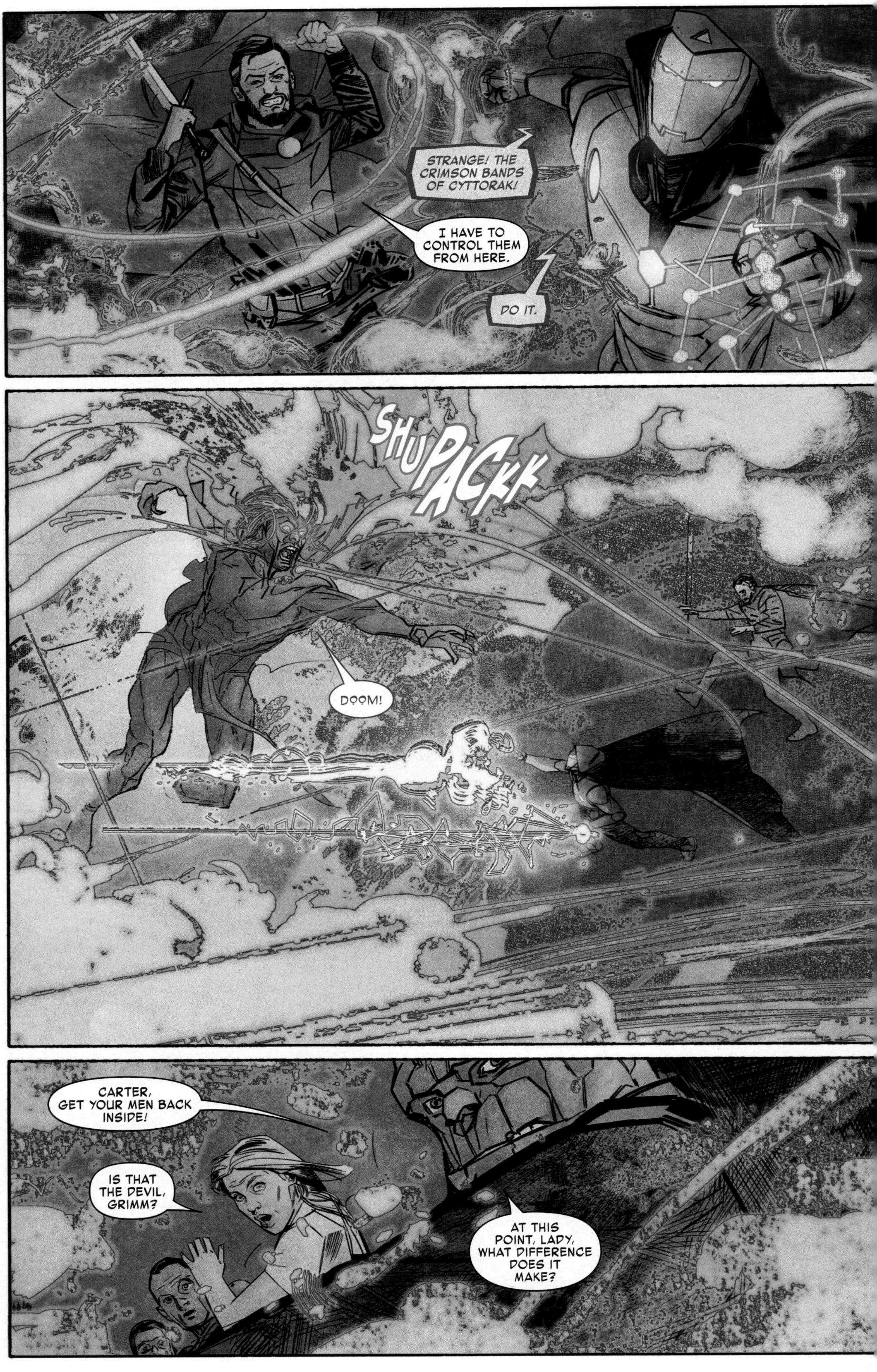
STRANGE! THE CRIMSON BANDS OF CYTTORAK!
I HAVE TO CONTROL THEM FROM HERE.
DO IT.
SHUPACKK
DOOM!
CARTER, GET YOUR MEN BACK INSIDE!
IS THAT THE DEVIL, GRIMM?
AT THIS POINT, LADY, WHAT DIFFERENCE DOES IT MAKE?

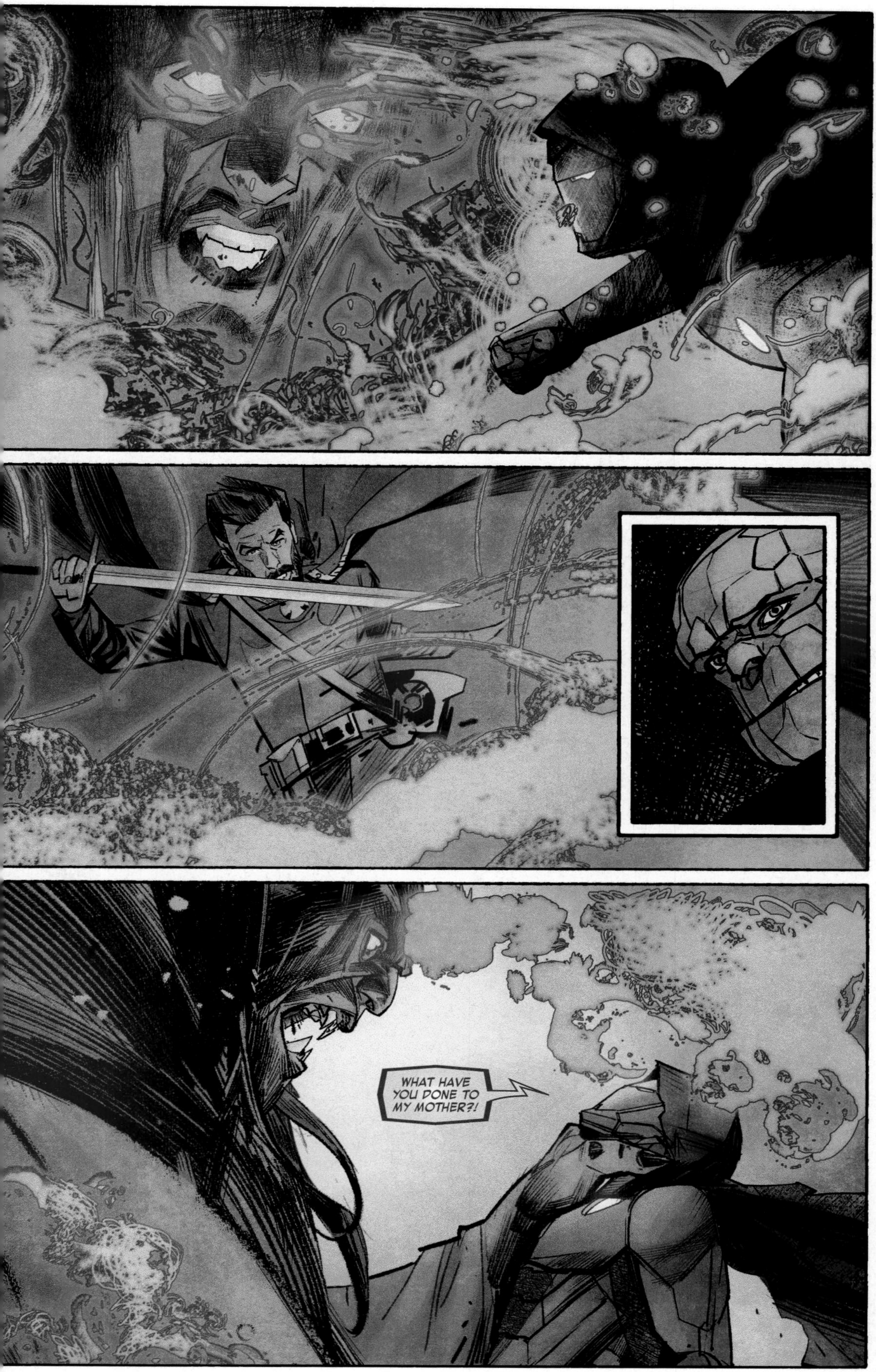
WHAT HAVE YOU DONE TO MY MOTHER?!

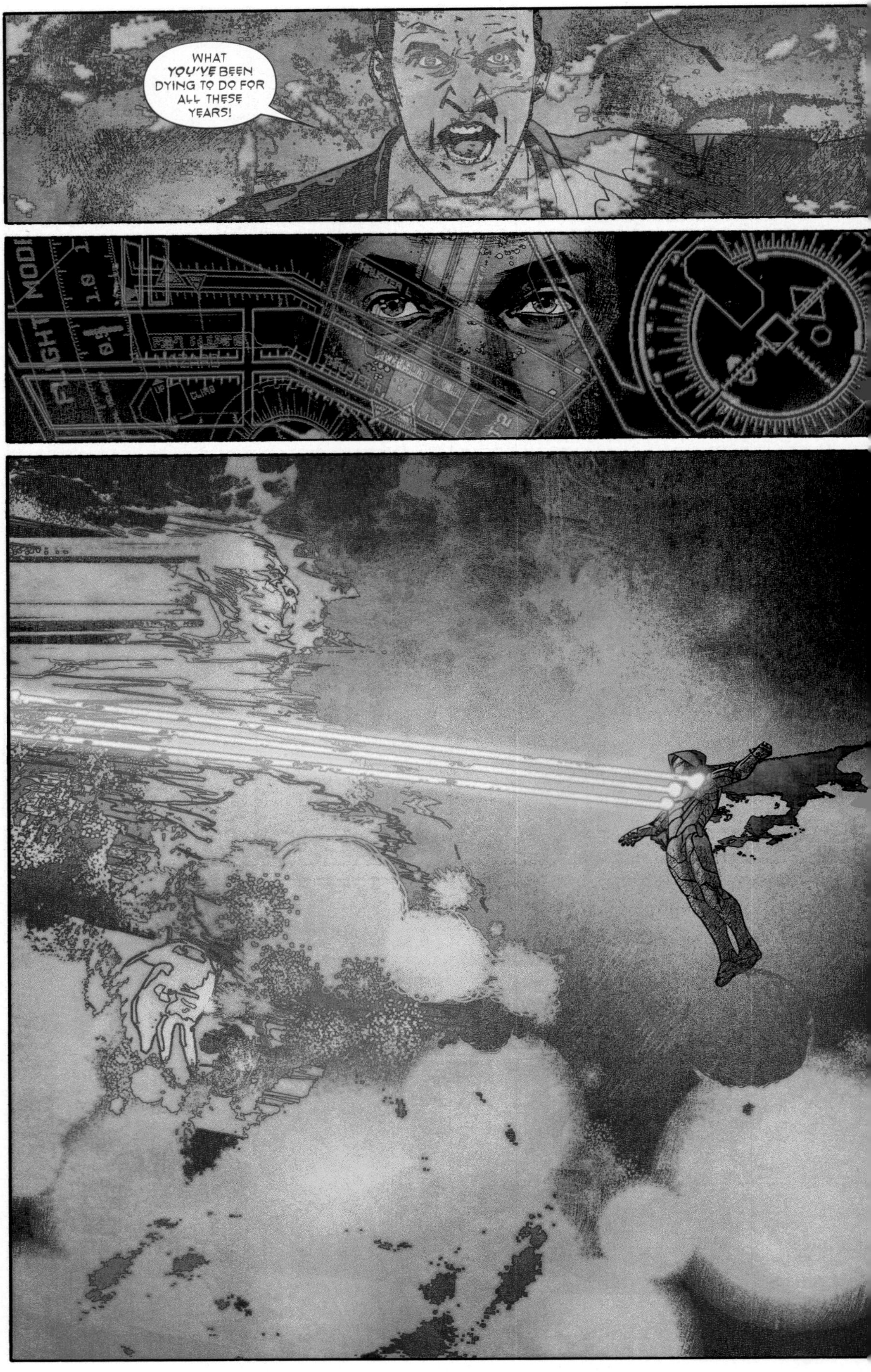
WHAT YOU'VE BEEN DYING TO DO FOR ALL THESE YEARS!

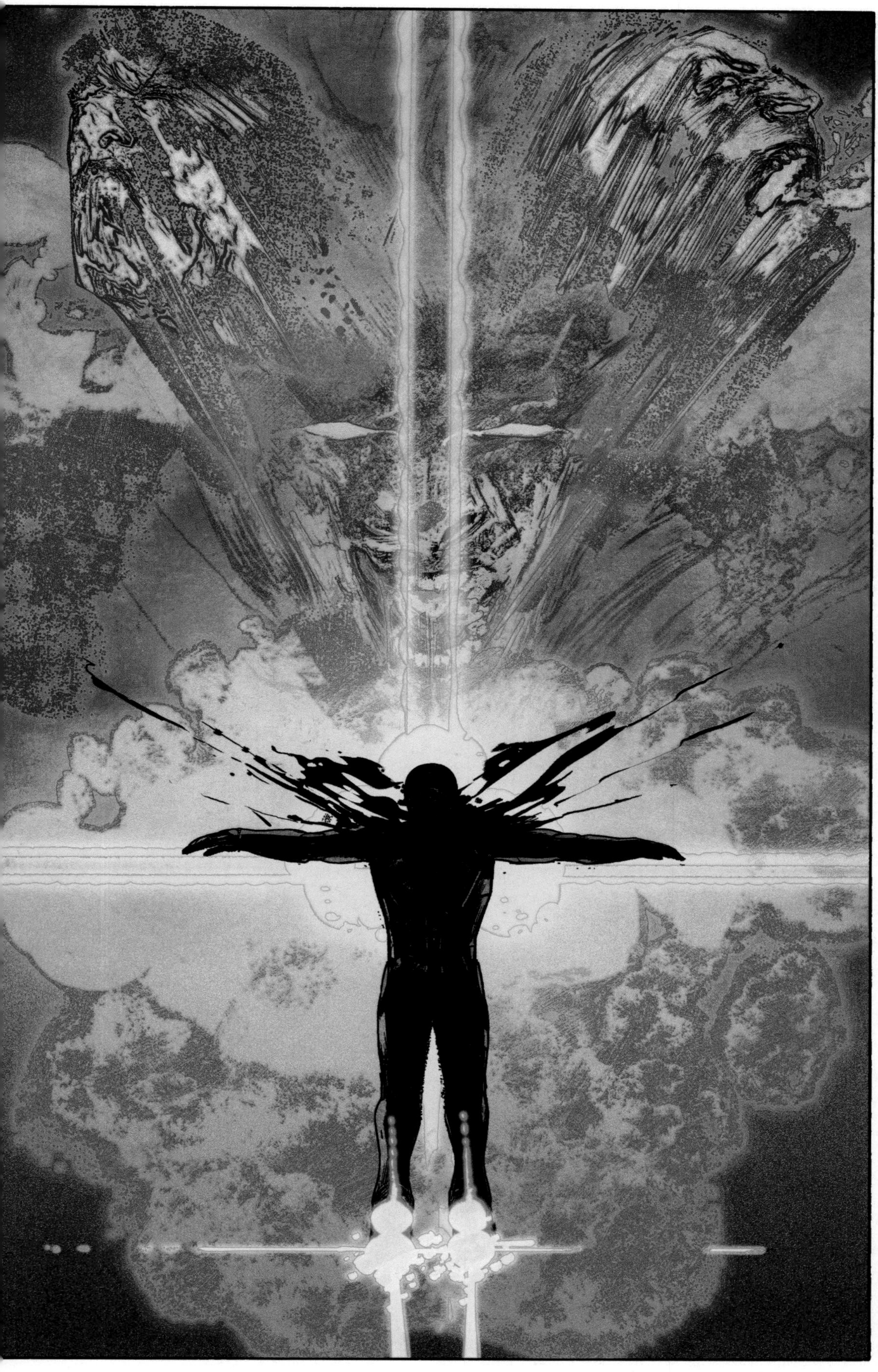

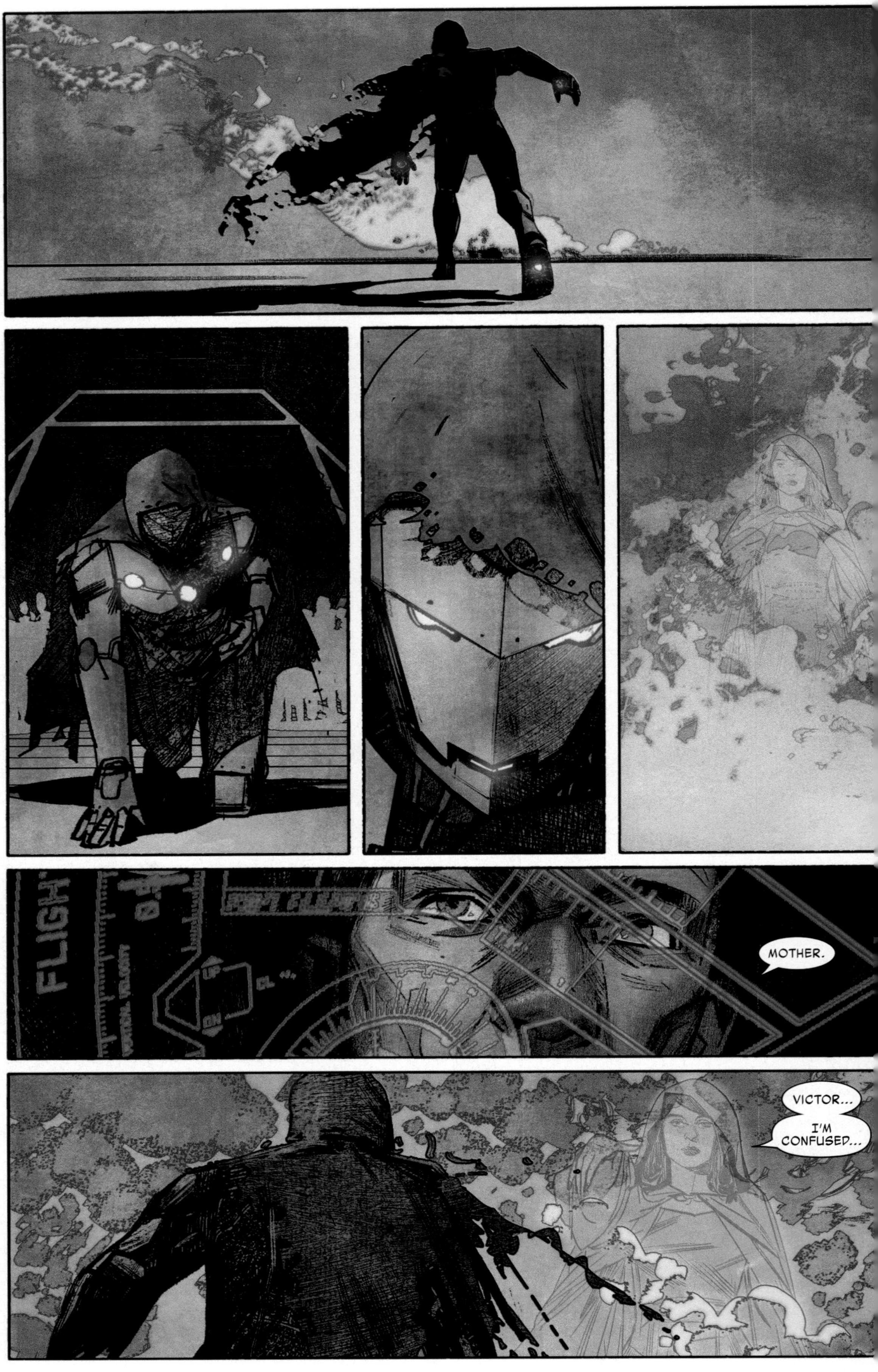
MOTHER.
VICTOR...
I'M CONFUSED...

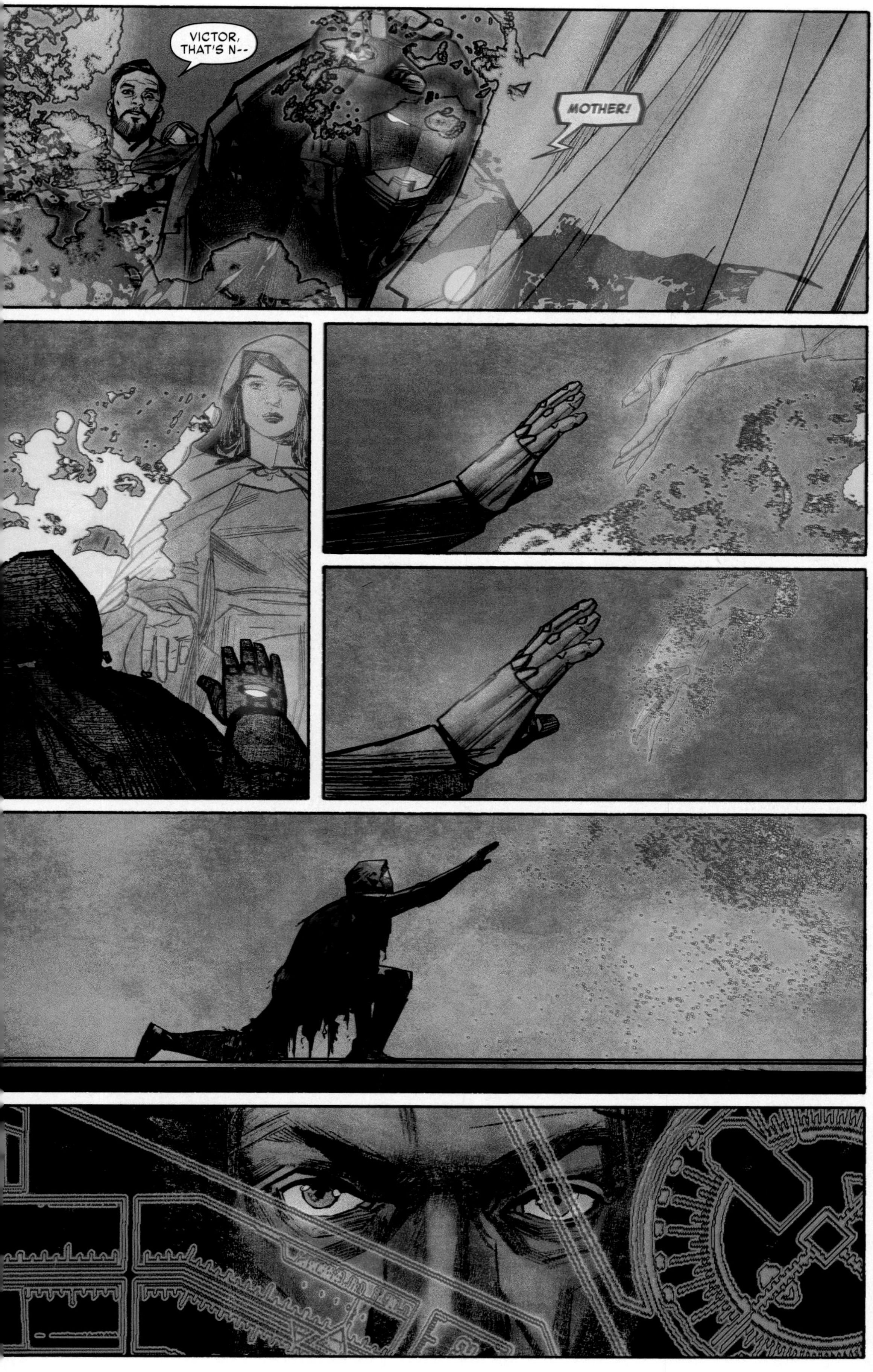
VICTOR, THAT'S N--
MOTHER!

THAT WAS... UNPLEASANT.

THANK YOU FOR YOUR ASSISTANCE, DOCTOR.

OBVIOUSLY, IT WAS NEEDED.

YOU'RE WELCOME, VICTOR.

DOOM... I HAVE TO INCARCERATE YOU.

I UNDERSTAND HOW THAT WOULD BE YOUR FIRST INSTINCT, COMMANDER CARTER.

OR, TO GO ALONG WITH THE 42 POWERED CRIMINALS I HAVE RECENTLY INCARCERATED FOR YOU...

...WHAT IF, TONIGHT, I BROUGHT DOWN A WORKING HYDRA SCIENCE ISLAND OFF THE COAST OF BRAZIL?

THAT IS WHAT I WOULD HAVE BEEN DOING IF NOT FOR THIS...DISTRACTION.

TONIGHT?

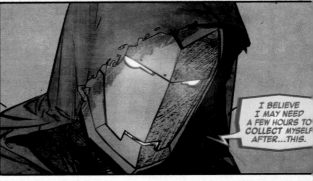

I BELIEVE I MAY NEED A FEW HOURS TO COLLECT MYSELF AFTER...THIS.

A HYDRA SCIENCE ISLAND?

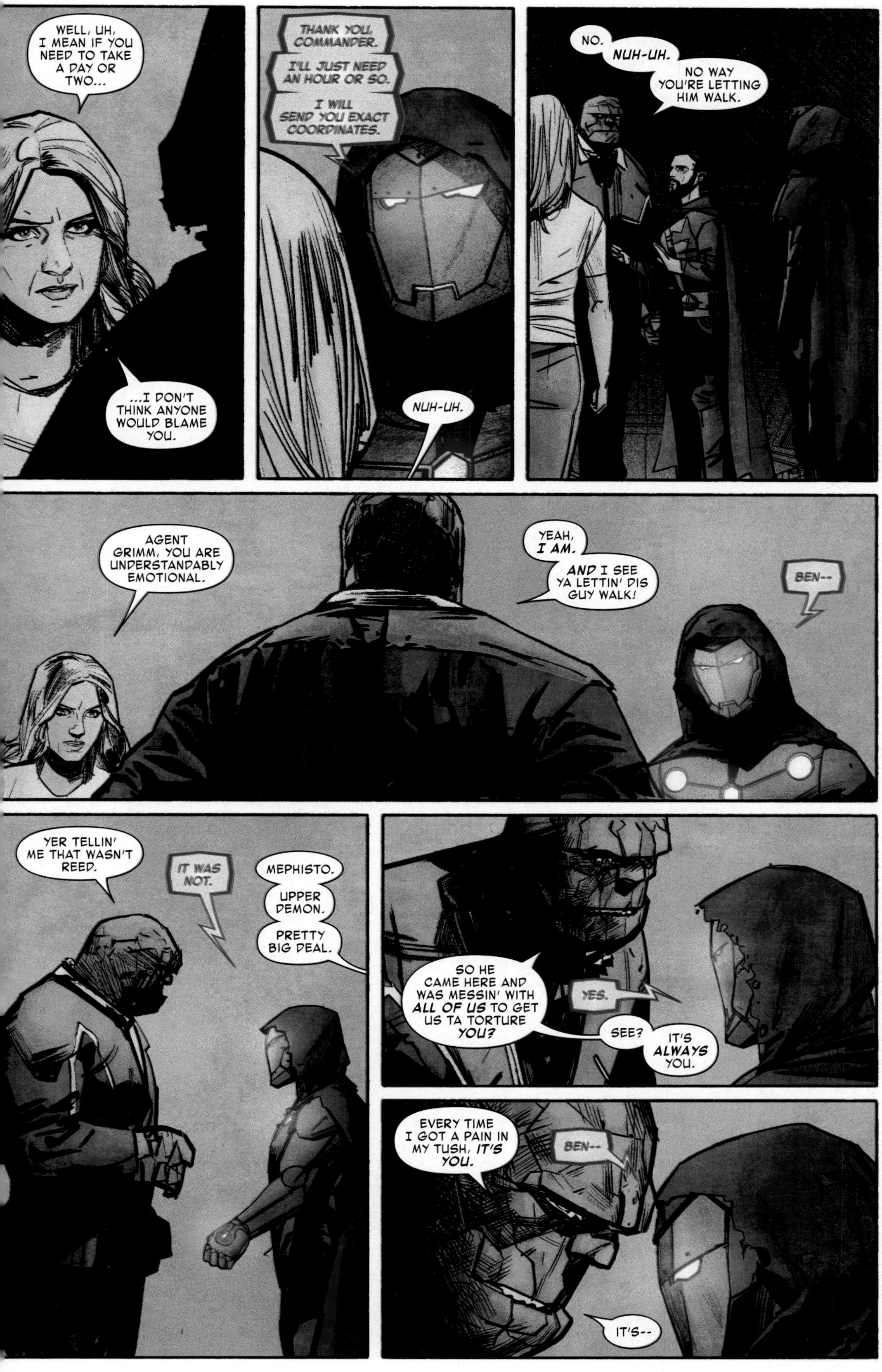
WELL, UH, I MEAN IF YOU NEED TO TAKE A DAY OR TWO...
...I DON'T THINK ANYONE WOULD BLAME YOU.
THANK YOU, COMMANDER.
I'LL JUST NEED AN HOUR OR SO.
I WILL SEND YOU EXACT COORDINATES.
NUH-UH.
NO.
NUH-UH.
NO WAY YOU'RE LETTING HIM WALK.
AGENT GRIMM, YOU ARE UNDERSTANDABLY EMOTIONAL.
YEAH, I AM.
AND I SEE YA LETTIN' DIS GUY WALK!
BEN--
YER TELLIN' ME THAT WASN'T REED.
IT WAS NOT.
MEPHISTO.
UPPER DEMON.
PRETTY BIG DEAL.
SO HE CAME HERE AND WAS MESSIN' WITH ALL OF US TO GET US TA TORTURE YOU?
YES.
SEE?
IT'S ALWAYS YOU.
EVERY TIME I GOT A PAIN IN MY TUSH, IT'S YOU.
BEN--
IT'S--

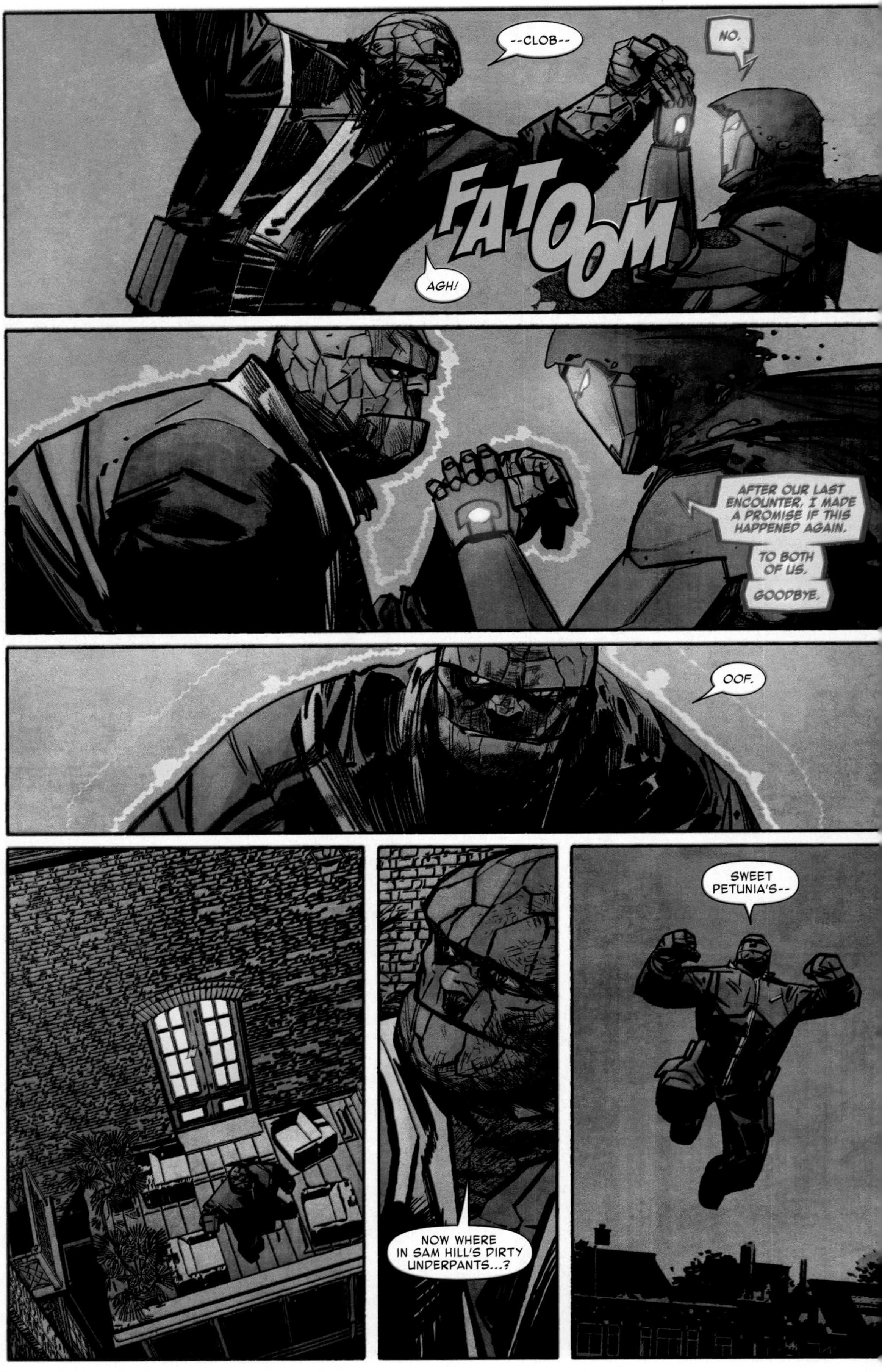
--CLOB--
NO.
FATOOM
AGH!
AFTER OUR LAST ENCOUNTER, I MADE A PROMISE IF THIS HAPPENED AGAIN.
TO BOTH OF US.
GOODBYE.
OOF.
NOW WHERE IN SAM HILL'S DIRTY UNDERPANTS...?
SWEET PETUNIA'S--

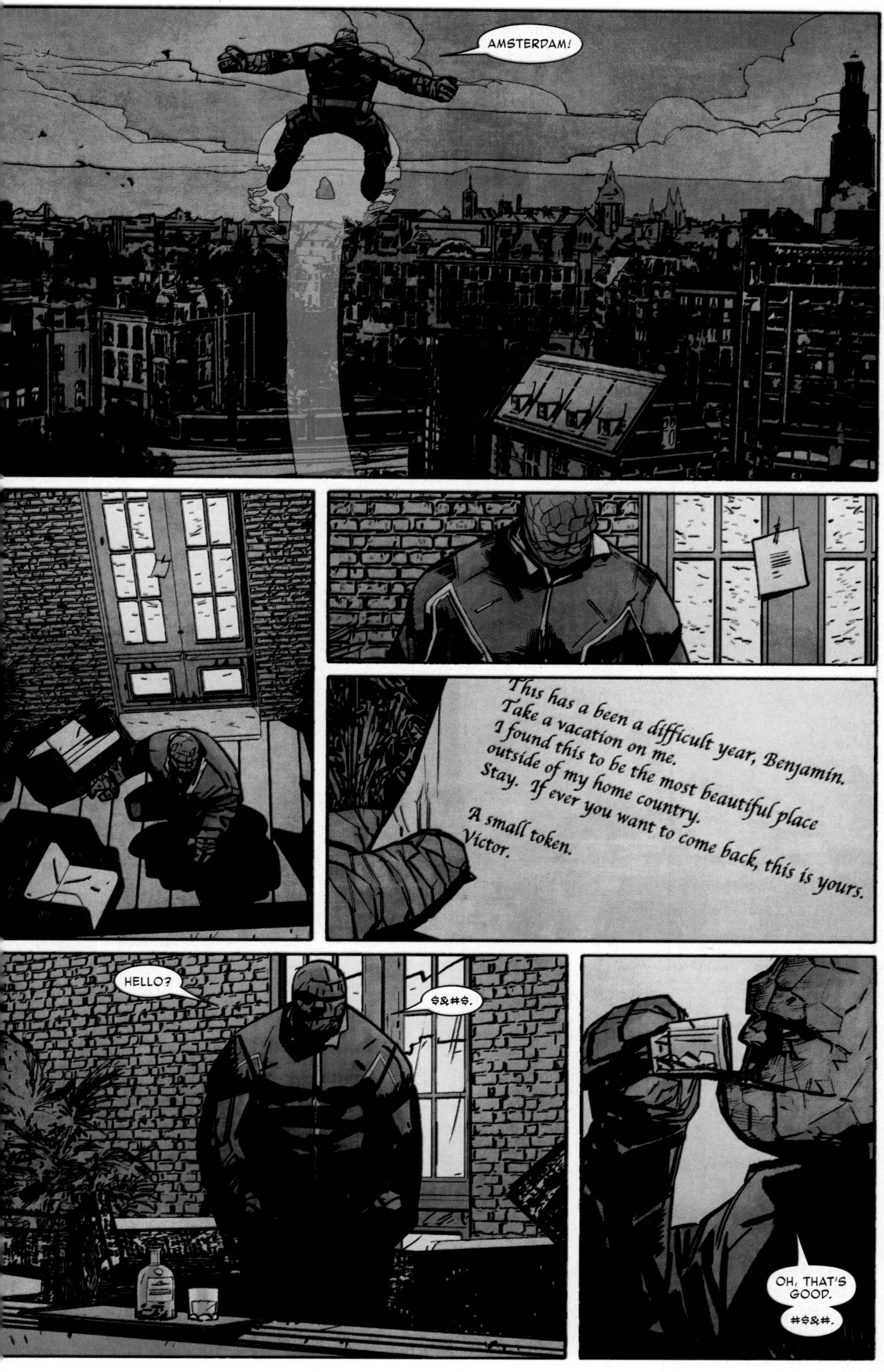
AMSTERDAM!
This has a been a difficult year, Benjamin.
Take a vacation on me.
I found this to be the most beautiful place
outside of my home country.
Stay. If ever you want to come back, this is yours.
A small token.
Victor.
HELLO?
$&#$.
OH, THAT'S GOOD.
#$&#.

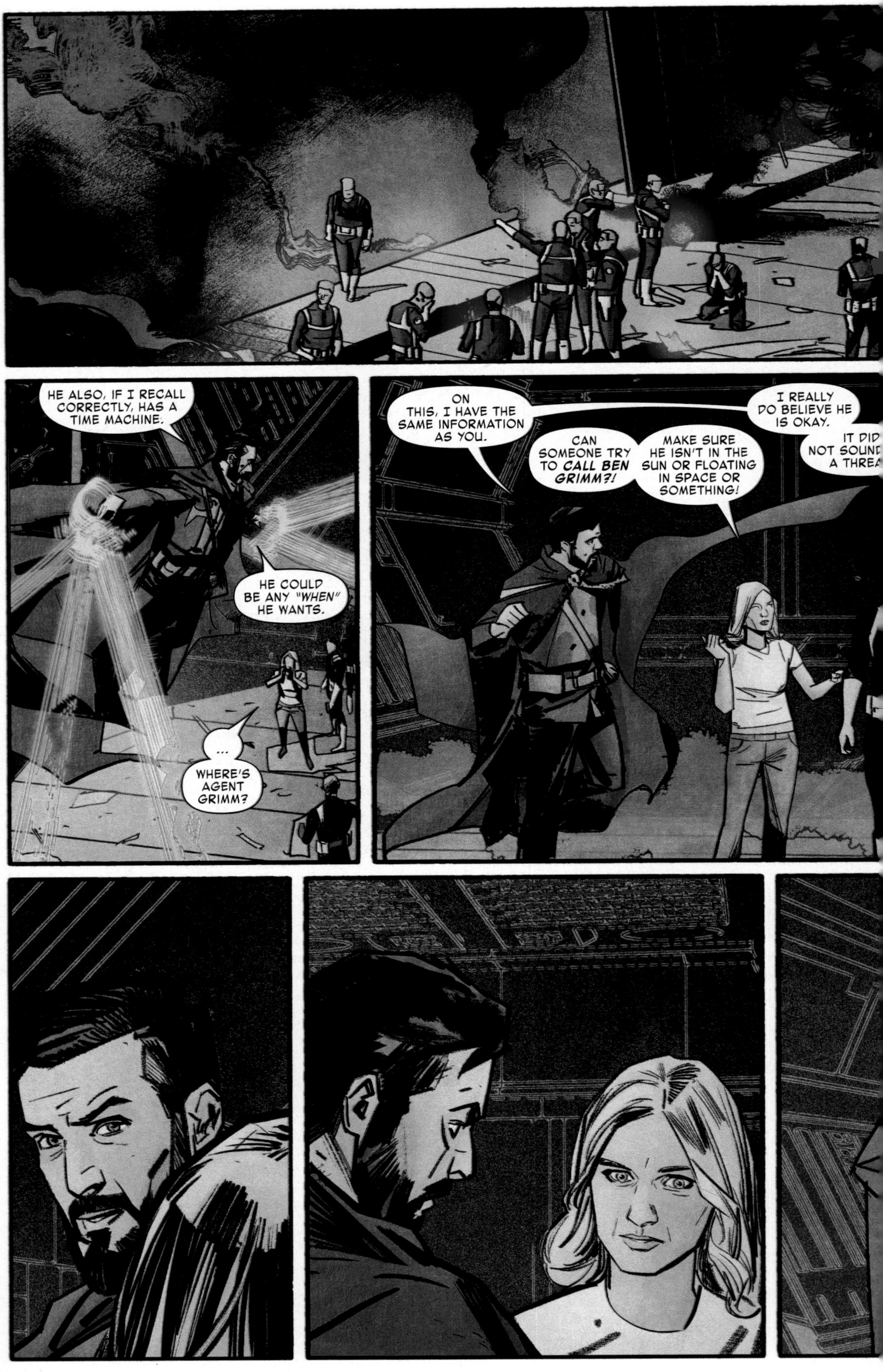
HE ALSO, IF I RECALL CORRECTLY, HAS A TIME MACHINE.
HE COULD BE ANY "WHEN" HE WANTS.
...
WHERE'S AGENT GRIMM?
ON THIS, I HAVE THE SAME INFORMATION AS YOU.
I REALLY DO BELIEVE HE IS OKAY.
CAN SOMEONE TRY TO CALL BEN GRIMM?!
MAKE SURE HE ISN'T IN THE SUN OR FLOATING IN SPACE OR SOMETHING!

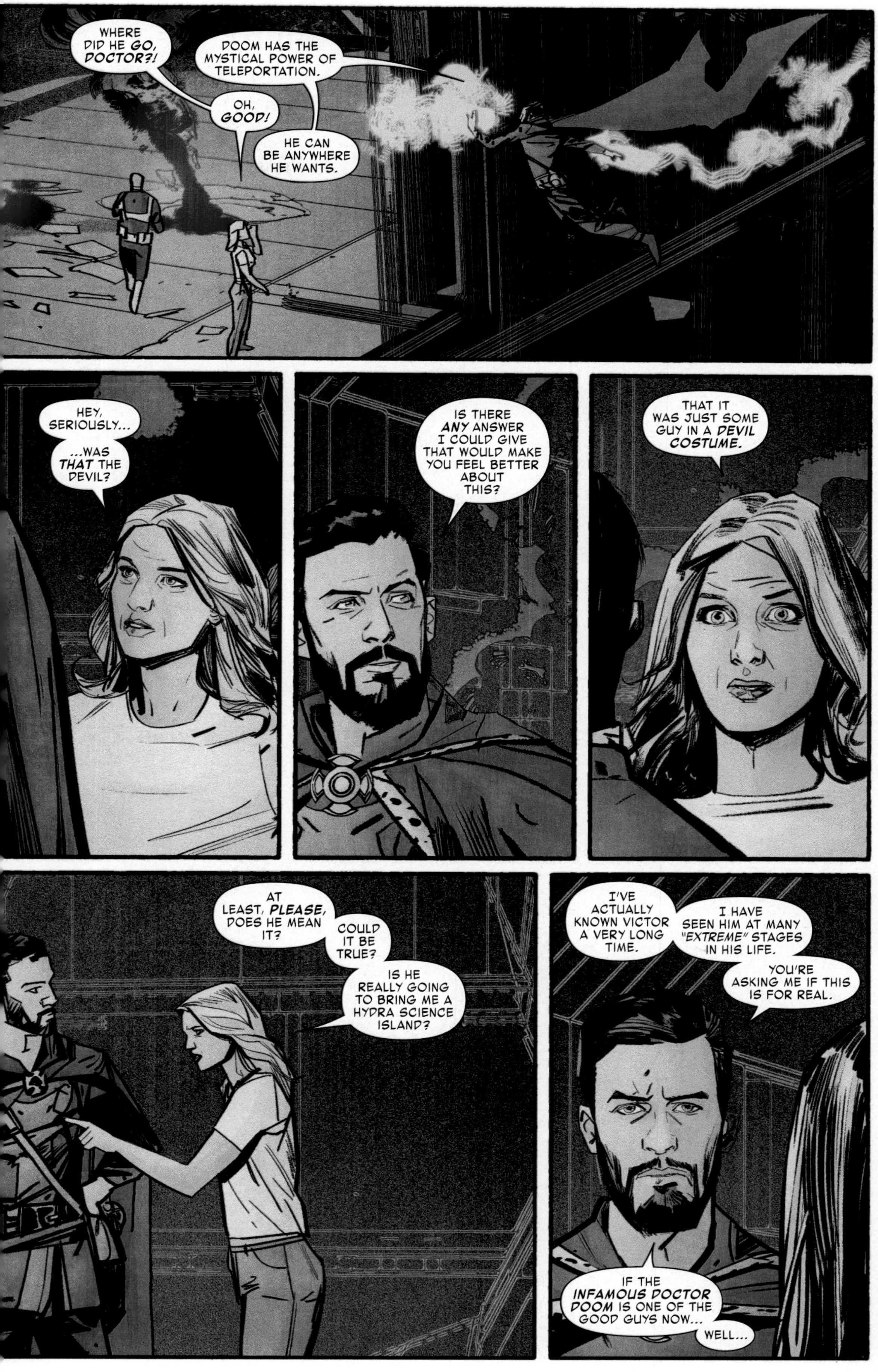
WHERE DID HE GO, DOCTOR?!
DOOM HAS THE MYSTICAL POWER OF TELEPORTATION.
OH, GOOD!
HE CAN BE ANYWHERE HE WANTS.
HEY, SERIOUSLY...
...WAS THAT THE DEVIL?
IS THERE ANY ANSWER I COULD GIVE THAT WOULD MAKE YOU FEEL BETTER ABOUT THIS?
THAT IT WAS JUST SOME GUY IN A DEVIL COSTUME.
AT LEAST, PLEASE, DOES HE MEAN IT?
COULD IT BE TRUE?
IS HE REALLY GOING TO BRING ME A HYDRA SCIENCE ISLAND?
I'VE ACTUALLY KNOWN VICTOR A VERY LONG TIME.
I HAVE SEEN HIM AT MANY "EXTREME" STAGES IN HIS LIFE.
YOU'RE ASKING ME IF THIS IS FOR REAL.
IF THE INFAMOUS DOCTOR DOOM IS ONE OF THE GOOD GUYS NOW...
WELL...

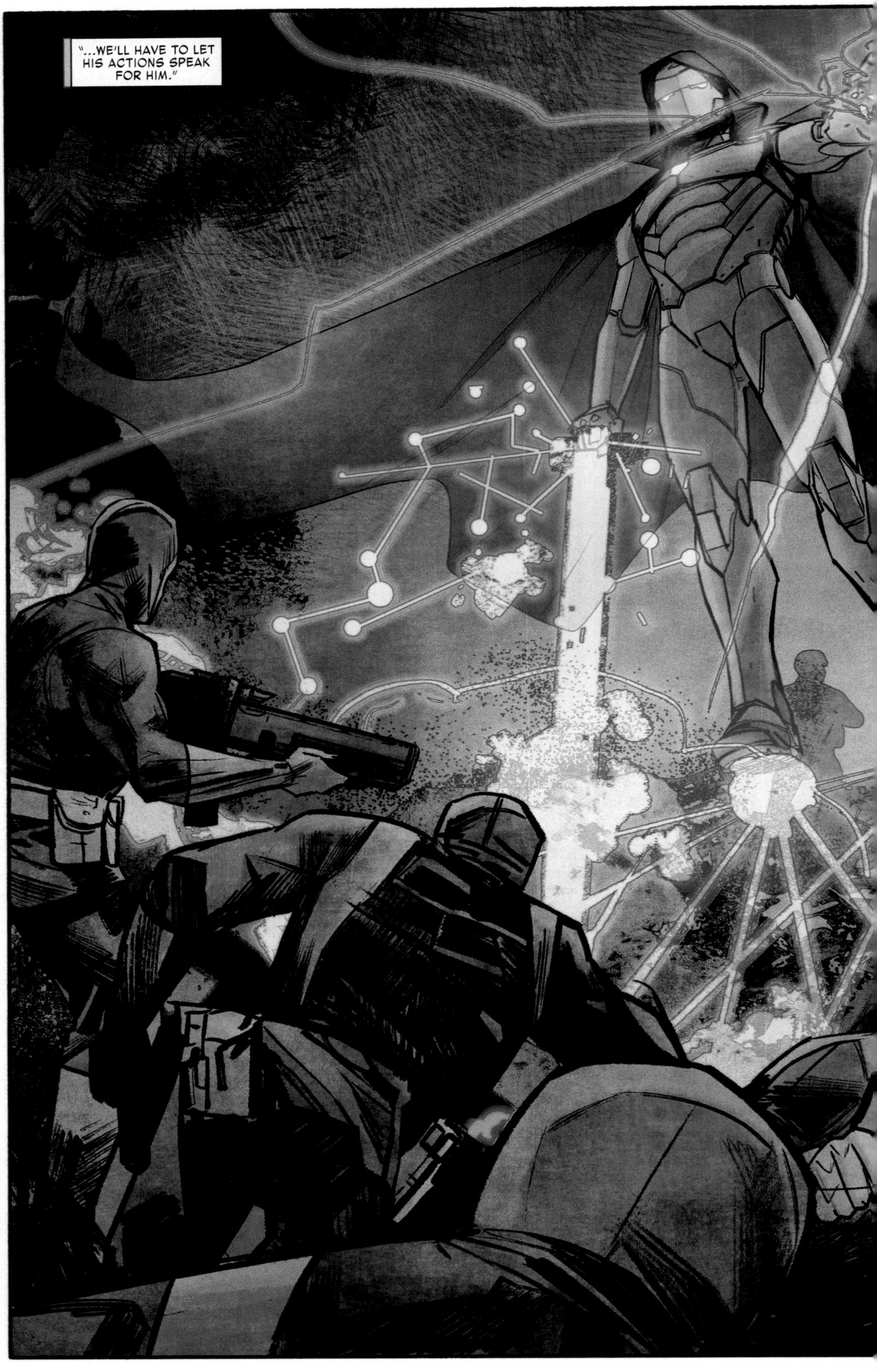
"...WE'LL HAVE TO LET HIS ACTIONS SPEAK FOR HIM."

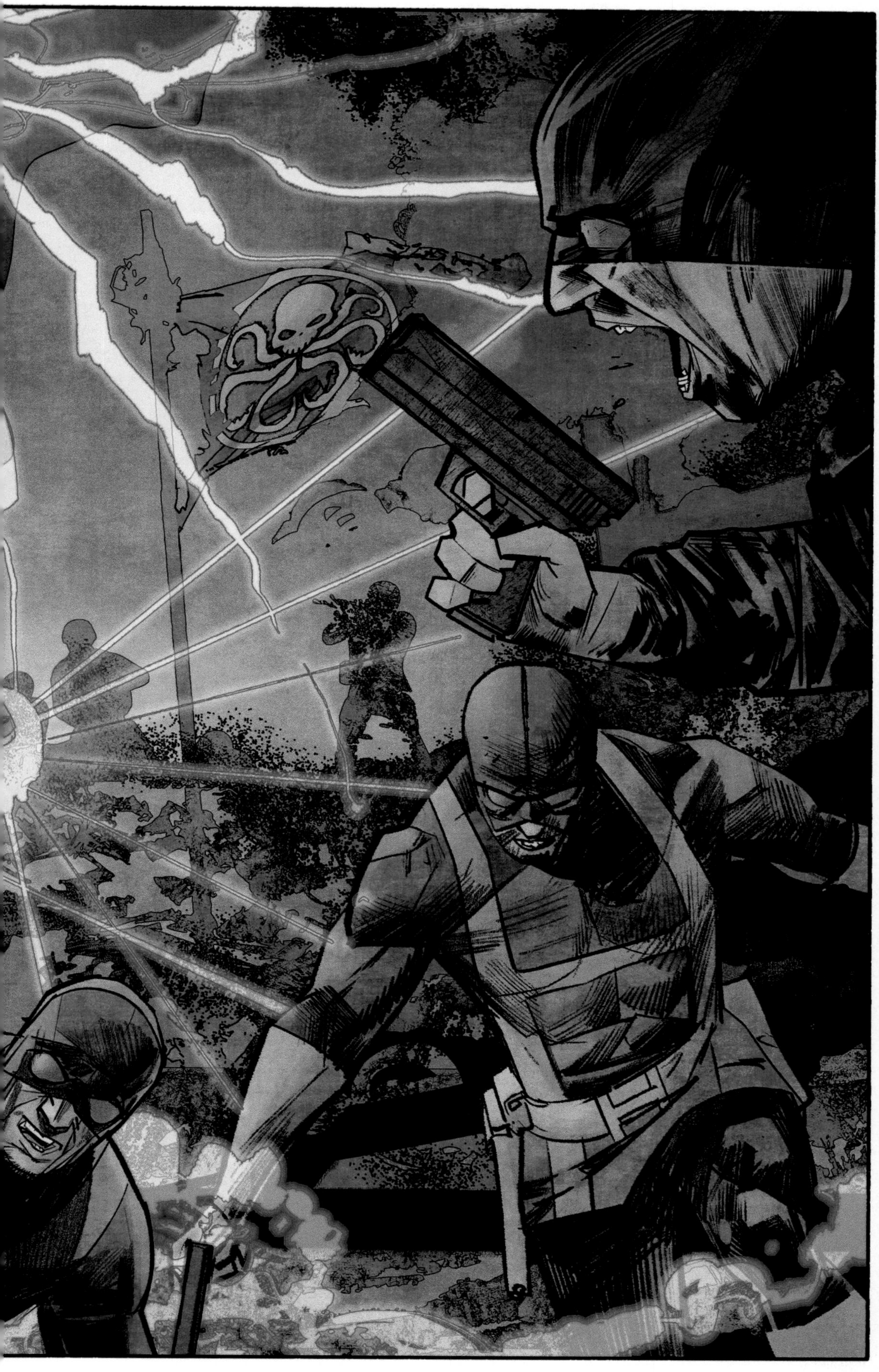

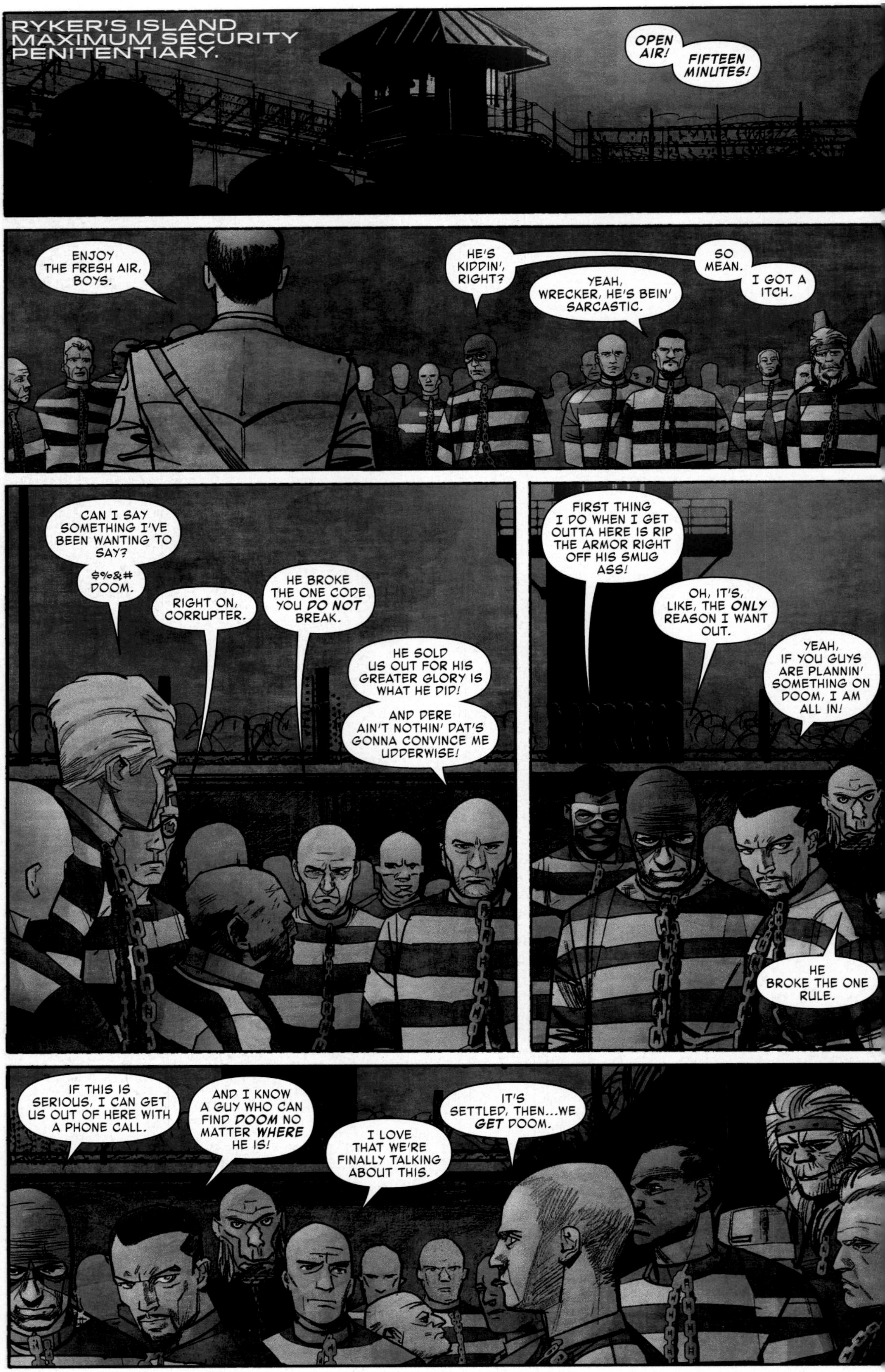
RYKER'S ISLAND MAXIMUM SECURITY PENITENTIARY.
OPEN AIR!
FIFTEEN MINUTES!
ENJOY THE FRESH AIR, BOYS.
HE'S KIDDIN', RIGHT?
SO MEAN.
YEAH, WRECKER, HE'S BEIN' SARCASTIC.
I GOT A ITCH.
CAN I SAY SOMETHING I'VE BEEN WANTING TO SAY?
$%&# DOOM.
RIGHT ON, CORRUPTER.
HE BROKE THE ONE CODE YOU DO NOT BREAK.
HE SOLD US OUT FOR HIS GREATER GLORY IS WHAT HE DID!
AND DERE AIN'T NOTHIN' DAT'S GONNA CONVINCE ME UDDERWISE!
FIRST THING I DO WHEN I GET OUTTA HERE IS RIP THE ARMOR RIGHT OFF HIS SMUG ASS!
OH, IT'S, LIKE, THE ONLY REASON I WANT OUT.
YEAH, IF YOU GUYS ARE PLANNIN' SOMETHING ON DOOM, I AM ALL IN!
HE BROKE THE ONE RULE.
IF THIS IS SERIOUS, I CAN GET US OUT OF HERE WITH A PHONE CALL.
AND I KNOW A GUY WHO CAN FIND DOOM NO MATTER WHERE HE IS!
I LOVE THAT WE'RE FINALLY TALKING ABOUT THIS.
IT'S SETTLED, THEN...WE GET DOOM.

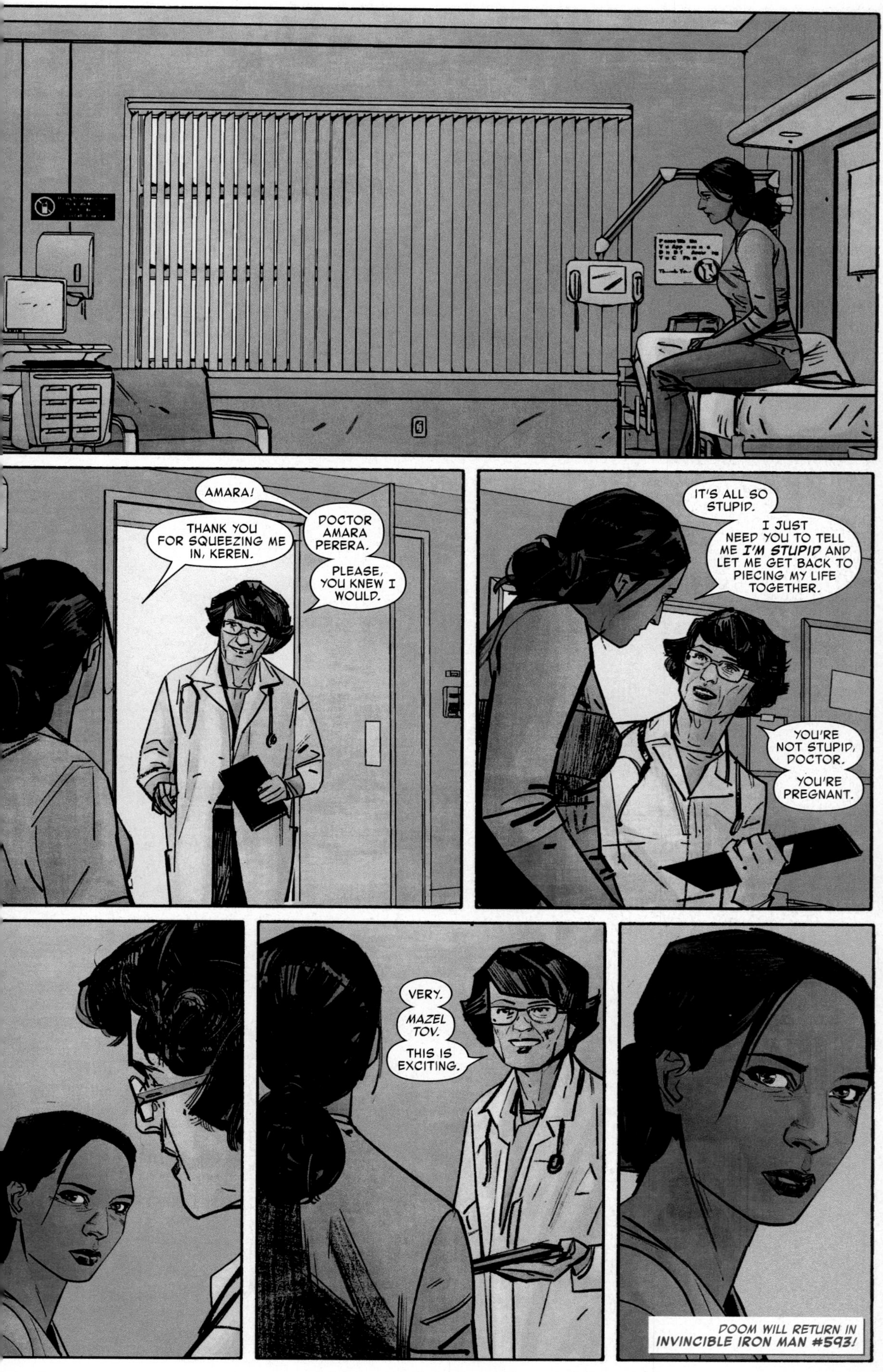
AMARA!
THANK YOU FOR SQUEEZING ME IN, KEREN.
DOCTOR AMARA PERERA.
PLEASE, YOU KNEW I WOULD.
IT'S ALL SO STUPID.
I JUST NEED YOU TO TELL ME *I'M STUPID* AND LET ME GET BACK TO PIECING MY LIFE TOGETHER.
YOU'RE NOT STUPID, DOCTOR.
YOU'RE PREGNANT.
VERY.
MAZEL TOV.
THIS IS EXCITING.
DOOM WILL RETURN IN INVINCIBLE IRON MAN #593!

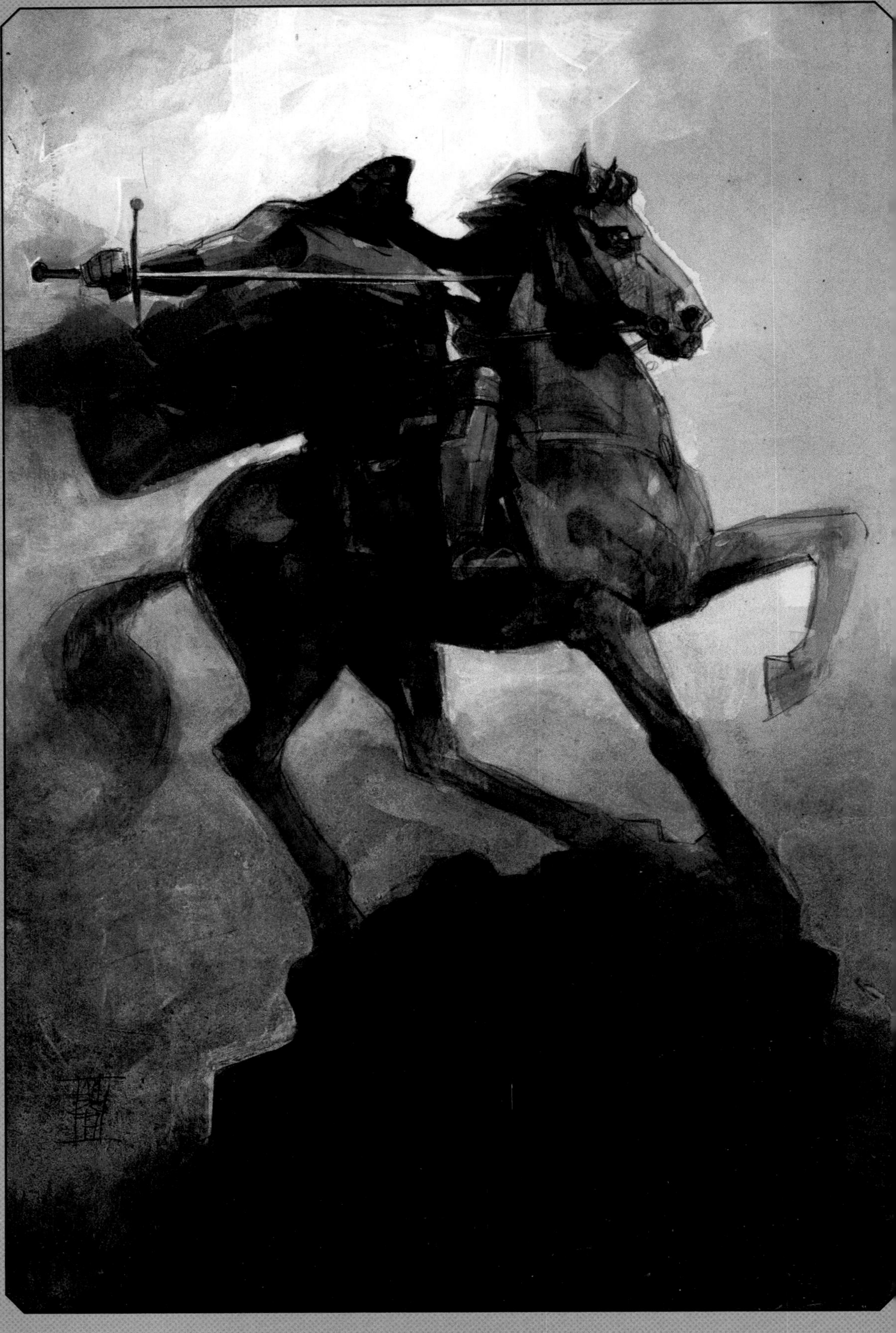

ALEX MALEEV

12 VARIANT